FROM PILGRIMAGE TO PACKAGE TOUR

FROM PILGRIMAGE TO PACKAGE TOUR

Travel and Tourism in the Third World

David L. Gladstone

Routledge
Taylor & Francis Group
New York   London

Published in 2005 by
Routledge
Taylor & Francis Group
270 Madison Avenue
New York, NY 10016

Published in Great Britain by
Routledge
Taylor & Francis Group
2 Park Square
Milton Park, Abingdon
Oxon OX14 4RN

Printed in the United States of America on acid-free paper
10 9 8 7 6 5 4 3 2 1

International Standard Book Number-10: 0-415-95062-7 (Hardcover) 0-415-95063-5 (Softcover)
International Standard Book Number-13: 978-0-415-95062-6 (Hardcover) 978-0-415-95063-3 (Softcover)

Library of Congress Cataloging-in-Publication Data

Gladstone, David L.
    From pilgrimage to package tour : travel and tourism in the Third World / by David L. Gladstone.
        p. cm.
    Includes bibliographical references (p.   ) and index.
    ISBN 0-415-95062-7 (hb : alk. paper) -- ISBN 0-415-95063-5 (pb : alk. paper)
    1. Tourism--Developing countries. I. Title.

G155.D44G53 2005
338.4'791'091734--dc22   2005005278

Taylor & Francis Group
is the Academic Division of T&F Informa plc.

Visit the Taylor & Francis Web site at
http://www.taylorandfrancis.com

and the Routledge Web site at
http://www.routledge-ny.com

Contents

Acknowledgments

Because this book has been many years in the making and is the culmination of my experiences as a scholar-tourist on five continents, it would be well-nigh impossible for me to list all the people who helped me out in various ways and, in some cases, in very substantial ways. In most cases I do not even know their names and in other cases I promised not to publish their names. So to the hundreds if not thousands of travel professionals, scholars, innkeepers, hospitality workers, government officials, fellow travelers, pilgrims, sadhus, motorcycle mechanics, long-distance taxi drivers, and friends in Oaxaca, Chiapas, Mexico City, Quintana Roo, New Delhi, Mumbai (Bombay), Kolkata (Calcutta), Chennai (Madras), Rajasthan, Uttar Pradesh, Himachal Pradesh, Peru, Mauritius, Bolivia, Austria, Germany, the Netherlands, Russia, Kazakhstan, Australia, the United Kingdom, New York, New Jersey, California, Louisiana, and lots of places in between, thank you, dhanyavaad, graçias, danke, añay, dank u, merci, mersi, cheers, nandri, todah, shukran, spaseeba.

There are a number of people, however, to whom I owe a special debt of gratitude and without whom this book in its present form would certainly not have been possible.

In the United States there are my friends, teachers, and colleagues at Rutgers University, Columbia University, the University of New Orleans, and other academic institutions who in one way or another have encouraged me to parlay my love of travel into a career of researching and writing about tourism in its various forms. First and foremost is Susan Fainstein, who was the first person to suggest that I could actually write about tourism in an academic fashion. Susan has collaborated with me on a number of research projects over the years and has continued to encourage me in my academic endeavors. Dennis Judd has also encouraged me to write about tourism and has made many useful comments about my research on Third World tourism and other topics. Hooshang Amirahmadi, Meredeth Turshen, and Briavel Holcomb all helped me learn how to place Third World tourism, and the Third World more generally, in a broader theoretical framework. Robert Lang and Karen Danielsen encouraged me to pursue an academic life in the first place and have served as unofficial academic advisors ever since. My current and former colleagues in the College of Urban and Public Affairs at the University of New Orleans have made working at UNO a real pleasure, encouraged my work in various ways, and have allowed me the flexibility to continue my investigations of global travel and tourism. My students have likewise made, and continue to make, working at CUPA a very pleasurable and rewarding experience.

In Mexico I would like to thank Daniel Hiernaux-Nicolas and Manuel Rodriguez Woog for sharing their knowledge of Mexico's tourism industry with me.

My research in India would have been much more difficult, if not impossible, without the friends I met along the way. Foremost among them are Parag Pradhan and the late S. Alam Habeeb, who answered what must to them have seemed like my interminable questions about India, let me tag along on their business outings, introduced me to some very interesting people, and generally looked after me. Parag and Habeeb opened my eyes to an India I had not known very well prior to meeting them and for that I will always be most grateful. I would also like to thank Parag's parents, Mr. Suresh Pradhan and Mrs. Rohini Pradhan, and his wife, Dr. Amita Pradhan, for their gracious hospitality. Many thanks are also due to Samson Suryawanshi, who helped me out on numerous occasions and taught me quite a lot about his country in the process. I would also like to thank my old friend and Hindi teacher Kailash Sagar and his family who likewise taught me things about India I would never have discovered on my own.

In Austria I would like to thank Jürgen Dolezal for reading the parts of my manuscript dealing with Zipolite and making many useful comments.

I must extend a special note of thanks to Dave McBride at Routledge who shepherded the book along from beginning to end. I would also like to thank Dave's associates: Angela Chnapko at Routledge, who played an instrumental role in making the book a reality; Julie Spadaro, project editor at Taylor & Francis; Scott Suckling at MetroVoice Publishing Services; and copyeditor Marti Jones.

Last but certainly not least I would like to thank my sister, Deborah Woodard, my brothers Lee Fineberg and Louis Fineberg, and my friends Beat Barblan, Tanya Van Order, Bennett Paris, Alda Costa, Alidad Mafinezam, and Aimee Préau for their unflagging support over the years.

I owe the greatest debt of all to my wonderful mother, Sheila Gladstone, and I dedicate this book to her.

Preface

The Varieties of Touristic Experience

Flights into Delhi's Indira Gandhi International Airport generally arrive in the early hours of the morning. Returning nationals, those visiting Delhi on business, nonresident Indians (known universally in India as *NRIs*), and a smaller number of foreign tourists filter through passport queues, customs checks, and bank counters before exiting the arrivals hall and officially entering the country. Most of the travelers disappear into the early morning darkness in Ambassador taxis and waiting cars, with some paying a few rupees for the Delhi Municipal Corporation bus and others paying a bit more for a special tourist bus that connects the international airport to the city's many starred hotels. I buy a ticket on the tourist bus for 30 rupees (about U.S.60¢), but not before observing a taxi driver charge two unsuspecting foreign tourists more than eight times the official price for the ride into the city. The smoky air is warm and moist, permeated with the odor of bidi cigarettes, diesel fumes, and mildew. The smell is a familiar one and brings back a lot of memories. This is my eighth trip to India in twelve years.

After picking up passengers at the domestic terminal, the bus heads into the city. Delhi consists essentially of three parts, a planned "new" Delhi constructed under British rule, an unplanned "old" Delhi (Shahjahanbad) that was once the capital of the Mughal Empire,[1] and a third part made up of numerous additions to the city, mostly in the form of residential sprawl. We head first into the newer, planned part of the metropolis, consisting of tree-lined avenues, low-density residential areas, government buildings, and foreign embassies. As the bus lurches along the Ring Road, I observe the shadowy outlines of the numerous posh, gated communities that have sprung up in recent years in south Delhi, enclaves of wealth that Delhiites often refer to as the "new" New Delhi (in contrast to Lutyens's "old" New Delhi). The conductor comes through the aisle checking tickets and fielding questions about where people want to go. I ask to be let off at the New Delhi railway station and settle in for the thirty-minute ride to my destination.

There are not many passengers on the bus: a couple of airport workers on their way home, an Indian businessman who asks to be let off at the Ashok

Yatri Niwas Hotel, and a small group of English tourists. It is still very early in the morning, and the streets are deserted, apart from some wayward cattle, the police, and groups of homeless people wandering up and down the otherwise empty sidewalks.

The bus slows down as it goes past the Taj Palace Hotel, then the Maurya Sheraton, one of the poshest five-star hotels in the capital, where rooms go for more than U.S.$400 per night. Most luxury hotels in India are fortresslike, and the Sheraton is no exception. Set back from the road, the architecture excludes; anyone seeking entry must run a gauntlet of security guards, doormen, and maîtres d'hôtel. The entire complex is gated and surveilled with video cameras twenty-four hours a day. Ordinary Indians and scruffy foreigners are not allowed inside. A similar scene awaits us as we pass some of Delhi's other five-star hotels: the Ashok, the Claridges, the Oberoi, and the Meridien. I know them all, having taken refuge in their air-conditioned splendor on more than one occasion during the sweltering Indian summers. The Meridien Hotel, in particular, stands out in my mind as the epitome of exclusionary architecture, its fully enclosed glass towers forming a world of their own, complete with restaurants, coffee shops, retail stores, hairstylists, atriums, and banquet halls.

The bus stops in front of the government-owned Ashok Yatri Niwas, a high-rise hotel just a few blocks from Connaught Place, New Delhi's commercial center. The hotel was constructed in the late 1970s, expressly designed for the Indian middle class and foreign budget tourists. It has deteriorated markedly since its opening; the entire complex has fallen into various stages of disrepair, its cave-like hallways reeking of mildew, buckets positioned strategically to collect dripping water, bare electrical wires hanging loose, and periodic electrical outages. Even in its deteriorated state, however, the Ashok Yatri Niwas continues to attract a large number of tourists because of its central location and its relatively inexpensive room rates (about U.S.$15 per room, 1997).[2] The other lodging alternatives are, on the upscale side, the dozen or so five-star hotels dotting the capital or, on the down-market side, the thousands of guesthouses, *dharamshalas* (pilgrims' rest houses), dormitories, and small hotels found in the alleys running off of Connaught Place, in Pahar Ganj, and in Old Delhi.

The bus pulls away from the Ashok Yatri Niwas and turns down Janpath, a major radial road running off of Connaught Place. We first pass the Kanishka Hotel,[3] a luxury government-owned facility, then the Imperial Hotel, one of the city's first five-star luxury hotels. As the bus turns onto the outer radial road of Connaught Place, the conductor asks the remaining passengers, at this point only the English tourists and myself, where we will be getting off. Finally we reach our destination, the New Delhi railway station, and file out of the bus into a group of touts (commission agents), who have obviously been waiting for us.

To a chorus of "Cheap hotel," "Cheap tickets to Kashmir," "Where do you want to go?" and, in Hindi, "Come to my hotel, sister-fuckers," I hurry past the crowd of touts who quickly part once I speak a few relevant words of Hindi, explaining that the hotel I am going to does not pay commission. Upon hearing this, they realize that I am not worth pursuing and refocus their attention on the other foreigners. The English tourists have by now taken out their guidebooks, a sure sign that these *Angrezi* (English persons) have only the vaguest idea where they are going. As I walk away from the railroad station into Pahar Ganj, I can hear the touts arguing among themselves about who will get what commission from what hotel proprietor for showing up with these particular tourists. Most likely, the price of the rooms will be inflated to include the touts' commissions.

It is still early in the morning. Apart from some stray dogs and a herd of cows, the streets are empty. Pahar Ganj is probably not the safest place in the city. I have personally been held up at knifepoint here, and I have known many other tourists who have been mugged and robbed here. I cautiously take in the surroundings as I walk the half-kilometer or so past numerous hotels, restaurants, and shuttered retail shops to my destination, a small, family-owned guesthouse in the center of the bazaar. The night manager and I recognize each other, and after a couple of cigarettes and a few minutes of conversation, I head for my room. .

I have known about this particular hotel for over a decade and usually stay here when I am in Delhi. By most Western accounts, the place would surely rate as a dive; crumbling paint on the walls, bed bugs in some of the rooms, squat toilets, and dirt everywhere. I stay here because it is inexpensive and, in a way, extremely entertaining. Most of the hotel's current residents are foreigners, which I confirm by checking the hotel registry. Many hotels in Pahar Ganj rent only to foreigners, but this particular hotel caters to Indians and non-Western foreign tourists, as well. Room rates start at about U.S.$2 per night for a single room with a common toilet and shower, and run as high as U.S.$3 for a double room with an attached bath. The hotel is officially illegal because it operates without the proper permits and licenses, a fact not lost on the local authorities, who routinely threaten to shut it down unless the owners pay them a "fine."

As I relax on the bed, I think to myself how different this place is from the half-dozen or so five-star hotels that we passed on the way from the airport— as different from each other as the West is from India and the Third World in general. In a way, five-star hotels such as the Meridien and the Hilton represent islands of the West in the heart of the Third World, enclaves of power and privilege surrounded by guard posts and, at times, barbed-wire fences. There is perhaps no greater contrast to these enclaves, I think, than the type of hotel in which I am staying. Here, I feel like I am in India. In the Meridien, however, I could be anywhere. My hotel certainly represents one end of the Indian hospitality industry, and the Hiltons, Hyatts, and Sheratons represent the other. Indeed, there are clearly two distinct tourism sectors in India, a formal sector of starred hotels and exclusive restaurants and an informal sector of small guesthouses and cheap *dhabas* (greasy spoons). But what is the relation between the two ends of the spectrum? Is there a relation? If so, does it hold across countries? What impact does each sector have on the economy and the society? Is there a large middle sector?

I knew already that this particular characteristic of the Indian tourism industry—upscale five-star luxury at one end of the spectrum, cheap lodgings and food at the other—is not unique to India. The pattern is replicated in countries as diverse as Thailand, Mexico, Nepal, Indonesia, Guatemala, Cuba, and China. One variable that seems to differ across countries, however, is the relative size of the two sectors. In India, for example, the informal tourism sector is much larger than the formal tourism sector, with few all-inclusive resorts and a small number of luxury hotels in the major cities. In Mexico, by contrast, the formal tourism sector appears much larger, with planned resort cities such as Cancún and Huatulco drawing millions of tourists a year, whereas smaller beaches and cultural centers attract far fewer tourists. Countries such as Thailand fall somewhere in between, with both a large upscale tourism industry and significant informal tourism facilities, ranging from cheap guesthouses in Bangkok to beach bungalows along the coast and on many of the country's islands.

I wake up the next morning soaked through with perspiration. Indian summers are notorious for their combination of oppressive heat and high humidity, and this one was proving no exception. None of the rooms in my hotel are air-conditioned. Air conditioning is a rarity in most Indian hotels, particularly those that cater to domestic travelers and international budget tourists. Most rooms have a fan, though, and when the power is on, they usually do the trick. Delhi and other Indian cities are prone to power outages, however, so for at least several hours a day, usually in the early morning, there is no power, no fan, and for many tourists that means a great deal of discomfort.

I soon discover that the shower in my room is not working. There is a bucket in the bathroom, however, so I fill it up with cold water and bathe in the traditional Indian way, squatting down and drawing water from the bucket with a small cup. Water is in extremely short supply in Delhi and sometimes runs out. "*Nahin pani ata hai*" ("there is no water") is an exclamation often heard in the type of hotel in which I was staying, as is "*nahin light ata hai*" ("there is no power").

I have always marveled at how well the Indians conserve resources by using them sparingly. The "bucket method" of showering is a perfect example. From the point of view of water conservation, I think, these small Indian hotels compare quite favorably with India's luxury hotels that re-create the West in a Third World context, right down to their needless waste of natural resources. My particular hotel had sunk a well, however, and water is usually available twenty-four hours a day. The hotel workers use an electric pump to transport water from the well to a holding tank on the roof. That way, in the event of a power outage, the upper floors are not left without water. The water tank is very dirty; one of the owners told me it has never been cleaned. Inevitably, some tourist drinks the tap water and gets sick. The owners of the hotel boil their drinking water, as do most residents of Pahar Ganj, and most tourists buy bottled water from the *choti ducan* (small shop) just outside the hotel entrance in the small *chowk* (square).

The cool water feels good in the heat. I pull out an Indian-tailored *kurta pyjama* (loose-fitting Indian clothing) from my knapsack, throw it on, and head out into the main bazaar. The tourist season had ended months before (in March) and would not pick up again until early October. (India receives most of its international visitors from October through March.) International tourist arrivals drop precipitously during the summer months. Even so, I still notice quite a few Western tourists in the bazaar. Most are probably going to or coming from the mountains in the north of the country. Ladakh, Manali, McLeod Ganj, and other tourist destinations are popular with many foreign travelers, and travel agencies in Pahar Ganj sell inexpensive bus tickets to these and other destinations. A couple of Israeli youngsters with Indian-made Enfield motorcycles drive past me, weaving their way in and out of the crowd. In typical Israeli-tourist fashion, they have custom-made handlebars fitted to their bikes, chopper-style. Touring India on an Enfield has become increasingly popular among foreign tourists, particularly those who come to India for extended periods of time. It is common to see foreign tourists riding motorcycles on India's busy national highways: National Highway 8 from Delhi to Ajmer, National Highway 1 from Delhi to Chandigarh, National Highway 21 from Chandigarh to Manali, and all along the Grand Trunk Road. Indeed, markets for secondhand Enfields are now found in Pushkar, Manali, Delhi, Goa, and other destinations popular with younger international travelers.

I have not eaten since I arrived in India, so I walk the half-kilometer or so to the station area where the bus had dropped me off the previous evening. The bazaar is busy, and I walk to a chorus of "Change money?" "Anything to sell?" "Carpets?" "Hashish?" "Brown?"[4] "Do you want to go to Kashmir?" Most of the people asking are either shopkeepers—who double as moneychangers—or commission agents working for someone else with a shop or office in the bazaar. Money is changed fairly openly, even though it is illegal. India has a large black market, and places such as Pahar Ganj are where tourists find out about it, mostly through changing money but also through buying and selling electronic items, whisky, *charas* (hashish), and other contraband goods.

I turn down an alleyway near the railway station featuring a half-dozen or so small South Indian cafes. I sit down in one and order a *masala dosa* (a rice-flour pancake filled with potatoes and spices) and a cup of *chai* (Indian tea). As I sit there eating, I offer greetings in Hindi to the man sitting next to me. He smiles but does not answer. The restaurant manager and the man exchange a few words, then the manager tells me that the man sitting next to me is from the south and does not speak Hindi. He had just arrived from Madras with his family. They are on their way to Haridwar, Rishikesh, then on to Badrinath, the source of the Ganges. Hindus revere each of these places, and millions of Indians from all over India travel to these holy pilgrimage centers each year. I finish my breakfast, pay the manager, and head back out into the bazaar.

As I walk back to my hotel, I think about the kinds of tourists who travel through Pahar Ganj. Most are neither stereotypical "ugly Americans" nor equally stereotypical camera-toting Japanese or Germans traveling in groups. Indeed, those kinds of tourists are rarely seen in Pahar Ganj. In all the years I had been coming to India, I had never seen a foreign tour group in Pahar Ganj or places like it. I do know, however, that Pahar Ganj attracts many Western tourists. Most of them are young people from Europe, Israel, and North America. Many are staying in my hotel and in dozens of similar hotels and guesthouses. In this respect, Pahar Ganj is a kind of tourist ghetto, a place with a very high concentration of foreign tourists (Calcutta, Kathmandu, Bangkok, and other cities I had traveled to also featured similar tourist ghettos). But even these foreign tourists are not typical of the type of tourist found in Pahar Ganj. Most tourists are like the man I met in the restaurant. Most are domestic tourists, not foreigners. Most are poor or middle class and certainly not wealthy in Western terms. Most travel on extremely limited budgets, often less than U.S.$3 a day. And without a doubt, such travelers are representative of the vast majority of tourists in India today.

Pahar Ganj, I think, is not some special tourist enclave that caters solely to scruffy foreigners, as a number of guidebooks claim. Pahar Ganj and similar tourist spaces are the rule in India and other Third World countries, not the exception. Its cheap restaurants and inexpensive lodging are what the vast number of Indian travelers can afford. How many Indians can pay over U.S.$300 per night to stay at the Oberoi, the Sheraton, or the Hyatt? After all, most Indians earn less than U.S.$2 per day, and even highly educated persons (engineers, lawyers, and other professionals) earn less than a few hundred dollars a month. Clearly, five-star luxury is out of the question for most Indians, and that is precisely why Pahar Ganj and places like it exist: because they cater to the travel needs of mainstream, ordinary Indians.

Tourist spaces such as Pahar Ganj, however, are rarely mentioned in the vast literature on tourism in Third World countries. Indeed, judging from the thousands of journal articles, books, and monographs on Third World tourism, one is almost forced to conclude that the only facilities catering to tourists are the relatively small number of five-star hotels, integrated resorts, wildlife game parks, and other "attractions" designed for domestic elites and international tourists from the wealthy countries. This investigation was therefore undertaken with a view to furthering our knowledge of the "other" forms of tourism in Third World countries. Who travels in low-income countries? For what reasons? What impacts do different groups of tourists have on the communities they visit? These are some of the questions I have attempted to answer in the following pages.

A methodological caveat: The Third World spans five continents, includes diverse cultures and peoples, and currently contains about two-thirds of the world's population, which is one of the reasons some people (Jeremy Seabrook, for instance) refer to it as the "Two-Thirds World." It is certainly true that low-income countries differ from each other in significant ways.[5] What is true of India may not necessarily be true of China, and what is true of China may not apply to Brazil. The problem of generalizing the findings of research conducted in one or two low-income countries to all the others is certainly fraught with difficulties, particularly if the research involves case studies in a small number of countries. I have tried to keep this in mind while completing the present study, especially when making general statements about tourism in the Third World as a whole.

Although I have traveled to many low-income countries over the last two decades, I have spent the most time in India and Mexico, two of my favorite places in the world, and continue to visit both countries on a fairly regular basis. Because of my familiarity with the two countries, I have referred mostly to them or specific places within them to illustrate the major points of the book. I have spent more time in India than in Mexico, which, including my latest trip in the winter of 2005, is roughly four years. I undertook my first journey to Mexico in 1997 and, with the exception of one year, have returned annually. Although I use mostly 1990s census and other data to support most of the points I make in the book, the observations and understandings that inform most of the case studies extend from the mid-1980s to 2005. Needless to say, despite many similarities, India and Mexico are two low-income countries with very different social, economic, and cultural systems. Whereas I observed a similar structure in the tourism industries of these two countries, they also differed in significant ways, most notably in the relative importance (magnitude) of different types of tourism and tourist facilities. Nonetheless, the conceptual framework developed in the present study applies to both countries and, to the best of my knowledge, to most countries in the Third World.

CHAPTER 1

An Overview of Tourism in the 2000s

The value of goods and services consumed by tourists and tourism-related firms exceeds U.S.$1.2 trillion annually and accounts for nearly four percent of gross world product (GWP), making travel and tourism one of the largest industries in the world in terms of value-added (World Travel and Tourism Council 1999, 2002). It is also among the world's largest export industries: In 2001, international travelers spent more than U.S.$465 billion on lodging, food and beverages, entertainment, transportation, and souvenirs—an amount exceeding total world exports of food (U.S.$437 billion), raw materials (U.S.$110 billion), iron and steel (U.S.$130 billion) and nearly equal to world exports of automobiles (U.S.$565 billion), fossil fuels (U.S.$616 billion), and chemicals (U.S.$595 billion) (World Trade Organization 2002; World Tourism Organization 2002a). In addition, the travel and tourism industry is a major source of employment worldwide; 71.9 million people work in tourism-related firms and another 126.7 million people are employed indirectly by firms supplying the travel and tourism industry with good, services, capital equipment, and infrastructure (World Travel and Tourism Council 2002).

Fueled by declining transport costs and globalization of both business and cultural activities, tourism has grown rapidly, relative to other industries. Between 1950 and 1996, international tourist arrivals and expenditures registered 7 and 12 percent average annual growth, respectively (World Tourism Organization 1997). International arrivals grew even faster during the 1990s, from 457.3 million in 1990 to 687.3 million in 2000, an average annual increase of over 7 percent (World Tourism Organization 2002a). When domestic tourists—who outnumber international tourists ten to one in the high-income countries and one thousand to one in many of the low-income countries—are taken into consideration, it is clear that tourism is an immense global phenomenon, easily exceeding 10 billion tourist arrivals per year (table 1.1).

The economic and demographic magnitude of tourism is important and its effects on the places where it occurs are equally significant. Cities, coastlines, and entire regions have been altered beyond recognition by the growth of the leisure industry. Miami Beach, Atlantic City, and Las Vegas, perhaps America's quintessential resort cities, owe their very existence to the tourism phenomenon (Gladstone 1998). Likewise, the Spanish Costas, Greek isles, many Caribbean and South Pacific microstates, Australia's Gold Coast, Brazil's Nordeste, Mexico's two coastlines, and scores of other places on every continent have become resort landscapes of hotels, marinas, time-share developments, and retail strips catering almost exclusively to tourists (figure 1.1). Tourism is also one of the major industries fueling urban growth in the 2000s. Convention centers, hotels, festival marketplaces, sports stadiums, historic preservation, and other developments are now part of many cities' urban revitalization efforts (Judd and Fainstein 1999).

Tourism development is not confined to the First World and the glitzy Third World resorts that Bob Shacochis (1989) refers to collectively as "Gringolandia." The wealthy countries of Europe, North America, and the Asia-Pacific region account for the largest share of world tourism expenditures but they do not account for the largest share of tourists, especially if we adopt the World Tourism

Table 1.1
Arrival of Overnight Visitors from Abroad, 1950–2000

Year	Total (thousands)	Index 1950 = 100	Receipts (U.S. $ millions)	Index 1950 = 100
1950	25,282	100	2,100	100
1960	69,320	274	6,867	327
1965	112,863	446	11,604	553
1970	165,787	656	17,900	852
1975	222,290	879	40,702	1,938
1980	285,328	1,129	105,313	5,015
1985	326,697	1,292	117,879	5,613
1990	457,647	1,810	268,310	12,777
1995	563,605	2,229	401,475	19,118
2000	687,300	2,719	473,400	22,543

Source: World Tourism Organization (1998a; 2005a; 2005b).

Figure 1.1 Cancún, Mexico

Organization (WTO) definition of a *domestic tourist* as "any person residing in a country who travels to a place within this same country" (World Tourism Organization 2002b). In India alone, pilgrimage centers such as Vrindavan, Haridwar, and Pushkar attract millions of visitors annually, and the 2001 Kumbha Mela festival held at the confluence of the Ganges, Yamuna, and legendary Saraswati Rivers in the city of Allahabad—the largest gathering of human beings in history—drew upward of 60 million visitors. In Mexico, the world's eighth most popular international tourist destination, domestic tourists make over 94 million business or leisure journeys each year, nearly five times the number of international arrivals reported in 2001 (Secretaría de Turismo 1996; World Tourism Organization 2002c). If we classify such travelers as tourists, the effects of tourism are as pronounced in the Third World as they are in the First, perhaps even more so.

Who Is a Tourist?

The United Nations-affiliated WTO defines an *international tourist* as "any person who travels to a country other than that in which s/he has his/her usual residence but outside his/her usual environment for a period not exceeding twelve months and whose main purpose of visit is other than the exercise of an activity remunerated from within the country visited" (World Tourism Organization

1998, 263). The WTO's definition is easily expanded to include domestic tourists, defined as any resident of a country traveling to a place within the same country for more than twenty-four hours and less than one year and within which they do not receive work-related remuneration (World Tourism Organization 2002a). As geographer and tourism researcher Douglas Pearce (1995) points out, the difference between domestic and international tourism is not one of distances traveled; Europeans making international journeys rarely travel further than the average domestic journey made by Americans on their vacations (1,335 kilometers).

The WTO also distinguishes between excursionists (day-trippers) and overnight tourists, defining an *international same-day visitor* as "a visitor who does not spend the night in a collective or private accommodation in the country visited" (World Tourism Organization 1998b, 263). International excursionists include cruise ship passengers and ship employees who return to the ship each night to sleep on board as well as overland travelers visiting a country for fewer than twenty-four hours. As with the WTO's definition of an international tourist, its definition of an excursionist is readily adapted to domestic tourism; domestic excursionists are residents of a country visiting a place other than their own for less than twenty-four hours and for reasons unrelated to employment in that place. Although most tourism statistics exclude same-day visitors, excursionists represent an important market for many international and domestic travel destinations. For instance, most tourists visiting Atlantic City and Manhattan are day-trippers, and a large percentage of Mexico's international tourist traffic takes the form of cross-border, day-long journeys (Port Authority 1994; Secretaría de Turismo 1996). There are approximately three times as many international excursionists as international tourists worldwide but in countries as otherwise diverse as Switzerland, Kuwait, and Slovenia, excursionists outnumber overnight tourists more than ten to one.

Tourist Typologies

Although travel and tourism involves very large flows of people both within and between countries, not all tourists share the same motivations for travel. The stereotype of the camera-toting American, European, or Japanese tourist in Bermuda shorts and a loud shirt is undoubtedly accurate with respect to a great many pleasure travelers from the wealthy countries, but a large number of people also travel on business or to visit family and friends. Even so, the distinction between business and leisure travelers is not hard and fast: Business travelers often combine a business trip with one or more days of pleasure travel, and both business and pleasure travelers stay with family and friends at their destinations. Confounding attempts to typologize tourists are the scores of pilgrims and other religious travelers who do not travel for business reasons and have little in common with most Western holidaymakers.

Or so it may seem. Anthropologists have long held that pleasure travel serves the same functions in industrial societies that pilgrimage serves in more traditional cultures (Graburn 1989; Turner 1973; Turner and Turner 1978). Leisure travel, like pilgrimage, is often liminal (it allows us to relinquish our ordinary social roles and expectations), it is socially and culturally sanctioned, and it often serves as a marker of social status. As anthropologist Nelson Graburn (1989, 28) notes, "For traditional societies the rewards of pilgrimages were accumulated grace and moral leadership in the home community [but] the rewards of modern tourism are phrased in terms of values we now hold up for worship: mental and physical health, social status, and diverse, exotic experiences."

Notwithstanding the parallels anthropologists have drawn between religious pilgrims and leisure tourists, most tourist typologies apply only to tourists from high-income countries and neglect the majority of travelers in the Third World. For example, Erik Cohen, a sociologist who has written extensively on tourism, classifies a tourist's experience on the basis of how travel relates to that person's "life-center," or orientation toward the values of Western industrial society. For most people in the First World, travel is recreational and usually undertaken for purposes of enjoyment or pleasure. The weekend trip to Las Vegas or Atlantic City, a week spent cruising around the Caribbean, and other experiences typical of Western tourists are, for Cohen, much akin to watching television or going to the theater. Such activities are consciously intended to "re-create" a person fully committed to the values of his or her own society, or life-center; thus, "recreational tourism is a movement away from the center, which serves eventually to reinforce the adherence to the center" (Cohen 1979, 185). A New York City investment banker returning from a two-week vacation in the Caribbean may very well exclaim that she feels like a new person, ready to rededicate herself to her career and her family with a renewed vigor and sense of purpose.

For smaller numbers of Western tourists alienated from the norms and values of their own societies, travel "becomes purely diversionary—a mere escape from the boredom and meaninglessness of routine, everyday existence, into the forgetfulness of a vacation, which may heal the body and soothe the spirit, but does not 'recreate'—i.e., it does not re-establish adherence to a meaningful centre, but only makes alienation endurable" (Cohen 1979, 185–186). Diversionary tourists travel not to re-center their lives in a taken-for-granted and existentially acceptable social and cultural reality but rather out of a sense of ennui and boredom.

An even smaller number of travelers, whom Cohen divides into experiential, experimental, and existential categories, differ markedly from mainstream leisure travelers and diversionary tourists. Experiential tourists are alienated from the norms of Western industrial society but look for meaning in the lives of others, seeking out what they take to be authentic places in cultures other than their own. Experimental tourists are similar, but

> While the traveler in the "experiential" mode derives enjoyment and reassurance from the fact that *others* live authentically, while he [*sic*] remains "disinherited" and content merely to observe the life of others, the traveler in the experimental mode engages in that authentic life, but refuses to commit himself to it; rather, he samples and compares the different alternatives, hoping eventually to discover one which will suit his particular needs and desires. (Cohen 1979, 189)

Cohen, who began writing about tourism in the 1970s during the heyday of the "hippie trail" from London to Kathmandu, points to drifter tourists, or young budget travelers from the West, as the largest contingent of experimental travelers.

Finally, existential tourists are people "fully committed to an 'elective' spiritual center, one external to the mainstream of [their] native society and culture" (Cohen 1979, 190). Examples of existential tourists are "the person who encounters in his visit to an Israeli kibbutz a full realization of his quest for human communion; the seeker who achieved enlightenment in an Indian asrama; the traveller who finds in the life of a remote Pacific atoll the fulfilment of his cravings for simplicity and closeness to nature" (Cohen 1979, 190). For Cohen, existential tourism is most similar to the traditional religious pilgrimage, with the important difference that pilgrims are traveling to a hallowed place, or center, of their *own* cultures and societies. Existential tourists, in contrast, adopt a center other than the one into which they were born or, as Cohen puts it, "[their] pilgrimage is not one from the mere periphery of a religious world toward its centre; it is a journey from chaos into another cosmos, from meaninglessness to authentic existence" (Cohen 1979, 191).

Cohen's is neither the only typology of tourists nor even the only one he has formulated. In an earlier work, he categorizes tourists on the basis of the environmental bubble in which they travel, defined as the degree of novelty or strangeness that a tourist is willing to accept while away from home (Cohen 1972). Mass institutional tourists, who demand the kinds of food, accommodation, and transportation most in keeping with what they are used to at home, stand at one end of the spectrum. Drifters are at the other end, a group of tourists most likely to adopt the practices and lifestyles of the people in the places they visit. Independent tourists and explorers are intermediate tourist types, with the former more closely resembling mass institutional tourists and the latter more similar to drifters.

In yet another tourist typology, travel and tourism consultant Stanley Plog classifies Western tourists according to their psychological dispositions (Plog 1974). The most adventurous and outgoing among them, the "allocentrics," are the first people to discover a destination and make do with what rudimentary tourist facilities they find there. To the extent that a tourist destination attracts only allocentric tourists, the total number of arrivals remains small, and the tourist infrastructure is relatively undeveloped. As a destination begins to develop its tourist facilities, it begins to attract more mainstream tourists, or "midcentrics," and the total number of arrivals begins to increase, slowly at first, then rapidly. Midcentric tourists are characterized by their willingness to experience some degree of novelty at their chosen destination, perhaps sampling different types of food or foregoing some of the comforts of home in exchange for a unique travel experience. "Psychocentrics," the least adventurous type of traveler, closely resemble Cohen's mass institutional tourists. They generally travel on chartered tours, stick to the same kind of food and accommodations they are used to at home, and travel for relatively short periods of time.

An Alternative Formulation of Third World Tourism

Because most tourist typologies deal only with tourists from Western industrial societies, they are hard to apply in China, India, Iran, Mexico, and other Third World countries where many travelers are pilgrims or temporary migrants and do not have the same motivations for travel as tourists from the United States, Western Europe, Australia, New Zealand, and Japan. Consider, for instance, the Himalayan pilgrimage center of Badrinath in the Indian state of Uttar Pradesh. Because it is the source of the Ganges, a river revered by devout Hindus, Badrinath receives hundreds of thousands of tourists annually, even though it lacks any international standard hotels and restaurants, and its tourism infrastructure is in general undeveloped. According to Plog's typology, we should expect most visitors to Badrinath to be adventurous and outgoing allocentrics, with perhaps a few midcentrics and virtually no psychocentric travelers. But virtually the exact opposite is the case: Whereas Plog's typology may be applicable to Western tourists visiting Badrinath, it is clearly inapplicable to Indian visitors, the majority of whom are poor and middle-class Indians who best fit into the midcentric and psychocentric tourist categories.

What then is an appropriate way of typologizing not only international travelers but *all* tourists in Third World countries? Because most tourists in low-income countries are domestic tourists, Cohen's idea of an environmental bubble has only limited relevance; hosts and guests share a similar culture, and any culture shock experienced by tourists will be minimal. In other words, there is never any choice but to remain within a cultural framework common to both host and guest.[1]

Dividing domestic tourists in Third World societies into a privileged sector of Westernized elites and a traditional sector of everyone else (religious pilgrims, informal-sector business travelers, poor people visiting family and friends, and leisure tourists on extremely limited budgets) goes far in accounting for all travelers in low-income countries. It is a typology based essentially on relative wealth and the entrée to the global consumer society that access to such wealth buys in the Third World. In this it differs from the typologies of Western tourists I considered earlier that do not take occupational status, class position, or income levels into account when discussing the varieties of tourist experience and the factors that motivate people to travel in the first place. It is easily extended to business travel, with Third World corporate executives and higher-level government officials more likely to frequent upscale hotels and other formal-sector tourism establishments, whereas informal-sector entrepreneurs and low-level government workers and more likely to patronize budget hotels and other informal-sector tourism businesses.

Typologizing domestic tourists on the basis of how their travel relates to a cultural or religious center is also useful in understanding the motivations of travelers in Third World countries, particularly those with long traditions of religious pilgrimage, such as India, Iran, and Mexico. Cohen employs this approach in his analysis of First World tourism through the concept of a social and cultural life-center, but his typology does not allow for the possibility that tourists might seek out religious centers in their own societies. They are either re-creating adherence to their own societies' ultimate values in leisure pursuits, alienated from those values in diversionary travel, or they are preoccupied with some other culture's values as experimental, experiential, or existential tourists.

Although pilgrimage in Western society is far from an extinct cultural form, relatively few tourists from First World countries go on pilgrimages to religious centers. Indeed, Cohen's tourist typology explicitly assumes that sizable numbers of Westerners are alienated from their own socioreligious traditions; experimental, experiential, and existential tourists are all in one way or another looking for or adopting the values of another culture or subculture. In the Third World, however, large numbers of people are not alienated from their own social and religious traditions and many undertake journeys for spiritual reasons. In India, an entire industry has grown up around this form of travel, complete with specialized travel agencies, particular types of accommodation (*dharamshalas, chattis, sarais, gurudwaras*[2]), specific kinds of eating places, and an array of gift and souvenir shops specializing in religious paraphernalia. The search for authenticity in the lives of others through tourism simply does not play a large role in the Third World, or at least not yet.

There is of course a sense in which a large number of people in low-income countries are adopting the ultimate values of an alien culture, one that has definite implications for how they view leisure and tourism in the most general sense (figure 1.2). The ultimate value is consumerism, which Winin Pereira and Jeremy Seabrook (1994, 221) describe as a new creed, the embodiment of "a conspicuous and garish culture now being projected worldwide, [one] that implicitly bears the promise to the people of the Two-Thirds

Figure 1.2 Connaught Place, New Delhi, India

World that they too can enjoy the material levels of consumption of the West." It is widely acknowledged by scientists, planners, and even the propagators and chief beneficiaries of the consumer society itself—the large transnational corporations (TNCs) based in the West—that only a minority of the world's citizens can partake of a standard of living now enjoyed by the middle classes of the rich countries. Quite simply, the rampant consumerism most people in the West take as their birthright is outstripping the regenerative capacities of the earth's ecosystems. Even so, the number of people in the Third World who can aspire to such consumption levels is now sufficiently large for TNCs to profitably promote the mythos of the consumer society to them, too.

Designer clothes outlets, Kentucky Fried Chicken, McDonald's hamburger restaurants, subcompact automobiles, and other markers of middle-class existence have become highly visible components of urban landscapes from São Paulo to New Delhi. The ideology embraced by the Third World consumers of such items is identical to the one propagated to and generally accepted by their Western counterparts. It should come as no surprise, therefore, that middle-class individuals in Third World societies increasingly view leisure time as an additional item of consumption. Indeed, family vacations taken "to get away from it all" are on the increase in India and other low-income countries, especially among the salaried employees of the large corporations and those in upper-level government positions, and a network of destinations has sprung up in the Third

World to cater to this growing market segment. I will consider the connections between a growing middle class and tourism in chapter 5.

Where Does It Occur?

Scholarly estimates of the magnitude of tourism are a lot like the story of the man looking under the streetlight for his lost car keys. Even though he lost them somewhere else, he looks under the light because it is easier to see there. Similarly, most studies of tourism focus on international tourist flows and assume that these represent a true indicator of the growth of the tourism industry because few domestic tourism statistics are available, especially in low-income countries. I have therefore divided the following discussion of tourism's demographic magnitude into two parts. The first part deals with the flow of international tourists, and the second part will take up the question of domestic tourism.

International Tourism

It is safe to say that every country in the world has tourists from abroad traveling within its borders who need to eat, drink, and sleep. Thus, every country has some kind of international tourism industry. Even so, international tourists and the businesses and institutions that serve them are not evenly distributed in space. Certain regions are more specialized in tourism than others, and countries and regions differ in their role as generating regions or markets for international tourism goods and services.

The WTO collects data on international tourist arrivals and departures, tourism receipts, and total tourist expenditure. According to the WTO, the vast majority of tourists, about two-thirds of the total, originate in the Organization of Economic Cooperation and Development (OECD) countries, with most coming from the United States, Western Europe, and Japan. The market for Third World tourism exports is highly concentrated and bears a strong similarity to the structure of other international export markets. Like petroleum, semiconductors, and textiles, the First World accounts for nearly 80 percent of the market for world tourism exports, with the United States and Western Europe together accounting for about 50 percent of all international tourism spending. In other words, tourism production in the Third World is geared to the metropolitan markets of First World countries. An analysis of concentration ratios, a measure of the share of a country's international tourism market accounted for by its three or four largest source markets, underscores this point very clearly and demonstrates that many tourism destinations in the Third World depend on just a few, mainly Western markets for the bulk of their tourism revenue (table 1.2).

Not surprisingly, the same countries supplying most of the world's international tourists also account for most of the world's tourist arrivals and expenditures. The high-income market economies of North America, Western

Table 1.2

First World Arrivals in Select Third World Countries, 1999 (All Figures % of Country's Total Arrivals)

Region	Canada	United States	Northern Europe	Western Europe	Southern Europe	Europe	United Kingdom	Japan	Australia	New Zealand
Bahamas	4.9	82.8				8.9				
Barbados	11.1	20.4				47.6				
Costa Rica	4.4	38.1				14.1				
Cyprus			59.7	19.8	4.8	95.0	47.5			
Fiji	3.3	15.2				16.4		8.4	36.1	21.1
Jamaica	8.0	69.7				16.8				
Kenya			0.2	0.3		0.6				
Mexico		91.7								
Morocco			5.9	31.7	10.5	49.2				
Saint Lucia	5.1	32.1				37.8				
Sri Lanka			20.4	37.0		64.6				
Tunisia			7.2	49.4		71.6				

Northern Europe = Denmark, Finland, Iceland, Ireland, Norway, Sweden, UK; Western Europe = Austria, Belgium, France, Germany, Luxembourg, Netherlands, Switzerland; Southern Europe = Greece, Italy, Portugal, Spain, Yugoslavia.

Source: World Tourism Organization (2001).

Europe, Japan, and Australia host about 60 percent of the world's international tourists, with the G-7 countries (the United States, Canada, Japan, the United Kingdom, France, Germany, and Italy) accounting for close to 40 percent of the total. Eight of the world's top ten tourism destinations are high-income countries (the exceptions are China and Mexico), and eight of the world's top ten tourism earners are likewise in the First World (here, the exceptions are China and Hong Kong; table 1.3). Accordingly, most tourist flows are between the core capitalist countries; the world's most traversed international boundary is the U.S.–Canadian border, followed by travel between the West European countries (Pearce 1995).

A clear distance decay function is also at work in the movement of international tourists, with people from the major tourism markets more likely to

Table 1.3

World's Top Twenty International Tourist Destinations, 2002

Country	Arrivals (millions)	Rank	Earnings (U.S.$ billions)	Rank
France	77.0	1	32.3	3
Spain	51.7	2	33.6	2
United States	41.9	3	66.5	1
Italy	39.8	4	26.9	4
China	36.8	5	20.4	5
United Kingdom	24.2	6	17.6	7
Canada	20.1	7	9.7	11
Mexico	19.7	8	8.9	13
Austria	18.6	9	11.2	8
Germany	18.0	10	19.2	6
Hong Kong (China)	16.6	11	10.1	9
Hungary	15.9	12	3.3	32
Greece	14.2	13	9.7	10
Poland	14.0	14	4.5	25
Malaysia	13.3	15	6.8	19
Turkey	12.8	16	9.0	12
Portugal	11.7	17	5.9	20
Thailand	10.9	18	7.9	15
Switzerland	10.0	19	7.6	17
Netherlands	9.6	20	7.7	16

Source: World Tourism Organization 2005c; 2005d.

travel shorter distances and less likely to venture further afield (Pearce 1995). Thus, the United States represents the largest market for the Caribbean and Mexican tourism industries, whereas relatively few Americans but many West Europeans travel to North Africa. Similarly, Germany represents the largest market for Greece but not Mexico or the Caribbean. There are some exceptions (for example, the United States is Israel's largest tourism market), but proximity to major First World markets is an important factor explaining the relative development of the tourism industry in Third World countries, a factor I will explore more fully in chapter 2.

Although the tourism industry in Third World countries has grown rapidly over the last fifty years, not all countries and regions have grown at the same rate and, for many low-income nations, arrivals have grown significantly faster than tourism revenues. Africa and East Asia have increased their share of international arrivals, and North America and Western Europe have seen their shares decline. Overall, Third World international arrivals have grown faster and First World arrivals slower than the growth of world arrivals since 1950, which is not too surprising, given the relatively small number of international visitors to Third World countries prior to the advent of long-haul jet aircraft.

Receipts from tourism have grown more slowly than arrivals in many Third World countries and regions. Africa, for example, increased its share of international arrivals but saw its share of total tourism receipts decline from 1980 to 1993. The same is true of Mexico, one of the world's leading tourist destinations. One explanation for the Third World's declining share of international tourism receipts and rising share of international arrivals is greater competition among receiving countries for a growing but still limited number of First World tourists. Another is the structural adjustment programs imposed on debtor nations by ruling elites in concert with the International Monetary Fund, the World Bank, and other international economic institutions. Over 100 countries in the Third World have adopted some form of structural adjustment since the early 1980s. The purpose is to reprogram the economies of debtor nations to transfer income to the large banks and financial institutions based in the North. In essence, structural adjustment policies depress domestic consumption and investment through currency devaluation and the maintenance of high interest rates. At the same time, exports expand, and the foreign exchange so generated is transferred to the country's foreign creditors. Because international tourism is an export, it should come as no surprise that more people travel from the First World to indebted Third World nations to take advantage of the travel bargains found there. At the same time, total revenues fall because exchange rates and the terms of trade often favor people in high-income countries.

Mexico provides a good example. The impact of structural economic reforms in Mexico, especially the devaluation of the peso, is clearly evident in the country's ranking among international tourism destinations. In 1985, Mexico was the world's ninth most popular destination and the tenth largest tourism exporter; by 1996, it had become the world's seventh most popular international destination but had fallen to sixteenth place in terms of international tourism receipts. Devaluation has had a marked effect on the demographic structure of the country's tourism industry. For example, prior to successive devaluations during the "lost decade" of the 1980s, Cancún, which is currently Mexico's most popular international tourist destination, attracted mostly domestic tourists; it was not until a sharp fall in the price of the peso that Cancún became a center of international tourism.

In summary, the picture that emerges from WTO data is one of a truly global but highly concentrated industry. Most international tourists are from the First World countries, and most of these tourists head for destinations in other First World countries. The vast bulk of tourist dollars originate in the OECD countries, the same places where they are spent. Most international tourists to the Third World are from the First World, and the Third World today accounts for a small but growing share of total international arrivals, although with the exception of East Asia, its share of tourism receipts is either stagnating or declining.

Domestic Tourism

International tourism is only the tip of the iceberg as far as total global tourist arrivals are concerned. An accurate assessment of global tourism must include domestic tourist flows as well, a problematic contention, given the paucity of data on domestic tourism worldwide. As Pearce notes, despite its magnitude, "comparatively little research has been undertaken into domestic tourism flows" (Pearce 1995, 67). He refers here to domestic tourism in the First World nations. In the Third World, even less is known of the patterns and magnitude of domestic travel. At least a part of the problem in measuring domestic tourism inheres in the very nature of the tourist commodity: Unlike most other commodities, tourism goods and services are largely defined in terms of who consumes them. Because both residents and tourists eat in restaurants, shop in retail stores, stay in hotels, and visit museums, it has been notoriously difficult for social science researchers and industry officials to accurately separate and measure the impact of tourists, particularly domestic tourists. Despite the lack of data, however, it is clear that domestic tourists greatly outnumber international visitors, especially in large Third World countries such as China, Mexico, or Brazil. In this section, I outline the dimensions of domestic tourism in the Third World, paying particular attention to India, a country with a very large domestic tourism component.

Although it is primarily concerned with the collection and publication of international tourism data, the WTO publishes statistics on domestic tourism for select countries and estimates domestic tourism arrivals worldwide as ten times greater than international arrivals, or about 7.5 billion arrivals per year in 2004. For at least two reasons, this is a gross underestimate of the total number of domestic tourists.

First, the WTO does not collect its own data but relies instead on national reporting agencies to supply it with their tourism statistics. International tourism arrivals data are usually compiled on the basis of landing cards passengers complete at the port of entry. Few countries keep records on domestic arrivals, however, and in very few cases do governments or tourism ministries standardize and regularly tabulate data on domestic tourism. Some countries require hotels to report their arrivals to data collection agencies but even in these cases, travel not involving an overnight stay in a hotel or similar establishment is not recorded. What is not recorded is not reported to the WTO.

Second, WTO data include domestic tourism activity in large, formal-sector establishments and exclude informal-sector tourist activity. This is perfectly understandable because one of the hallmarks of informal economic activity is its unregulated, and hence unenumerated, nature. In Mexico, for example, *posadas* (inns) do not generally require guests to register, and in many cases even the owners do not know how many tourists have stayed at their hotels in a given year. Those who do know rarely report the figures to the federal authorities.

India provides a very good example of how a large domestic tourism industry is compatible with a country that attracts relatively few international tourists. (South Asia as a whole, which includes India, accounts for less than 1 percent of the world's annual international tourist arrivals.) The WTO does not provide any statistics for India's domestic tourism industry, but based on the WTO's domestic arrivals figures for other countries, we might take 20 million tourists per annum as a first approximation of India's domestic tourist arrivals, ten times the country's 2 million annual international tourist arrivals in 1998.

Data provided by both the Indian Railways and the Indian Census Administration, however, indicates that 20 million tourists is a gross underestimate of India's annual domestic tourist traffic. According to Indian Railways, approximately 5 million tourists per *day* make an overnight journey on a train somewhere on the subcontinent. Recalling the WTO's definition of a tourist as anyone traveling away from home for a period exceeding twenty-four hours, then based just on India's rail ridership figures, the country registers close to 2 billion domestic tourist arrivals per year. Even if we assume that bus journeys in India carry half the traffic of the railroads (probably an underestimate, because buses serve most of the areas that are not accessible by rail and many that are), then domestic tourist arrivals in India exceed 3 billion per year, or 1,500 times the number of foreign tourists the country hosts annually. If we include excursionists in the equation, the number of Indian domestic tourists approaches 3,000 times the number of foreign tourists visiting the country annually.

Perhaps even more revealing is the huge discrepancy between international standard tourism establishments and the country's total number of tourism-related enterprises. Government-approved hotels in India, ranging from a no-star rating to a five-star deluxe rating, total just over 2,000 establishments. If we include hotels awaiting government approval, the number increases to 2,500. Such facilities cater overwhelmingly to foreign tourists and the Indian upper classes and are found disproportionately in the country's major cities.

According to the Indian census, however, there are over 400,000 hotels, guesthouses, *dharamshalas*, *sarais*, *chattis*, and other accommodation facilities in India, more than 150 times the number of approved hotels. There are more than 6,000 accommodation facilities in Bombay alone. If we assume that these facilities cater overwhelmingly to domestic tourists, it is easy to see how large the domestic tourism component is in India relative to the international tourism sector.

The WTO's estimate that domestic tourist arrivals worldwide are approximately ten times the number of international arrivals implicitly assumes that poor people who live in Third World countries do not travel and hence are never tourists, an assumption shared by many First World tourism researchers. David Harrison (1994, 719), for example, concludes, "very poor societies do not attract tourists and investment in infrastructure and international-standard accommodation and other facilities are prerequisites for a successful tourism industry." This assumption is completely unwarranted, however, as the Indian case clearly shows. India, Mexico, Brazil, Indonesia, and other countries with large populations of poor people also have enormous domestic tourism industries, although few hotels, restaurants, and transport facilities measure up to the standards demanded by most international travelers. Once we recognize that poor people in Third World nations do in fact make frequent journeys for various reasons, our concept of the relative magnitude of global tourism changes considerably.

What Does It Mean? The History and Cultural Significance of Tourism

If one accepts the WTO's definition of tourists as people who travel away from their homes for less than a year without receiving compensation from individuals or businesses in the places they visit, it is clear that tourism has been around for quite some time and possibly for as long as people have had homes. Most historians of tourism, however, usually focus on leisure travel and date the phenomenon to eighteenth-century England, when increases in national wealth associated with the industrial revolution allowed the landed gentry to travel through continental Europe on what came to be known as the Grand Tour (Cormack 1998). Some historians are even more precise in the date they assign to the beginning of modern leisure travel. Fred Inglis (2000), for example, claims modern tourism began with the end of the Seven Years War in 1763, when peace in Western Europe made travel there safer and easier than it had been before the cessation of hostilities. Perhaps not coincidentally, the word *hotel* in its current usage dates to 1765 (Cormack 1998). Regardless of the date one assigns to the beginning of leisure travel, however, it is clear that for most of the world's population, travel before the modern era was arduous, difficult, and dangerous. One author, writing in 1891, comments of travelers in the days before the railroads, "They took solemn leave of their friends and relations; they made their wills, and requested the prayers of the congregation that they might reach their destination and return home in safety" (Rae 1891, 5).

It would take nearly a century after the close of the Seven Years War for mass tourism to become a viable proposition in Europe. The person scholars most often point to as bringing tourism to the people is Thomas Cook, an English wood-turner and missionary who organized the first group tours on England's emerging railway system. Cook began by offering cheap excursion tickets to working- and middle-class individuals and their families, first in England itself, then to Wales and Scotland, which, despite their close proximity to England, were for the most part unknown to most English residents.[3] Tours to continental Europe and the Middle East followed, and within fifty years of operating his first excursion tour from Leicester to Loughborough, Cook's firm had become one of the world's leading travel agents, with offices on four continents, a fleet of steamers on the Nile, and even a branch office in India organizing tours to Mecca for Indian Muslims. Three factors that more than anything else fueled increased tourism in England and other European and North American countries were a slowly rising standard of living for the working and lower-middle classes, increased leisure time, and the rapid growth and declining cost of rail travel (Cormack 1998; Inglis 2000; Rae 1981).

From a cultural perspective, one of the interesting things about the early history of tourism in Europe and North America is the development of attitudes and practices that closely parallel those of later years. Disdain for the mass tourist is certainly one. Perhaps because of the sharply defined class structure of nineteenth-century England, it did not take long for upper-class individuals to develop negative stereotypes of middle- and working-class leisure travelers. As early as the 1860s, a "Cook's tour" was the object of ridicule, associated with the idea of herds of tourists despoiling what had been pristine and picturesque places (Rae 1891). Another theme common to both the nineteenth and twenty-first centuries is the toll that mass tourism often takes on destination communities. In connection with Cook's early tours to Scotland, Cook chronicler W. Fraser Rae (1891, 39) noted how quickly the excitement of hosting tourists from England dissipated: "There was no continuance of the enthusiasm which the first party of pleasure-seekers from England excited when its members reached Glasgow and Edinburgh. Bands did not play on the arrival of every party, neither were there speeches made in their honour." Other themes resonating through the centuries are romantically inspired drifting and sex tourism, both of which I discuss in later chapters.

Most histories and anthropological studies concerned with the meaning of tourism deal exclusively with First World tourists, focusing on tourism in Western society or on how an influx of people from high-income countries affects traditional Third World cultures. Dennison Nash (1996) points to three recurrent themes or research questions in his review of the anthropological literature on tourism. The first concerns the reasons people in the First World countries become tourists. What role does tourism, the liminal act of separating oneself from one's daily routine, play in re-creating the individual? A second and related group of studies deals with the political, cultural, and economic conditions in First World countries that give rise to tourism in the first place. What is it, these authors ask, that generates such large numbers of travelers in First World countries? A third group of studies deals with the effects of tourism on host societies in the Third World. Anthropological analysis is particularly germane to this type of investigation because it often involves an understanding of how Third World cultures adapt to an influx of Western tourists. Although the following discussion of what tourism means in the contemporary world is largely based on scholarly studies of the tourism phenomenon in the First World and in Third World tourism resorts catering to mostly First World travelers, it has increasing applicability to domestic tourism in Third World countries, a theme I will elaborate on more fully in chapters 5 and 6.

Tourism and Postmodernism

A good place to begin a discussion of the meaning of tourism is with the idea of commodification. Throughout the post–World War II period, rising incomes, increasing leisure time, and decreasing transport costs have combined to spur the growth of the tourism industry, particularly in the high-income nations of Western Europe, North America, and Australasia. Although in the past, only the elite could partake of tourism in the tradition of the European grand tour, now the vast majority of First World tourists are middle class. Just like automobiles and refrigerators, tourism goods and services have become mass-produced commodities that most families want and can afford. To the degree that travel and tourism in the First World are commodified—a very great degree in the late twentieth century—hosts and guests in a tourist exchange become buyers and sellers, a development underscoring an important aspect of late modernity: Places and the cultures specific to them are bought and sold in the market like any other commodity (Watson and Kopachevsky 1994).

Tourism lends itself so readily to postmodern theorizing precisely because of its semiotic qualities and the many ways in which the tourism industry manipulates, decontextualizes, and at times even creates mass culture. Professor and cultural critic Todd Gitlin, for example, characterizes postmodernism as a cultural form that

> self-consciously splices genres, attitudes, styles. It relishes the blurring or juxtaposition of forms, stances, moods, cultural levels. It disdains originality and fancies copies, repetition, the recombination of hand-me-down scraps. (Gitlin 1988, 1)

Gitlin provides a number of examples of postmodern places, including Disneyland, Las Vegas, suburban strips, and shopping malls, to which we might add reconstructions of heritage sites, New York City's Times Square redevelopment, downtown festival marketplaces, and residential theme parks. The de/recontextualization of tourist space so remarked on by postmodern theorists and critics of mass tourism blurs the distinction between signifier and signified, copy and original, so much so that, as Eco puts it, "really real is the absolute fake" (Eco 1986, 7).

Such postmodern spaces of consumption are no longer, or perhaps have never been, confined to the high-income countries of the North. Entire Third World spaces have been rewritten, reconfigured, even created from scratch to match up with the cultural expectations of middle-class North Americans, Europeans, and Japanese. The people who planned the Mexican resort city of Cancún, for example, consciously modeled it after a Disney World exhibit, seeking to re-create on the resort island a sense of "Mexicanness" familiar to tourists from the United States (Alarcón 1997). Bob Shacochis (1989, 42) calls it *Gringolandia*, "the network of fun-in-the-sun destinations, the honeyed cash traps, the Otherly fantasylands erected up the mountains and down the coasts of what we call the Third World or the developing world or the post-colonial world." Shacochis focuses on Mexico's publicly subsidized, built-from-the-bottom-up integrated tourist cities of Cancún, Ixtapa, and Huatulco but other examples abound in the Caribbean, Asia, Africa, and Latin America (see figure 1.3). I will consider Mexico's megaresort complexes and their impact on local, regional, and national populations in chapter 3.

Tourism and Authenticity

As noted above, many tourism researchers and cultural critics point to the commodification of the tourist experience as the key to understanding how and why culture and history are prepackaged and manipulated in many tourism destinations. Hospitality and entertainment corporations are in the business of selling experience of different kinds, so that the representation

Figure 1.3 Hilton Cancún Beach and Golf Resort

of the experience becomes as important as the experience itself. By playing on individuals' desire to consume images and representations of the places they visit or, in other words, by orchestrating the spectacle, tourism firms are able to translate consumers' anticipation of experience into the sale of actual tourism commodities, which is why advertising and other forms of marketing play such an important role in promoting the tourism industry worldwide.

The routine manipulation of tourist environments is also germane to the issue of authenticity, another recurrent theme in the study of tourism. Since the early 1960s, when author and cultural critic Daniel Boorstin chided the tourism industry for purveying—and mass tourists for pursuing—hollow images rather than reality, sociologists and anthropologists have dealt at length with the issue of authenticity and how it relates to culture, not only of tourists but also of the societies they visit. One line of argument is that because many tourism-related activities are staged solely for the benefit of tourists, tourists' experience is inauthentic and devoid of any real meaning. Critics of mass tourism point to the manufacture of tourist spectacles, the "staged authenticity" that extends from contrived "native" dances in the Third World to the multibillion-dollar theme parks in the high-income countries. Tourists' search for authenticity is ultimately confounded, however, by the commodification of tourism in modern societies: Authenticity is replaced by staged authenticity—by inauthentic production for the market—and the alienation tourists seek to escape is reproduced in their experience as tourists (MacCannell 1976). It is ironic but not surprising, therefore, that "while modern tourists typically hanker for leisure as a respite from deeply alienating, routine work, and presumably as an effective counterbalance to the pressures of work, in the very nature of the commodification of modern tourism, the sense of alienation seems to follow the travelers into their touristic adventures" (Watson and Kopachevsky 1994, 649).

More recently, critics have made similar arguments about culturally and environmentally sensitive forms of travel, known variously as *alternative tourism, responsible tourism, green tourism,* or *ecotourism.* They point to the same commodification of the tourist experience found in more traditional forms of tourism, the only difference being the nature of the commodity and the relative size of the market. Affluent Westerners now enjoy "unique travel experiences" and "tourist-free, out-of-the-way destinations," where "large numbers of middle- and lower-class tourists are not welcome, nor are 'hippies' in any number, but small numbers of affluent, well-educated and well-behaved tourists" (Butler 1992, 40). In this view, the commodification and inauthenticity of the tourist experience proceeds apace with the new tourist forms, despite the fact that promoters of alternative forms of tourism often tout them as authentic travel experiences.

Given the fact that many activities falling under the "tourist gaze" are contrived, artificial, and inauthentic, the question still remains: Is inauthentic experience necessarily bad and something that people should avoid? Or are staged spectacles and cultural events authentic in their own right, that is, are they authentically inauthentic? This kind of question gets at the heart of Marxist debates surrounding false consciousness, ideological hegemony, and similar concepts. The problem is largely reducible to one of standpoint: From whose standpoint are we to judge some experiences authentic and others inauthentic? Is one's experience of Disney World any less valid than one's experience of "authentic" cultural events, whatever they are? In short, the distinction between authentic cultural experience and inauthentic tourist experience begs the much larger epistemological question of what constitutes authentic knowledge and what does not. The debate on authenticity in the tourism literature does not, I feel, adequately deal with this admittedly philosophical problem.

There is, of course, an argument against framing the authenticity question in epistemological as opposed to commonsensical terms. By claiming that even inauthentic experiences are valid, we tend to bypass the question of what kinds of travel experience impart a greater feel for the life of the places we visit as tourists. This is especially true in the Third World, where the living arrangements of tourists staying in upmarket hotels differ completely from those of ordinary citizens. For example, which tourist experience is more likely to impart a better feel to the Western tourist for the culture and society of India: (1) staying at the Sheraton, Intercontinental, Hyatt, Hilton, or other five-star hotel in a cordoned-off enclave with mostly other tourists of the same socioeconomic station; traveling in air-conditioned buses and taxis, and eating Western food in deluxe restaurants or (2) staying in a modest guesthouse, bathing with a bucket of cold water, eating at local restaurants (and perhaps getting a stomach bug), and traveling on rickshaws and local buses and trains? Clearly, the answer is the latter, if by "authentic" we mean a travel experience providing the most insight into the living conditions of the vast majority of hosts—in this case, Indians. Indeed, if travel is supposed to bring about cultural understanding—perhaps a dubious claim—then enclaves of wealthy, white Europeans with no meaningful contact with the "natives" other than as people to fetch some tea or clean the room cannot possibly further this goal.

We must, however, immediately qualify the preceding statements, because it is possible to make exactly the opposite argument under a different set of conditions. For example, who is more likely to gain insight into the "real" India: a wealthy Nepali businessman who can communicate with Indians in their own language and who understands many aspects of Indian culture but who stays at a five-star hotel and travels in air-conditioned taxis; or a young American tourist who bathes with a bucket and stays in an inexpensive guesthouse but who has no knowledge of Indian customs, cannot speak any Indian languages, and has no idea why Indians harass her for wearing religious garments inappropriately? That we seem to know in each case who is more likely to have an authentic experience points to both the slipperiness of the authenticity concept and the fact that Western and non-Western tourists may have very different experiences in Third World countries.

Even so, there is still a problem with simply saying that any experience is an authentic one, even an inauthentically authentic experience, and it is closely related to the "anything goes" attitude of postmodern theorists. In arguing against any kind of critical reference point or grand narrative, as they put it, and in their insistence on the social construction of reality, postmodern epistemologists are often all too accepting of the status quo. Thus, in the postmodern sense of "any tourist experience is an authentic experience," enclave resorts are as good as any other type of tourist facility, even those that conform more closely to the living conditions of the local population. In validating these kinds of tourist experiences, however, the entire edifice of economic, social, and environmental domination that enclave resorts are founded upon are likewise validated as "part of the experience," right down to the beggars and child prostitutes who await the tourists just outside the gates. Arguments of the relative nature of authentic experience thus form a crucial link in the ideological structures of imperialism, what political scientist Linda Richter seems to have had in mind when she observed that underdevelopment may serve to bolster a country's tourism industry: "Nations which are veritable hellholes for most of their citizens are sold as 'unspoiled paradises' to outsiders" (Richter 1992).

It is the manufactured and staged qualities of tourist attractions that critics point to when discussing authenticity in tourism. For Dean MacCannell and many other tourism scholars, the concern with authenticity is characteristic only of Western societies or, more correctly, with Western tourists who travel to the Third World in search of authenticity. But is the authenticity debate relevant only to the experience of Western tourists? Is it, like postmodernism, only a part of the cultural logic of *late* capitalism (Jameson 1984)? Or does it apply to the touristic experiences of Third World people as well? In other words, can pilgrims in India have inauthentic experiences or are their experiences by definition always authentic?

Tourism scholars have generally not addressed these or similar questions. They are important questions to ask, however, because so many of the world's tourists live in low-income countries, and I will address them when discussing the impact of Third World domestic tourism in chapters 5 and 6. In the next chapter, I turn to the task of conceptualizing the impact of tourism in the Third World, incorporating findings from this chapter that indicate the broad reach of the tourism phenomenon, not just in high-income countries but in low-income countries as well.

CHAPTER 2

Conceptualizing Travel and Tourism
in Third World Countries

Las Bahías de Huatulco, *Huatulco* for short, is a relative newcomer to Mexico's burgeoning tourism industry. Located about four hundred kilometers south of Acapulco in the poor southern state of Oaxaca, Huatulco is the latest in a series of megaresorts planned by the Mexican government for the express purposes of diversifying export production and generating regional economic growth. Set against a backdrop of the Sierra Madre, Huatulco stretches along Mexico's Pacific Ocean coastline for over thirty kilometers, encompassing nine tranquil bays. The project is ambitious by just about any standard. With the first phase of construction nearly complete, the resort city already attracts hundreds of thousands of tourists annually, has more than 3,500 hotel rooms, and features the world's largest Club Méditerranée holiday resort. There is a new international airport, recently expanded to accommodate Boeing 757 aircraft. When finished in 2018, Huatulco will spread out over 52,000 acres, host more than 2 million tourists annually, and feature more than 35,000 hotel rooms, exceeding even Cancún in its geographic scope and total number of tourist arrivals.

Less than twenty-five years ago, however, what is today Huatulco was an isolated stretch of coastline with no electricity, sewage system, or phone lines. About a thousand people lived there, and most residents were either smallholding farmers or fisherfolk. There were neither paved roads nor concrete structures, and the only access to the region was along a rugged dirt path. As a part of its plan, the National Fund for the Promotion of Tourism (FONATUR), the government agency responsible for developing Huatulco, evicted the residents from their homes near the water and relocated them inland. FONATUR planned and constructed a separate town for the workers who built the resort and for those who would eventually work in the hotels, restaurants, and other tourism establishments. The population of the region soared, with many of the new residents migrating from Oaxaca City, Mexico City, and points even further afield. Many came looking for work. Others came to open businesses. Still others came to work in the government ministries and for FONATUR itself, which remains actively engaged in building the massive resort complex.

Vrindavan is a small Indian town halfway around the world from Huatulco. Located about 150 kilometers south of New Delhi in a predominantly poor, agricultural region, it is known all over India as the playground of Lord Krishna, one of the more popular Hindu deities. Along with Goverdhan, Radhakund, Mathura, and numerous other towns and villages, Vrindavan forms part of a larger region known as Braja Mandal, an area that attracts millions of religious pilgrims and Krishna devotees every year (figure 2.1).

The religious imprint is everywhere to be seen in Vrindavan. The town, with a population of 50,000 year-round residents, is built along the Yamuna, a holy river revered by devout Hindus. Temples and *ashramas* (monasteries) line the river's banks (Vrindavan is reputed to contain over 5,000 Hindu temples). In its waters, hundreds of people and sometimes thousands during particularly auspicious times perform ablutions throughout the day. *Bhajans* (religious

Figure 2.1   Vrindavan India

songs) blare from loudspeakers, and the sweet smells of *agarbathi* (incense) are everywhere. During religious festivals, the town is literally choked with foot traffic and *tongas* (horse-drawn carriages), the areas around the major temples virtually impassable.

The local economy is based almost completely on the tourist trade, just as it has been from times immemorial. Every morning dozens of tourist buses from Delhi, Agra, and other cities turn off the main highway and make their way into Vrindavan's dusty center, their passengers soon disappearing into the hustle and bustle of the town's central market area. Many will stay in *chattis* and *dharamshalas*, simple accommodation facilities located near the major temples. Gift shops and souvenir stands line Vrindavan's bazaars, and in the back streets of the town and surrounding areas, scores of *mukut wallahs* (adornment-makers for temples) ply their trade. A large number of *dhabas* (inexpensive restaurants) cater to the pilgrims, as do dozens of *chai* (tea) shops and *paan* (betel nut) stands. *Dudhwallahs* (milk sellers) do a brisk business as well, selling both hot sweetened milk and *rabri*, a sweet made from boiled milk and spices.

In just about every respect, the growth of tourism has completely transformed and continues to transform both Huatulco and Vrindavan. The social, cultural, economic, and physical impact of tourism in these two places is immense. Yet the kind of tourism in each place is very different. Huatulco attracts a large number of foreign tourists. Vrindavan attracts relatively few international tourists. Mexican state authorities planned Huatulco and continue to funnel public subsidies into its development. The development of Vrindavan was completely unplanned and receives little in the way of public subsidies. When it is finished in 2018, FONATUR expects Huatulco to attract over 2 million tourists annually. Vrindavan already attracts over 2 million tourists per year. Huatulco features many international-class, five-star hotels. Vrindavan has none. Most tourists in Huatulco are motivated primarily by secular concerns. Most tourists in Vrindavan are religiously motivated. Formal-sector enterprises predominate in Huatulco. Informal-sector enterprises are the norm in Vrindavan.

In short, although Vrindavan and Huatulco are both major Third World tourist centers, they differ enormously with respect to the organization of their tourism industries and the impact that tourism development has had and continues to have on each of them. Although both Vrindavan and Huatulco attract travelers throughout the year and their economies depend almost exclusively on them, many scholars of Third World tourism cannot distinguish Huatulco from Vrindavan because they do not recognize Vrindavan and places like it as tourist centers. In this chapter, I will address the oversight by developing a conceptual framework within which to view the impact of tourism development in the Third World, one that will attempt to account for all tourism development and not just Western-style resorts catering exclusively to national elite groups and foreign tourists. It is a conceptual framework based on both the type of tourist that frequents a destination (domestic or foreign) and the predominant type of tourist establishment found there (formal sector or informal sector). In subsequent chapters I will then seek to evaluate and compare the impact of four distinct kinds of tourism destinations in low-income countries: international formal-sector (IFS) destinations, international informal-sector (IIS) destinations, domestic formal-sector (DFS) destinations, and domestic informal-sector (DIS) destinations (figure 2.2). In the balance of this chapter, I will further develop a conceptual framework that builds on the tourist typologies presented in chapter 1 and theories of formality and informality in the Third World.

Tourists

The previous chapter dealt with tourist motivations and how these differ among different types of domestic and international tourists. I will offer only a few additional comments here, with specific reference to the conceptual schema represented in figure 2.2. To begin with, dividing Third World tourism destinations into two groups—one oriented to international tourists and another oriented to domestic tourists—has a certain prima facie validity to it. Whereas tourist destinations such as Cozumel and Cancún in Mexico, Phuket in Thailand, and most Caribbean resorts attract mostly international tourists, others, such as India's hill stations, the Tabasco coast in Mexico, and most pilgrimage centers, cater overwhelmingly to domestic travelers.

It is inaccurate, however, to view the tourism industry in low-income countries as consisting solely of a domestic, low value-added sector of inexpensive

Figure 2.2 Formal and informal tourism sectors in low-income countries

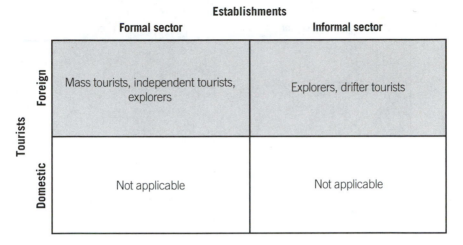

Figure 2.3 Cohen's tourist typology applied to Third World societies

accommodation and low-cost transportation and an international, high value-added sector of large hotels and jet aircraft. Many domestic tourists in Third World countries frequent upscale facilities, often exclusively, and a large part of the tourism industry in low-income countries caters to backpackers and other low-budget international travelers. In other words, not every domestic tourist is poor, and not every international tourist travels on package tours and stays in luxury hotels and resorts. The tourist typologies discussed in the previous chapter may thus be incorporated into the international/domestic formal/informal conceptual schema (figure 2.3). Among international travelers, institutional mass tourists are those most likely to patronize "international standard" tourism establishments because these provide an environmental bubble shielding tourists from any meaningful contact with the resident population. Independent tourists and explorers are more likely to move out of the environmental bubble, perhaps eating at informal-sector restaurants, occasionally riding on a local bus, or even staying at an informal-sector hotel or guesthouse. Drifters, those tourists most willing to seek out local culture, are also more likely to patronize informal-sector establishments and least likely to frequent international-standard hotels and eating establishments.

Similarly, psychocentric travelers, the least adventurous and outgoing group of tourists, are those most likely to frequent formal-sector establishments (figure 2.4). The most outgoing and adventurous tourists, allocentrics, are those most likely to eschew formal-sector accommodation and eating places altogether and to seek out more traditional, informal-sector guesthouses and restaurants. Midcentric tourists, like independent tourists and explorers, fall

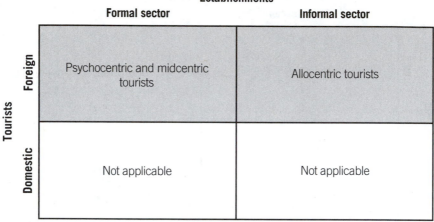

Figure 2.4 Plog's tourist typology applied to Third World societies.

somewhere in between, perhaps staying at a formal-sector hotel but "going native" with respect to local transport and cuisine (figure 2.5).

As noted in the previous chapter, none of the tourist typologies found in the tourism literature are directly applicable to domestic tourists in low-income countries, even though they may be applicable to the relatively small number of Third World tourists who travel to First World countries. We saw, however, that Third World travelers are by no means a monolithic group of people. They range from traditional pilgrims to middle class tourists motivated by many of the same factors as their First World counterparts. In addition, there are a large number of business travelers ranging from corporate executives to informal-sector entrepreneurs and many people who travel to visit family and friends. Incorporating the typology of Third World domestic tourists developed in chapter 1 into the conceptual schema outlined in figure 2.2 reveals that more traditional, low-budget Third World travelers, including pilgrims and temporary migrants, are more likely to utilize informal-sector accommodation and tourist facilities, whereas middle class tourists and elite groups are more likely to frequent formal-sector establishments (figure 2.6).

Tourist Establishments

Dividing the tourism industry into domestic and international parts is necessary but not sufficient for purposes of understanding its complexity and its impact on specific places and communities. In low-income countries, it is also important to distinguish among the types of enterprises found at each destination. The assumption here is that Third World tourist destinations generally fall into one

Figure 2.5 Top: Cancún, Mexico. Bottom: IIS Tourists, Koh Pha Ngan, Thailand.

of two broad categories: a relatively small group of tourist centers that feature large numbers of international-class hotels and well-developed infrastructures and a much larger group of destinations where small, labor-intensive, locally owned and managed enterprises predominate. Again, prima facie evidence

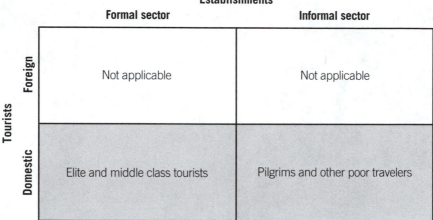

Figure 2.6 Third World domestic travelers.

suggests that some destinations are characterized by upscale resorts serving domestic and international travelers while many others lack international-standard accommodation and other exclusive tourist facilities (figure 2.7). A second assumption is that tourist centers characterized by small-scale, labor-intensive, locally owned and unregulated tourism-related businesses will differ in important ways from resorts and other destinations characterized by capital-intensive, internationally owned and managed, and highly regulated tourism-related firms.

For analytical purposes, therefore, it is useful to incorporate the conceptual categories of formality and informality, and the related concepts of formal- and informal-sector establishments in any discussion of tourism, and especially the impact of tourism, in low-income countries. Because measures of formality and informality are widely applied in studies of Third World societies generally and because there is some disagreement concerning their definitions and operation, I have included a brief discussion of the concepts here.

Formal and Informal Economic Sectors in Low-Income Countries

A rather vast literature has grown up since the early 1970s that seeks to describe and explain the unregulated, unmeasured, small-scale, labor-intensive, and at times marginal economic activity found in most Third World, and to a lesser degree First World, cities. Such activity is extremely diverse and extends from household production of essential commodities, including shelter, to street hawking and vending to transportation services of various kinds to small-scale manufacturing to the illegal production and sale of controlled

Figure 2.7 Top: Holiday Inn Crowne Plaza, New Delhi, India. Bottom: Chander Dharamshala, New Delhi, India.

substances. In a pioneering study of ethnic minorities in Ghana's urban areas, anthropologist Keith Hart (1973) refers to these activities as the urban informal sector, a term adopted by the International Labour Organisation (ILO) and other international institutions.

Theories of the informal sector in Third World societies are intellectually rooted in the notion of dualism, common to most analyses of the Third World in the immediate postwar period (Boeke 1978; Hirschman 1964; Lewis 1958). Early accounts of the dual nature of Third World economies generally focus on the vast disparities between the modern industrial sector in the urban areas and the traditional or "backward" agricultural sector in the countryside. Development economists of the 1950s and early 1960s theorized economic development as the transfer of surplus labor out of rural, agricultural areas, where its marginal productivity was zero or close to zero, and into urban areas where a modern proletariat would staff the new factories and propel underdeveloped countries forward into the twentieth century. The modernization school, particularly influential at the time, also held that Western cultural attitudes and institutional practices would accompany the transition from Third World to First World status.

This particular concept of development was based on the historical experience of Western Europe, the United States, and Japan. Accordingly, many development theorists view the modern, Westernized sector of capital-intensive, state-regulated, high-productivity industries as a progressive social force and an engine of growth. The modern sector includes the branch plants of multinational corporations, the production facilities of the national bourgeoisie, plantation cash-crop agriculture, and most state-run enterprises and parastatals. In contrast, development theorists often view the traditional agricultural sector, the urban self-employed, most of the service sector, petty traders, and home-based industry as limiting growth, constituting precapitalist forms of economic activity that will pass away with the transition to higher forms of social organization. According to the dualist perspective, the traditional sector acts as an obstacle to growth because of its low productivity and underutilization of labor.

Most discussions of Third World urban development cite rural-to-urban migration as a key factor in the growth and continued presence of informal-sector activity in Third World cities. And for good reason: due to wage differences between urban and rural employment, population growth and environmental degradation in the countryside, and the collapse of traditional agricultural systems, rural-to-urban migration in the Third World has assumed immense proportions since the 1950s, even in regions such as South Asia and sub-Saharan Africa that remain predominantly rural. Even though economic considerations drive many people to leave their ancestral villages for what they hope will be a brighter future in the city, many are unable to find good jobs, and the large numbers of farmers streaming into the cities of the Third World countries greatly outnumber the available employment opportunities in formal-sector establishments. One result has been the growth of a large urban underclass, or lumpen proletariat, and the rapid growth of the informal economic sector, the legions of street vendors, shoeshine boys, rickshaw drivers, and petty traders found in most Third World cities.

The Informal Sector Defined

Definitions of the informal sector generally fall into three broad categories: those that focus on the nature of employment, those that focus on characteristics of firms, and those that consider state regulation of labor, firms, and industries. Hart, who coined the term *informal sector* in the early 1970s in connection with his research in Accra, Ghana, defines *formal economic activities* as public and private employment "recruited on a permanent and regular basis for fixed rewards" (Hart 1973, 68–69). He classifies all other economic activity as informal and divides it into legitimate and illegitimate (illegal) sectors, ranging from agriculture to the production of tourism goods and services.

In addition to defining informality as a type of employment, or as a distinct *activity*, it is also possible to view informality as a characteristic of *enterprises*. In a 1972 study of Kenya's economy, researchers from the ILO discovered that a disproportionate number of the country's businesses are small, labor intensive, unregulated, highly competitive, family oriented, and reliant on indigenous resources and skills (International Labour Office 1972). The group of small informal-sector firms, which the ILO researchers termed the country's informal sector, stand in stark contrast to Kenya's formal-sector enterprises, large capital-intensive firms, usually corporately owned with high startup costs, dependent on imported capital, labor, and technology, and often operating in protected markets. An additional characteristic of informal-sector enterprises is their relationship to the state: Whereas governing authorities often subsidize the operations of formal-sector firms, they often act to curtail informal-sector activities, not only in Kenya but in other countries as well. Examples from around the Third World abound of state authorities bulldozing or otherwise clearing illegal housing settlements and unregulated market areas in order to make room for formal-sector development, including formal-sector hotel development (Halla 1997). Usually operating without the proper permits, informal businesses and residents of informal housing developments lead a very precarious existence.

A third group of researchers define the informal sector primarily in legal or regulatory terms. A key proponent of the regulatory view is the Peruvian economist Hernando de Soto (1989), who defines informal economic activity as the pursuit of legal ends in an illegal manner. Even though he often refers to a group or class of "informals," de Soto never refers to an informal economic sector, only informal economic activity:

> Individuals are not informal; their actions and activities are. Nor do those who operate informally comprise a precise or static sector of society; they live within a gray area which has a long frontier with the legal world and in which individuals take refuge when the cost of obeying the law outweighs the benefit. (1989, 12)

De Soto's concept of informality extends to the spheres of production and reproduction, including not only economic enterprises but also housing. In this regulatory view of the informal sector, excessive government regulations and administrative rules used to support and protect large and inefficient mercantilist enterprises *cause* informality. The process is circular. Because enterprises are informal, they cannot achieve the economies of scale necessary for legalization. Because they remain illegal, they continue to be informal; and so on. De Soto's prescription, much beloved by neo-liberal economists, is to eliminate excessive government regulations and create an institutional framework that would allow a true market economy to function.

A fundamental assumption informing de Soto's analysis is that informal producers are the real capitalists in Peru and other low-income countries, the ones most sensitive to market signals, efficiently combining labor and raw materials in ways that maximize their returns. Unlike the large rent-seeking formal-sector firms protected by mercantilist states, informal workers must rely solely on their entrepreneurial skills to survive. Indeed, they must often exercise extraordinary entrepreneurial talents because the state often enacts policies that positively discriminate against them.

De Soto is not the first to view the informal sector in dynamic terms. Hart (1973) stressed the dynamism of the self-employed in Accra, as did earlier Marxist theorists, such as Paul Baran and Bill Warren. The latter two theorists saw in the workings of the informal sector a submerged or lumpen bourgeoisie, infused with the spirit of capitalism and possessing a dynamic entrepreneurialism (Warren 1973). And Baran, after dismissing both the claim that underdevelopment is due to a deficit of risk-taking individuals and the tautological conclusion that "in the absence of industrial [formal] capital there are no industrial capitalists," goes on to state, "There is an abundance of entrepreneurial ability in the underdeveloped countries . . . all of them swarm[ing] with contriving, risking, and sharply calculating entrepreneurs determined to maximize their profits within the framework of existing opportunities" (Baran 1957, 236). For Baran and other Marxists, the real question is why "this abundance of talent" is confined to the spheres of circulation, to petty finance and the informal trading sector, rather than to the directly productive activities that would provide for the needs of the people.

Although the exact nature of the relationship may differ from country to country or even regionally within countries, formal and informal sectors do not exist independently of one another but are related both indirectly and directly. Indirectly, informality lowers the operating costs of formal-sector enterprises by reducing the cost of labor; a reserve army of the unemployed serves to depress wages in the formal sector while fiercely competitive informal-sector labor markets translate into lower prices for food and household services, which in turn lowers the cost of reproducing the formal-sector workforce.

Formal and informal enterprises are directly related through both forward and backward economic linkages (Bromley and Gerry 1979; Portes 1996; Thomas 1995). Forward linkages exist when the output of informal-sector firms becomes the input of formal-sector production processes: when, for instance, formal-sector firms subcontract out their production to informal-sector enterprises in an effort to reduce or displace the risks associated with market downturns. There is ample evidence of subcontracting links between formal- and informal-sector firms in the textile, electronics, apparel, and footwear industries (Portes 1996; Thomas 1995). Backward linkages occur when informal-sector enterprises utilize formal-sector products as inputs into their own production processes. Cigarettes, soft drinks, and other formal-sector goods sold by street hawkers in Third World cities are common examples, as are formal-sector cement and wood products used by informal-sector firms and households as intermediate goods or for informal housing construction, textiles for use in the informal apparel industry, and agro-industrial products utilized by informal-sector food stalls.

Thus, in most low-income countries, the informal sector forms an integral component of the economy. Informal export sectors, such as textiles, gems, jewelry, carpets, agriculture, and tourism, earn the foreign exchange that owners of formal-sector enterprises require to pay for the capital equipment and technology they import from firms in the United States, Western Europe, and Japan. Moreover, foreign exchange earned by informal-sector enterprises is instrumental in paying off a country's debts, a factor that has taken on increasing importance since the so-called Third World debt crisis erupted on the international scene in the early 1980s. As Lipietz argues in the case of Brazil, it is not the Fordist workers and the new middle classes in the large urban centers who bear the brunt of paying off the country's debts but rather the informal "women workers [who] suffer 'bloody Taylorization' in the electronics and textile industries [and] workers in the sugar cane plantations [who] are close to slavery" (Lipietz 1982, 46–47).

The Formal–Informal Continuum

Because definitions of the informal sector vary, classifying firms or economic activity as formal or informal raises a number of conceptual issues. Suppose a TNC builds a factory in a low-income country. If the TNC owns and operates the factory, it is by almost every definition a formal-sector enterprise. For instance, a General Motors assembly plant in Egypt and a Proctor & Gamble factory in India are clearly formal-sector enterprises. Few would disagree. But suppose a transnational corporation ties up with local subcontractors exploiting sweated labor. The Disney Corporation, Nike, The Gap, Liz Claiborne, and other firms based in the West have routinely subcontracted out their production to sweatshops in Latin America, Asia, and Oceania. Are assembly plants producing for Nike in Indonesia or Disney in Haiti, sweatshops that routinely flout national and international labor laws, formal or informal?

If such workers are included in the formal sector, it is clear that formal-sector workers are not always better off than their informal-sector counterparts. Most workers in the free trade zones, maquilas, and export platforms of the Third World are superexploited, often paid less than a subsistence wage for fourteen hours a day of intensive labor. Likewise, agricultural workers on the export plantations of low-income countries, many of whom are children, often face harsh working conditions, including long hours, poisoning from fertilizers and pesticides, and at times murder if they attempt to organize for better wages or working conditions.

A continuum thus runs from purely informal production (unregulated, locally owned, small scale, labor intensive, produced for local markets) to purely formal production (state regulated, foreign owned, large scale, capital intensive, produced for global markets). A formal, modern economy is one most development theory equates either implicitly or explicitly with the latter. Economic activity is either more or less informal or formal, but rarely is it one or the other. Bicycle rickshaw drivers in Delhi, for example, usually migrants from other parts of the country, represent the epitome of informality. Nevertheless, there is a rickshaw union, and rickshaws are licensed by the city (formal characteristics). At the other extreme are the giant TNCs based in the high-income countries. Through transfer pricing they are able to avoid paying taxes, and through subcontracting they are able to benefit from bloody Taylorization and related labor processes, many of which are technically illegal, in the Third World countries in which they operate.

Regardless of how the informal economy is defined, there is virtually near-universal agreement that it is a major factor affecting the life chances of most people in the Third World. In India, for example, over 90 percent of businesses are informal ("unorganized" in the parlance of Indian policymakers) and together account for more than 60 percent of the economy's value added (Visaria and Jacob 1996). In Latin America, more than half the workforce is engaged in informal-sector employment (Portes 1996). De Soto (1989) provides estimates for Peru, where the informal sector accounts for 30 percent of establishments and 60 percent of total hours worked. In places like India and Peru, therefore, perhaps the real question is not one of explaining how the informal sector comes about but rather one of explaining the origins and function of the *formal* economic sector (Breman 1996).

Formality and Informality in the Tourism Industry

Due in no small measure to the unregulated character of informal economic activity, we know fairly little about informality in the travel and tourism industry. Although a number of social scientists have applied the concepts of formality and informality in specific cases, few focus on the social dynamics of informal tourist space and concentrate instead on the informal economic sector within upmarket resort areas, such as the beach resort of Sosúa in the Dominican Republic and Pattaya, a seaside resort in Thailand (Kermath and Thomas 1992; Oppermann 1993; Wahnschafft 1982). Most adopt the ILO definition of informal-sector enterprises (small-scale, labor-intensive enterprises that are neither licensed nor enumerated and that pay no taxes or receive any kind of government subsidy), but each classifies formal and informal tourist enterprises differently, an outcome that is perhaps indicative of the imprecise definitions of formality and informality found in the development literature.

Research from Latin America, Asia, Africa, and the Caribbean indicates that in upmarket Third World resort areas, the informal sector tends to get crowded out and that the state plays an instrumental role in the process. There are many instances, however, where the informal sector has not only continued to exist alongside formal-sector enterprises but has managed to expand considerably. One example is the seaside resort of Kovalam Beach in the southern India state of Kerala. State authorities evicted many families from a site earmarked for hotel development, what had been until that time a small fishing village. An upmarket facility, the Ashok Beach Resort, was completed on the site in the mid-1970s, after which Kovalam Beach experienced an *informal*-sector tourism boom. Landowning families constructed small, unlicensed guesthouses, cafés, and restaurants on adjoining beaches. Families operate most of the businesses, although many workers come from other parts of southern India, especially the neighboring states of Karnataka and Tamil Nadu. Many of the new informal businesses are illegal, and they may occasionally pay bribes to local officials, although the amounts are not excessive and certainly cheaper than obtaining an official operating license.

How then are we to define formal and informal tourism sectors, and formal and informal tourism destinations in Third World countries? Although there is no universally agreed-upon definitions of formal and informal economic activities or enterprises, the broad outlines of the two sectors are readily apparent. The formal transportation and accommodation sector includes "star" hotels with access to computerized reservations systems, upmarket restaurants, airlines, registered/regulated transportation firms, and similar enterprises. The informal tourism sector is made up of small-scale enterprises, including small hotels and guesthouses, restaurants, and retail shops. It is generally unregulated, often illegal, unmeasured, and largely untaxed. In many cases, informal tourism enterprises are kinship and family based, require little investment, are operated efficiently, and have insecure tenure as a result of their illegality.

In short, the formal accommodation and transportation sector approximates the Western prototype while land-based travel, inexpensive eating places, and low-cost accommodation characterize the informal sector. The ownership of formal-sector enterprises rests either with the large national firms or with foreign capital. In India, Mexico, and other low-income countries, the Sheratons, Hyatts, Hiltons, Radissons, and other five-star hotels are rarely owned by the transnational hotel chains but by wealthy nationals who work out licensing and franchise agreements with the parent company. The company provides name recognition, management assistance, and most important, access to computerized reservations systems. In contrast, informal-sector tourism enterprises are almost always sole proprietorships, informal partnerships, or family owned and operated.

In low-income countries, most formal-sector hotels and resorts are enclaves of wealth and power, culturally and socially distinct from the larger society. The architecture of most five-star hotels in Delhi, Mexico City, Jakarta, Bangkok, and other Third World urban centers bears a striking resemblance to the defensible spaces of First World cities like the Bonaventure Hotel in downtown Los Angeles or the Renaissance Center in Detroit and for many of the same reasons. The hotels are generally cordoned off from the surrounding city through a series of roads, fences, and guard posts. The buildings are designed to face inward unto themselves rather than outward toward the rest of the city. Most have underground parking with direct access to the hotel lobby and restaurants. Some even feature video surveillance.

Author and social critic Jeremy Seabrook describes the ambience of five-star hotels in New Delhi:

> These hotels have become the object of a kind of cult, and with good reason. They are alien implants in the culture, microcosms of that human-made creation, the technosphere, in which the people of the West have been installed and which insulates them from the effects of their way of life on the biosphere; these hotels are illusions of universal escape, a promise that humanity can evade not merely the consequences of its actions, but also its destiny. The hotel is an enclosed glass bubble which separates its occupants from the environment. In such hothouses, fantasy luxuriates. You can see this in the dreamlike

way in which people behave in the hotels, gliding across carpets and marble floors, sunglasses in hand, flicking their hair, offering theatrical greetings, chinking the ice in long-stemmed glasses. Beyond the tinted windows the beggars exhibit their mutilations in vain; the rag pickers pass by with their sacks, the dust swirls in the hot air. In these air-conditioned refuges, nothing disturbs the purchased distance, the immense internal spaces that divide the people from a world outside that they scarcely acknowledge. (Seabrook 1996, 214–215)

The hotels Seabrook describes, however, are unlike the vast majority of tourism enterprises in India, where the typical accommodation unit is little more than a *charpoy* (traditional rope bed) and bed sheet without an attached bathroom. Unlike formal-sector hotels, informal tourist enterprises borrow from informal credit markets, hire informal labor, are minimally regulated, and cater overwhelmingly to the needs of domestic and international low-budget tourists. Informal tourism enterprises are more spatially and functionally integrated into the surrounding non-tourist space, and informal tourist destinations are, at least in their general outlines, more representative of the norm than resort enclaves and planned tourist cities.

I define informal tourism enterprises as those that operate in an illegal or quasi-legal manner *and* approximate the characteristics enumerated by the ILO in its 1972 Kenya Report (ease of entry, reliance on indigenous resources, family ownership of enterprises, small scale of operation, labor-intensive technology, skills acquired outside the formal educational system, and unregulated and competitive markets). Of course, not all of these characteristics are found in all informal tourism enterprises. For instance, informal hotels and guesthouses often entail high startup costs, particularly where the acquisition of real estate is involved. Many hotels and guesthouses operate on some kind of leasehold interest, however, and obtaining a leasehold interest is notably easier and certainly more affordable in India and other Third World countries than the outright purchase of land.

Like informal enterprises generally, informal-sector tourism enterprises are both directly and indirectly linked to formal-sector firms. Because tourism goods and services are almost always final consumption products and not intermediate inputs, the relationship between informal-sector tourism firms and formal-sector enterprises generally takes the form of backward linkages. Such linkages are extremely diverse and range from formal-sector goods sold in informal shops to formal-sector transportation services utilized by international low-budget tourists to building materials used in the construction of informal-sector accommodation facilities. A good deal of the products used by informal-sector firms involves backward linkages to other informal enterprises. Clothing shops in the Indian pilgrimage center of Pushkar, for example, purchase most of their stock from informal-sector manufacturing enterprises in Ajmer, Jaipur, Agra, and other Indian cities (see chapter 6). However, even in this case, the link to the formal sector is only once removed: The textiles used in producing garments sold informally are made in large formal-sector production plants in Bombay and Ahmedabad.

The informal tourism sector is also indirectly related to the formal economic sector. Workers in small-scale lodging facilities and restaurants are paid very little for laboring long hours in poor working conditions, particularly those workers in nontipping positions and those serving domestic tourists. For instance, hotel workers in informal-sector tourist establishments in Delhi's Pahar Ganj tourist district earn between 600 and 1,000 rupees (U.S.$12–20) per month and often work in excess of 80 hours per week. The large pool of unemployed and underemployed workers in both the informal tourism sector, and the informal sector generally, depress wages in formal-sector tourism enterprises, a fact not lost on India's five-star hotel managers, some of whom have pointed out the connection to me on numerous occasions.[1] Similarly, cheap informal-sector tourism goods and services provide an implicit subsidy to formal-sector employers by reducing the cost of recreation and travel for their employees, a cost savings that translates into lower formal-sector wages.

As an industry, therefore, the international tourism industry exhibits the full range of institutional structures characteristic of late capitalism.[2] At one end of the organizational spectrum lie the large multinational hotel, airline, and travel corporations that together form the core of IFS tourism. The formal-sector hospitality industry in most countries exhibits strong oligopolistic tendencies, particularly with respect to hotels, airlines, and tour operators. In the United States, the ten largest hotel chains account for more than 40 percent of total market share, and the five largest air carriers (American, United, Delta, Continental, and Northwest) control more than three fourths of the market for air travel (Ioannides 1995). Large booking agents such as Rosenbluth, Wagon-Lits, and American Express direct international and domestic tourist flows through extensive marketing of tourist commodities. The rapidly growing cruise industry is similarly dominated by a handful of firms that, due to merger and acquisitions activity, has grown progressively smaller (Klein 2002).

Although the international tourist trade is dominated by a handful of multinational corporations, a much larger number of smaller formal- and informal-sector firms cater to the needs of tourists as well. In addition, tourists everywhere demand goods and services from informal-sector enterprises. This is especially true of Third World countries, where both domestic and international travelers patronize informal-sector tourism-related enterprises. Street vendors, hawkers, touts, prostitutes, and drug dealers are ubiquitous sights at many Third World tourist destinations, as are unregulated or illegal transport and accommodation facilities. Large numbers of low-paid informal workers depress wages in the formal tourism sector while providing an incentive for the large formal-sector firms to contract out for producer goods and services.

From the Informal Tourism Sector to Informal Tourism Space

The tourism industry in low-income countries is characterized not only by formal and informal economic *sectors*; it also has a distinct *spatial* component. In other words, formality and informality in the tourism industry materialize differently in particular Third World places. I have defined the informal tourism sector as the sum total of tourism-related enterprises that operate in an illegal or quasi-legal manner and that approximate the characteristics enumerated by the ILO in its 1972 Kenya Report (ease of entry, reliance on indigenous resources, etc.). An informal tourist destination or informal tourist space, therefore, would be one characterized by the presence of a large number of informal tourism establishments. The definition needs qualification, however, because formal tourism destinations such as Cancún, Acapulco, and Sosúa not only feature five-star hotels and other upmarket facilities but also include a large number of unlicensed guesthouses, hawkers, food sellers, prostitutes, drug dealers, and other informal-sector micro-enterprises and activities. Conversely, spaces generally characterized by small-scale, unregulated accommodation facilities and eating places may also contain formal-sector elements, such as one or more formal-sector hotel and transportation facilities, travel agents, and stores well stocked with products manufactured in the formal sector, including tobacco products, canned goods, alcoholic beverages, and so on.

In other words, with few exceptions, there are no pure formal or informal tourist destinations, just as there are few Third World informal-sector activities or production processes undertaken without some connection to the formal sector, and vice versa. A mix of formal and informal elements characterizes most tourism space in the Third World; what distinguishes a formal tourist destination from an informal destination is the ratio of formal- to informal-sector activities. An informal destination is one in which informal-sector processes predominate, and a formal-sector destination is one in which formal-sector activities predominate. No two destinations will have precisely the same mix of formal- and informal-sector activities, but it is possible to differentiate destinations on the basis of where they fall on the formal–informal spectrum.

A key variable is the accommodation sector. Destinations with a large number of informal-sector hotels and guesthouses are almost always informal tourism destinations. Conversely, places dominated by large, formal-sector hotels, such as Hyatt, Hilton, and Club Méditerranée, are almost by definition formal tourism destinations. And although informal-sector ancillary services and businesses may develop to service the formal-sector hotels, rarely is it the case that formal-sector activities arise to service informal-sector accommodation facilities, although there are some exceptions, as noted above.

The difference between a formal and an informal tourism destination is primarily one of degree: Whereas formal tourism destinations in low-income countries almost always feature formal- and informal-sector enterprises, the formal sector is dominant. Often, the state acts to restrict or even eliminate informal-sector establishments and vendors on the grounds that they interfere with the profitability of formal-sector firms by creating "eyesores" or by harassing the tourists who patronize the large hotels. Conversely, informal tourism destinations may have some formal-sector participation, but the majority of enterprises will be small-scale and largely unregulated.

Size of the Informal Tourism Sector in Low-Income Countries

Determining the size of the informal tourism sector for an entire country is not an easy task. Few low-income countries keep accurate statistics on the informal sector generally, and to my knowledge none maintains a database on informal tourism establishments. Compounding the problem is the fact that countries that do compile statistics on the informal sector employ different definitions, making cross-national comparisons difficult if not impossible. Furthermore, the size of the informal tourism sector will vary from one country to the next, depending on a whole host of factors, including the general level of development, the level of income inequality, cultural traditions, the ratio of international to domestic tourists, and so on. At best, therefore, we can only estimate the size of the informal tourism sector for a given country. In what follows, I describe three techniques. The first estimates its size on the basis of domestic tourist arrivals, the second on the number of hotels outside the formal rating system, and the third on measures of value added in different industries based on the size of firms. I then construct a simple model to explain differences in the relative size of the formal and informal tourism sectors among low-income countries.

As noted in chapter 1, the WTO estimates the number of worldwide domestic tourist arrivals as a multiple of total international arrivals. One of the problems with this method is that the multiplier is not uniform across countries. Nations with a large number of domestic tourists relative to international tourists will have a much higher multiplier than countries with a relatively small number of domestic as compared with international tourists. In India, for example, a reasonable estimate of the domestic tourism multiplier is 1,500. In other words, domestic arrivals in India are 1,500 times higher than international arrivals. In the Bahamas, Cayman Islands, and other Caribbean microstates, however, the multiplier may be as low as 1/100: For each domestic arrival, there may be more than 100 international arrivals.

Another problem associated with identifying the informal tourism sector with a country's domestic tourist arrivals is that not all domestic tourists demand goods and services from the informal sector. Many stay in formal-sector hotels and resorts and rely on air transportation. The problem is compounded by the fact that the structure of the tourism industry in each country is different, so that we cannot assume that a certain percentage of domestic tourists in each country frequent informal-sector tourist establishments. What we can say with some certainty is that very large Third World countries such as India, Indonesia, Brazil, and China generate large numbers of domestic tourists and will have sizable informal tourism sectors. Delving more deeply into the actual number of informal tourism establishments would require detailed information for the country in question.

A second approach to estimating the size of the informal tourism sector is to base it some way on the number of hotels outside the formal rating system. The assumption here is that most nonrated accommodation facilities are informal-sector enterprises as I have defined them. This approach also underestimates the size of the informal tourism sector because it considers only accommodation facilities and does not take into account other parts of the tourist infrastructure. Once again, the problem is largely one of data availability because only a few low-income country governments maintain accurate databases on the total number of hotels found within their borders. I have pointed to the large discrepancy between rated hotels and those without any government-approved ratings. India, for instance, has nearly 300 nonrated accommodation facilities for every rated hotel. In Mexico, over half the country's accommodation facilities are nonrated, and most of these are presumably informal (Clancy 1996).

A third way of determining the size of the informal tourism sector is to place all small tourism-related firms in the informal sector and large firms in the formal sector. This approach is also problematic, however, because we lack data on firm size for most countries in the Third World. Some countries, however, do provide data indicating that the informal tourism sector is very large. In India, for instance, over 60 percent of the value added and 90 percent of the employment in the country's tourism industry is accounted for by firms employing fewer than twenty-five employees, what the Indian government refers to as the *unorganized tourism sector* (Visaria and Jacob 1996).

Explaining why the informal tourism sector is larger in some countries than in others is much easier than estimating its magnitude in a given country. The relative sizes of the formal and informal tourism sectors in a low-income country is largely a function of the role of the state, access to foreign markets, integration into the global economy, the nature and magnitude of domestic tourism, and that country's general level of development. I will consider each of these five factors in turn and show how they explain why the ratio of formal to informal tourism establishments is much larger in Mexico than it is in India.

The Role of the State

Because a hallmark of informality is its unregulated character, the state is central to any definition of informal economic activity. As we have seen, some theorists claim that through its onerous bureaucratic procedures and regulatory requirements, the state literally creates the informal sector (de Soto 1989; Portes 1996). A corollary to this view of the informal sector is that state-led development is by definition formal-sector development. A public-sector undertaking in India or anywhere in the Third World is always in the formal sector. The same is true for very large enterprises that are often subsidized by the state and for most transnational enterprises that work directly with the state. To the degree, then, that a low-income country's tourism industry entails a significant state-led component, either in the form of public sector enterprises or in the form of extensive state planning and state subsidies, that country's formal tourism sector will be larger.

Both the Indian and Mexican governments are directly and indirectly involved in their countries' tourism industries. The India Tourism Development Corporation (ITDC) is a public sector undertaking that operates thirty-three hotels in twenty-six Indian states and territories (ITDC 2005). In addition, most of India's state governments are also directly involved in the tourism business. For example, the Himachal Pradesh Tourism Development Corporation (HPTDC) operates fifty hotels in resorts throughout the state, as well as a bus transport company (HPTDC 2005). In addition, the ITDC and many of the state tourism development corporations maintain tourist offices in the country's largest cities.

In addition to its involvement as a direct investor and operator of hotels, both the central government and the individual states have also drawn up numerous tourism development plans for the country as a whole and for specific geographic regions. The state also provides incentives ranging from tax holidays to direct subsidies for hotel firms willing to invest per the plan requirements. Thus, the Indian state on both the national and subnational levels is actively involved in the country's tourism industry and accounts for a significant part of its formal tourism industry.

Compared with India, however, the Mexican government has taken a much more active role in the promotion of tourism. Particularly in the case of international tourism, the Mexican national authorities have taken a lead role in developing the integrated resort complexes of Cancún, Huatulco, Ixtapa, Loreto, and Los Cabos. In each case, the state planned for and constructed the vast infrastructure required for these tourist cities, resorts that attract millions of foreign tourists annually. Cancún's resorts alone attract more international tourists each year than does India, a country with over a billion people.

Although the Mexican government has operated hotel firms in the past (the Hotel Nacionalera group of hotels, the largest state-run hotel chain in Mexico, was privatized in the early 1990s), the state's role has largely taken the form of long-range planning and the provision of adequate infrastructure in each of the resort complexes (Clancy 1996; Hiernaux-Nicolas 1999). The active involvement of the state has all but eliminated informal-sector enterprises, particularly hotels and other types of informal accommodation, from the areas now home to the integrated resorts. This has occurred because of both strict enforcement of zoning provisions and a crowding out of the informal sector through the inflated land values accompanying the state-led development projects. The state's role has also paved the way for a large influx of international-class hotels, including Sheraton, Club Méditerranée, Hilton, Ritz-Carlton, and the like.

Access to Foreign Markets

Because most international tourists demand goods and services from formal-sector enterprises, a second factor with a direct bearing on the relative sizes of the formal and informal tourism sectors is proximity to foreign markets. Thus, to the degree that a country is able to attract large numbers of international tourists, its formal tourism sector will be larger. Conversely, low-income countries with comparatively fewer international tourists will have smaller formal tourism sectors. The process is circular: Because a country invests in more "international-class" tourist facilities, more international tourists will travel there; and because more high-spending tourists travel there, the country is more likely to invest in more formal tourist facilities, due to an enlarged market.

As I pointed out in chapter 1, a distance decay function is evident in international tourist flows (Pearce 1995). The closer a low-income country is to a major First World market, the more likely it is that tourists from the major market country will travel there. This is why Mexico receives more U.S. tourists than all other countries combined, why the United States is the leading market for Caribbean tourism, and why the European Community (EC) countries comprise a major market for West African tourism. The distance decay function also explains why half the international tourists visiting India are residents of other South Asian countries: Sri Lanka, Bangladesh, Nepal, Bhutan, and Pakistan.

Thus, an additional factor contributing to Mexico's relatively large formal tourism sector is proximity to the United States, the world's largest market for tourism exports. Even discounting cross-border traffic, over 7 million U.S. tourists visited Mexico in 2002, and 80 percent of the visitors to Cancún were U.S. citizens. Compared with Mexico, India is far from major markets. The United States is literally on the other side of the world, whereas Western Europe and Japan are six to eight hours away by jet aircraft. Due to their closer proximity, the Western European countries represent India's largest international tourism market after other South Asian countries and account for more than double the number of North American arrivals.

Integration into the Global Economy

A third factor that will determine the relative sizes of a country's formal and informal tourism sectors is the degree to which that country is integrated into the global economy. Third World countries that are more integrated into international trade and capital flows will tend to have larger formal tourism sectors. This is certainly the case with small island states and other countries heavily dependent on foreign tourism, where openness to the global economy and production of tourism goods and services are directly related (Milne 1992). Countries with more open trading systems are also more likely to host business travelers from high-income countries, a group of tourists most likely to demand international-standard accommodation and other formal-sector tourism goods and services.

One way of measuring global integration is by looking at imports and exports as a percentage of a country's gross national product (GNP). Another is to compare countries with respect to the volume of international capital flows and the rules governing foreign investment. Accordingly, countries with more liberal foreign investment climates will be more likely to attract international hotel and entertainment corporations. Those already characterized by significant levels of direct foreign investment (DFI) and international trade will also be more likely to feature formal-sector transport and accommodation facilities for foreign executives and business managers. With more low-income countries subject to IMF-style structural adjustment programs that force countries to "open up," we should expect an increasing formalization of Third World countries' tourism industries, all else being equal. Of course, all else is only rarely equal. Structural adjustment policies also cause increased levels of poverty within the low-income countries that adopt them. Higher levels of poverty translate into an enlarged informal sector, including, presumably, an enlarged informal tourism sector.

If we take total merchandise trade (exports and imports) and net private capital flows as indicative of the openness of an economy, Mexico's economy is certainly more internationalized than India's. Whereas India's total exports and imports as a percentage of the country's GNP was just over 30 percent in 2003, Mexico's was nearly 60 percent. Mexico's economy was also more open with respect to capital flows: In 2003, net private capital flows as a percentage of GNP was nearly 2.5 times higher in Mexico (1.7 percent) than in India (0.7 percent; World Bank 2005).

The General Level of Economic Development

A fourth determinant of formalization in the tourism industry in low-income countries is the general level of economic development. This is almost axiomatic in that *formality* and *development* are more or less synonymous terms. Countries with more highly developed infrastructures already have the essential prerequisites in place for a successful international tourism industry, including highways, airports, shipping terminals, and advanced telecommunication networks. Moreover, high-income countries are generally richer, at least on the basis of per capita income. Thus, provided that a high-income country does not have a grossly unequal income distribution, it will have relatively more people able to afford higher-priced formal-sector products. In other words, the national market for formal-sector tourism goods and services will be larger.

Mexico and India are both characterized by highly inegalitarian social structures. In India, the richest 10 percent of the population accounts for 30 percent of total income, and the wealthiest 20 percent receives nearly 45 percent of the nation's GNP. In Mexico, the figures are even more skewed: The richest 10 percent of the population receives 40 percent of the national income, and the richest 20 percent accounts for over 55 percent of the country's GNP (World Bank 1996). Expressed in dollar terms, the disposable income of the richest 20 percent of Mexicans (about 16 million people, roughly equivalent to the population of the Netherlands) is close to U.S.$12,000 per year, whereas the richest 20 percent of Indians earn on average just under U.S.$700 per year. These figures suggest that the domestic market for formal-sector tourism products is larger in Mexico than in India.

Measuring Tourist Impact: A Methodological Note

A large influx of tourists affects Third World tourist destinations—domestic and international, formal and informal—in numerous ways. For analytical purposes, in the chapters that follow, I have distinguished among tourism's economic, social, environmental, and cultural impacts. The economic variables considered in this study include employment, tourist expenditures, land, commodity, wage inflation, and import leakages. The social effects considered include residential displacement of local residents, migration, ownership (class) relations, changes in the living standards of local residents, and changes in the level of criminal activities. The cultural effects considered include commoditization of culture, growth of undesirable activities, hostility directed at tourists by the local residents, and the degree to which tourist behavior influences the culture of the local community. The environmental effects considered involve land use, pollution, deforestation, and sand/soil erosion. Each of the four tourism sectors (international formal, international informal, domestic formal, and domestic informal) differ markedly in their economic, social, cultural, and environmental impacts at both the sectoral and spatial levels. Whereas tourism's economic impact is easily quantified, the social, cultural, and environmental effects of tourism are more difficult to quantify and, hence, to measure. Although certain sociocultural measures are fairly straightforward, such as the number of crimes committed against tourists, numbers of prostitutes, and numbers of migrants, other indicators, including the degree of resentment tourists feel toward visitors, commodification of culture, and pollution attributable to the tourism industry, are much more difficult to operationalize.

It is important to understand that the effects of increased visitation to a place rarely operate in isolation. Tourism's environmental impact, for example, quite often entails social consequences and vice versa. For instance, the development of a large coastal resort may adversely affect local fisheries and result in the break up of traditional fishing communities. The creation of national parks to attract ecotourists may also interrupt social practices relating to the procurement of firewood and building materials, as in the case in Nepal. Similarly, the growth of a vibrant tourism industry in a particular place (economic impact) often impinges on the local culture as traditional practices become commodified—something to sell to tourists.

CHAPTER 3

The International Formal Sector

Megaresorts and National Tourism Planning in Mexico

My first visit to Cancún was in the spring of 1997. I had been traveling slowly along Mexico's Caribbean coast, from Chetumal, a large market town near the Belizean border, through the seaside villages of Tulum and Xpu-Ha, which at the time were international backpacker destinations noted for their uncrowded beaches, inexpensive campgrounds (or just places to pitch a tent), cabañas, and guesthouses. The coastline of Quintana Roo was still largely devoid of the massive tourism developments that have come to characterize it in more recent years, at least as far south as Tulum. What Mexican tourism officials call the Cancún *mega-proyecto* (megaproject) had yet to burst its bubble and produce wave after wave of tourism development along the Yucatán littoral. Even in 1997, however, signs of the coastal tourist boom were imminent, and nothing portended an ever larger influx of northern visitors more than a new four-lane highway under construction from Cancún to points further south. After passing through Xcaret, I stopped just south of Cancún in the older resort of Playa del Carmen and pitched my tent in a small campground near the center of town.

I found Playa del Carmen a very interesting place. Originally a Mayan village known as Xaman-Ha (Waters of the North), the town had become part seaside resort catering to Mexican nationals, part honky-tonk, part cruise ship port of

51

call and ferry launch to the upscale resort island of Cozumel, and part wintering destination for retired Québecois gentlemen "too old to take the cold," as one of them told me. The town's raison d'être was in nearly all respects tourism: The beaches were crowded with sun bathers from dawn to dusk; T-shirt and cheap souvenir shops, tattoo parlors, cafés, and restaurants lined the streets; and the seaside bars along the beach blaring a mix of ranchero music and rock and roll were full of tourists most of the day and night.

Many of the changes occurring along Mexico's Caribbean coastline, and indeed along the country's Pacific and Gulf coasts as well, were written into Playa del Carmen's evolving urban geography. Large hotels and international fast-food restaurants were displacing an earlier, less regulated, and smaller scale form of tourism still in evidence further south, in the villages of Xpu-Ha and Tulum, for instance, and along parts of Mexico's Pacific coast east of Puerto Escondido, in such places as Mazunte and Zipolite (see chapter 4). The campground where I pitched my tent, which also featured a barracks-like structure lined with rows of hammocks available for twenty or thirty pesos a night (U.S.$3) and rented mostly by young backpackers from Europe, Canada, and the United States, was literally a stone's throw away from a posh hotel complex. Just south of Playa del Carmen was the gated tourist community of Playacar, catering mainly to wealthier North Americans. Although I had not fully realized it at the time, what I had been passing through since leaving Chetumal were different types of tourist spaces; generally speaking, the closer I got to Cancún, the more organized, formal, and internationalized the spaces had become.

I spent about ten days commuting to Cancún from Playa del Carmen, mainly for purposes of photographing the tourist city, interviewing tourists, and, whenever possible, speaking with tourism resort workers. I soon learned that quite a few long-term tourists who stayed in Playa del Carmen, most of them from the United States, also commuted on a fairly regular basis to Cancún and earned money by begging from tourists on the beach. One of them, Bob,[1] told me he had been begging a few times each week since December and made enough money to live comfortably in Playa del Carmen. For Bob, "comfortably" meant enough money for beer, marijuana, two or three meals a day, daily rent for his hammock, and money for bus fare to and from Cancún. What I found surprising was how generous many of the better-off tourists seemed to be; on at least two occasions, Bob told me he had "hit up" a person for U.S.$20. When I asked him how much longer he intended to stay in Playa del Carmen and beg from tourists, he said he did not know for sure but would probably stay on until the late spring or early summer, when there were fewer tourists on the beach and the ones who were there were on bargain summer tours and less likely to part with their money. I also found it somewhat remarkable that Bob had developed a tourist typology much like the ones I had read about in the scholarly literature. He could spot a psychocentric tourist a mile away and knew almost instinctively who would give him money and who would not.

Although there were some less expensive places to stay in Cancún, most of them off the island proper in the part of the resort city Mexican tourist authorities had developed as a service center for the beachfront resorts, Cancún's tourist businesses catered almost entirely to short-term international visitors who had either come on prepaid package tours or were spending at least U.S.$100 per day for a room at one of the four- or five-star beachside hotels. Paul was one of the first tourists I spoke with in Cancún, a dentist and self-described "regular guy" from southern California. Paul and his family, which consisted of his wife Tammy and their two young children, were staying at one of Cancún's five-star hotels, the same place they had stayed the previous few years. They had been to some of the nearby tourist attractions, including a *cenote* (sinkhole), and went on excursions to Tulum and Chitzen Itza to view the Mayan ruins there. Paul was very intrigued with what he described as the "hippie scene" in Tulum, and he expressed a longing to be other than a "two-week-a-year tourist," as he put it. Despite his desire to expand his tourist horizons, however, Paul enjoyed his time in Cancún and told me he intended to return again the following year.

According the WTO, there are many Pauls roaming around the Third World. In 2001, nearly 700 million people undertook an international journey lasting more than twenty-four hours, up from just 25 million in 1950, and a fairly sizable chunk were First World residents visiting Third World destinations (World Tourism Organization 2002a). About two-thirds of them were pleasure tourists like Paul and his family, with the rest traveling on business or to visit family and friends. International tourist spending exceeded U.S.$450 billion in 2001, making tourism one of the world's largest export industries in terms of total receipts (World Tourism Organization 2002a). Although island nations in the Caribbean, South Pacific, and Indian Ocean regions are the most heavily dependent on international tourist spending, tourism receipts represent more than 25 percent of merchandise exports and more than 40 percent of commercial services exports in at least sixty-three countries in both the First and Third Worlds.

A large and growing body of evidence indicates that the rapid increase of First World visitor arrivals in Third World countries is associated with both positive and negative outcomes. Whereas it often leads to increased employment opportunities, regional growth, and an increase in foreign exchange receipts for the nation as a whole, the development of international tourist resorts and luxury accommodation facilities often proves disastrous for particular places and the people that inhabit them. Throughout the Third World, in both rural and urban areas, local residents are displaced by land grabbers, real estate speculators, state authorities, and others involved in the provisioning of international tourist space. In a number of low-income countries, the rapid growth of tourism has fueled, or perhaps has been fueled by, the growth of a large sex industry (Leheny 1995; Seabrook 1996; Truong 1990). In Bangkok's Patpong Road district, along Havana's Malecon, and in the beach resorts of Goa, the Dominican Republic, and Sri Lanka, among dozens of other places, it is now common to see middle-aged men from Western Europe, the United States, Australia, and Japan with local girls and boys as young as thirteen or fourteen and sometimes even younger (Davidson 1996; Seabrook 1995).[1] In places where it fails to eradicate the local culture and society completely, international tourism development commodifies and disrupts traditional cultures, degrades the environment, and often leads to increased criminal activity, rising levels of drug and alcohol abuse by local inhabitants, and social unrest.

The Political Economy of International Formal-Sector Tourism in the Third World

Until fairly recently, scholarly work on tourism had almost wholly neglected the relation of tourism to underlying forces of production and reproduction and focused instead on tourist behavior, economic costs and benefits, and microlevel impact (Ioannides 1995; Truong 1990). The same holds true for Third World tourism, where most studies fail to situate it within the larger debate on development and underdevelopment.[2] It is clear, however, that the rapid growth of international tourism has not occurred in a vacuum; political economy approaches to the subject prove useful in uncovering the global dynamics behind the growth of tourism, as well as provide a more critical perspective within which to view the costs and benefits of what has become a large global industry.[3]

With few exceptions, scholars have also failed to explore the state's role in regulating leisure activities, an important one because the capitalist state has proven instrumental in creating the legal, technological, infrastructural, and ideological basis for the rapid growth of the international tourism industry (Ioannides 1995). The state's regulation of the wage relation in the First World, including legislation regarding hours and vacation-time, was instrumental in the growth of a large middle class in the post–World War II period. State subsidies to the aerospace industry that allowed for the development of jet aircraft have both opened up long-haul travel markets and significantly reduced the cost of air travel. State-subsidized airport construction serves the same purpose. And because the international tourism industry is an information-intensive industry that relies on computerized reservations systems, government subsidies to information industries have likewise benefited the travel and hospitality industries. In addition, many governments in both the

First and Third Worlds have promoted the industry internationally through state-owned airlines, advertising campaigns, and the establishment of tourist offices in key overseas markets.

On the ideological plane, the capitalist state in the core countries, through such institutions as the World Bank and the International Monetary Fund, fervently champions a market-based ideology conducive to the development of tourism in Third World countries. According to mainstream development ideology, each country or region should specialize in the production of those goods and services for which it has a comparative advantage or those they are able to produce relatively more efficiently. As with the production of primary products, many Third World countries enjoy a comparative advantage in the production of labor-intensive tourism commodities. They have the sun, sand, sea, and sex demanded by international travelers, and they are often unable to compete with the OECD countries in the production of manufactured goods and advanced producer and consumer services. For these reasons, the World Bank and other development agencies have touted tourism as part of an overall development strategy for Third World countries.

Fordism Ascendant

One place to begin a critical discussion of IFS tourism is with the factors giving rise to such rapid growth of the international tourism industry. Foremost among these is the general increase in wealth and leisure time enjoyed by growing numbers of First World workers since the 1940s, a trend attributable to the dynamics of the post–World War II economic system, what political theorist Antonio Gramsci called *Fordism*. Fordist production systems or, in the parlance of French regulation theory, Fordist "regimes of accumulation," couple increases in investment and worker productivity with real increases in wages and leisure time, accomplished within the framework of a particular state-society relationship, or "mode of regulation," in which the state takes an active role in the economic system through its demand management policies and regulation of the wage relation (e.g., Keynesian fiscal and monetary policies, collective bargaining, etc.; Aglietta 1979; Lipietz 1987). Fordism effectively ties mass production to mass consumption and the realization problem, or what Marxists call the *problem of overproduction*, is solved internally, at least for large numbers of people in the First World. Prior to the advent of Fordism, the realization problem had been solved externally through war or imperial expansion (Harvey 1989; Lenin 1975; Luxemburg 1968).

Trade figures for the postwar period provide convincing evidence that Fordism had indeed solved the realization problem on the national level. Throughout the Fordist era, exports as a percentage of manufactured goods fell in all the core industrial economies while trade with the underdeveloped periphery remained negligible. The same is true of foreign investment: The decline of raw materials production in the peripheral countries relative to the metropolitan centers coincided with reduced investment in the periphery relative to the core. From the standpoint of central Fordism, the status of the Third World went from being an exploitable region to a largely irrelevant one.

As we have seen, the total number of tourist arrivals worldwide increased dramatically in the postwar period, from 25 million in 1950 to nearly 700 million in 2000, figures that underestimate the actual growth of tourism in high-income countries because they represent only international tourist flows (World Tourism Organization 2002a). During the same period, real wages in the OECD countries increased nearly fourfold. The First World countries, with their high spending consumers and well-developed travel infrastructure, represent both the largest market for and the largest suppliers of international tourism goods and services. The United States, Canada, Western Europe, Japan, and Australia currently account for more than 75 percent of the market for international tourism goods and services and for close to 65 percent of total value added in the industry worldwide (World Tourism Organization 1997). Because international tourism is a highly income-elastic commodity, the implication for the Third World was that tourist arrivals from the metropolitan countries would increase dramatically, particularly for those countries in close proximity to First World markets.

Travel-related technologies and declining transportation costs are additional factors that have fueled the growth of international tourism. The introduction of commercial jet airliners in the 1960s made relatively inexpensive long-haul travel to Third World countries increasingly feasible for larger numbers of First World tourists. Between 1960 and 1970, the decade in which the major airlines first began utilizing jet aircraft for most of their passenger flights, European incomes rose over 50 percent while the cost of jet air transportation fell by 9 percent in real terms (Peppelenbosch and Tempelman 1972). Computerized reservations systems, first developed in the 1960s by the major airlines in an effort to rationalize their ticketing procedures, have grown in scope and now integrate the international travel industry's air, hotel, rental car, and cruise-ship bookings (World Tourism Organization 1994). The Internet has further broadened the reach of First World travel consumers; there are now few countries to which one cannot book an air flight and hotel reservations from a desktop personal computer using a credit card.

Rising incomes, more advanced travel-related technologies, and cheaper transportation costs for First World residents mean that more of them travel to the Third World for business and pleasure. Between 1950 and 1990, tourist arrivals in low-income regions increased more than 40-fold, from 2.3 million in 1950 to 113.7 million in 1990, and grew more rapidly than international arrivals in First World regions and in the world as a whole (World Tourism

Organization 1992). Many Third World countries registered extremely rapid growth in international arrivals throughout the postwar period. The number of international visitors to Mexico, for example, increased from less than 500,000 in 1950 to over 19 million in 1997, or close to 4,000 percent (Jimenez 1993). Thailand's international arrivals grew from 800,000 in 1980 to 5 million in 1996, an average annual increase of 14.7 percent. During the same period, Indonesia's international arrivals grew even faster, averaging 20.6 percent annual growth, from less than 250,000 in 1980 to over 5 million in 1996. Indeed, Third World megaresorts such as Cancún, Nusa Dua, and Montego Bay would be unthinkable and certainly economically infeasible were it not for the large numbers of international, primarily First World tourists who choose to travel there. For example, Cancún, receives nearly 80 percent of its visitors from the United States and Canada. As we will see, Mexican planners designed the country's entire network IFS tourism resorts to provide for the recreational needs of international, primarily North American tourists.

Fordism in Decline

By the 1960s, the productivity increases underlying the success of central Fordism began to taper off. Profit rates declined, investment levels fell, and a period of stagnation set in for the core capitalist (OECD) countries. The problem was primarily one of wage rigidity: Productivity lagged behind real wage growth, and the share of income going to privileged sectors of society began to decline (Harvey 1989). Government spending continued to increase, however, a trend that would eventually lead to fiscal crisis and high levels of inflation (O'Connor 1973). The resulting "stagflationary" spiral, characterized by high rates of both inflation and unemployment, signaled something was wrong with the underlying economic system. In essence, a slowdown in productivity growth came into conflict with the mass purchasing power associated with a relatively higher wage (Aglietta 1979; Harvey 1989; Lipietz 1986).

At the same time, real reductions in the cost of transportation and communication made offshore investment more attractive. Entire industries relocated first to low-wage regions in the First World countries themselves, then overseas to the Caribbean, Latin America, and the Asia-Pacific region. Migrating industries included not only traditional, labor-intensive ones, such as textiles and footwear, but also high-technology industries, such as electronics, semiconductors, and automobile manufacturing. The rapid growth of export platforms and maquiladoras throughout the Third World in the late 1960s and early 1970s led some researchers to conclude that nothing less than a new international division of labor (NIDL) was taking shape (Froebel, Heinrichs, and Kreye 1979). Whereas the "old international division of labor" was characterized by an exchange of the primary products of the periphery for the manufactured goods of the core, the NIDL is based on the world market factory and the free export zone, the high-repression, low-wage export platforms of Third World countries. From the standpoint of the world economy as a whole, the NIDL is essentially a zero-sum game; as firms in the core countries move their production sites offshore to Third World locations, the industrialization of the periphery complements the deindustrialization of the core.

Tourism and Post-Fordism   The much-heralded transition to post-Fordist regimes of accumulation has had distinct consequences for the ways we conceive of leisure time and for the demand and supply of tourism goods and services. We may begin with a simple fact: Real wages have stagnated or declined since the 1970s, at least in the United States, and the average American worked three weeks more in 1996 than in 1982. The scrapping of hard-won labor legislation regarding hours and vacation time means that larger numbers of people work longer for lower wages. Americans consequently have less money to spend and less leisure time in which to spend it (Schor 1991). Moreover, the erosion of job security, another hallmark of the post-Fordist period, translates into reduced demand for tourism goods and services— especially long-haul tourism—because working people are more reluctant to deplete their meager savings on "inessentials" such as vacation time. Overall, the growth in outbound U.S. tourism has slowed considerably since the 1960s, which is not surprising in light of the rapid restructuring of the North American economy during the same period.[4] And because tourism is a highly income-elastic commodity, it is very sensitive to individuals' perceptions of economic well-being. During economic recessions, for example, world tourist arrivals decline sharply; people tend to travel less often, over shorter distances, and for shorter periods of time. Thus, as a result of Japan's current recession, Japanese outbound tourism has slowed considerably (to the detriment of Southeast Asian economies), whereas domestic tourism and travel to South Korea has increased (McDowell 1998).

In absolute terms, however, there are still more Americans than ever traveling overseas, an indication that countervailing effects of post-Fordist economic organization have influenced the demand for travel- and tourism-related goods and services. The shift to post-Fordism may indeed have served to polarize wealth and income in the First World countries further, but it may also have resulted, oddly enough, in more international tourism—or at least more high-end tourism—overall, due to the enlargement of upper-income groups and a growth in business travel stemming from an increasingly globalized economy. In other words, the "shrinking middle" may not matter, at least as far as the tourism industry is concerned. Real incomes are still rising for many people in high-income countries and for a much smaller number of people in low-income countries, and even though growth in international tourist arrivals slowed in the 1980s and 1990s, tourist expenditures continued to increase at a fairly high rate. In other words, relatively fewer Americans travel internationally, but those who do travel abroad spend more money. "Alternative tourism" and business travel are among the fastest growing segments of the international tourism industry, forms of specialized travel characterized by both the upper-middle-class origins of their practitioners and their relatively high price-tags, particularly when compared with traditional package tourism (Munt 1994; Whelan 1991).

An additional reason for the continued growth of outbound tourism from the First World is that travel itself has become less expensive, particularly to Third World destinations. Cheaper international travel stems in part from real reductions in the cost of air transportation and the cost economies achieved through computerization and the development of global distribution systems. It also stems from the structural adjustment programs Third World governments have implemented at the behest of the IMF and other international financial agencies. Because effective structural adjustment policies and, more recently, floating exchange rates dampen domestic inflation while sharply devaluing the national currency, the net result is cheaper imports for holders of dollars, euros, and yen, a fact not lost on those in the tourism industry who understand that falling exchange rates without corresponding increases in domestic inflation translate into lower prices for tourist experiences. As Susan Spano (1996), a travel correspondent for *The New York Times*, reports, "ever since the 1994 Mexican currency devaluation, I've been like a vulture as the peso has plummeted in value."

Increasing market segmentation in the tourism industry is another result of the shift to post-Fordist modes of economic regulation. Global restructuring and the rise of flexibly specialized regimes of accumulation have significantly altered class configurations in both high-income and low-income countries (Castells 1989; Harvey 1989). With the decline of mass-production industries and the Fordist mass consumption associated with them, tourism promoters must now tailor their product to a wider range of potential customers. Apart from package tours to traditional destinations, a whole host of "alternative" tourist destinations have sprung up, catering to a growing segment of elite tourists. The growth of new informational technologies such as the Internet and worldwide reservations systems has facilitated increased market segmentation: Tour operators can more easily customize holiday itineraries, and the travel options open to potential consumers have proliferated (Poon 1988; 1990). Today, anyone with a personal computer, a modem, and a credit card has direct access to computerized hotel and airline reservations systems such as Sabre. The growth in specialty tours and alternative travel has a special relevance for the Third World because most of the earth's "exotic" places are in the mountain ranges, rain forests, and savannas of Africa, Asia, and Latin America.

The appearance of new tourist practices is also in keeping with other aspects of a post-Fordist world; even more so than under Fordism, flexible accumulation entails the rapid growth of credit, the commodification of all aspects of life, and the need for faster turnover time of commodities and "fashions" through extensive advertising and the planned obsolescence of commodities (Harvey 1989; Urry 1990). Accordingly, new industries such as tourism are systemically important because in order to avoid devalorization of their assets, capitalists must continually devise new ways of creating and maintaining effective demand for a continuous stream of new products and commodities. The growth of tourism and other leisure activities has certainly provided capitalists with increased investment outlets, from a succession of "world's largest hotels" in Las Vegas and Atlantic City to the rapid growth of gaming facilities across the United States to Disney Worlds and other large entertainment centers in the United States, Europe, and Japan. A quick glance at any one of the many glossy travel and tourism magazines now available, not to mention the scores of new travel guides that appear every year, reveals that the industry is forever touting "new" and "must-see" destinations all over the globe.

The travel and tourism industry is itself well suited to the flexible employment practices and production techniques of post-Fordism, another way in which tourism contributes to the revalorization of capital. Tourism consultant Auliana Poon (1990, 113) contrasts what she calls the "mass, standardized and rigidly packaged tourism" of the 1960s and 1970s with a new tourism "driven by flexibility, segmentation, and diagonal integration." She points to the extensive use of information technologies, most notably computerized reservations systems, by tourism enterprises; airline deregulation; extensive networking among small tourism-related firms; and changing consumer tastes as key factors underlying a new "flexible" tourism practice in the Caribbean. Similarly, sociologist John Urry (1990) contrasts what he takes to be the "old" tourism of the mass-based seaside resort and holiday camp, "the quintessential example of Fordist holiday-making," with the "new" consumer-driven and individually tailored holiday where Fordist holiday camps become post-Fordist "holiday-worlds" (Urry 1990, 14). Urry also finds much of the academic discourse on flexibility prefigured in the tourism industry, where "the so-called restructuring strategy of the 1980s, the flexible use of labour, is something that has characterised many tourist-related services for some decades" (Urry 1990, 80).

Finally, it is important to note that Fordism is not yet a thing of the past. By almost any definition, the middle classes in the high-income countries are still the most numerous group. And whereas Europeans and North Americans have decreased their relative demand for mass-produced package tours in recent years, the absolute number of people who travel on package tours is still very large. More than 80 percent of British tourists traveling to Greece, for example, do so on a package tour; Dutch tourists to the Caribbean overwhelmingly purchase prepaid, mass-produced holidays; and Cancún, a middle-class holiday destination par excellence, is one of the most popular overseas destinations for U.S. tourists (Ioannides 1993). Indeed, as Daniel Hiernaux-Nicolas (1999, 131) observes, "at least until the mid-1980s, Cancún could be considered a paradigm of a totally Fordist tourist resort, if Fordism is defined as large-scale production of a uniform product according to inflexible organizational principles." Certainly, the mass-consumed tourism spectacle lives on in the likes of Orlando, Las Vegas, Disney World, Times Square, Australia's Gold Coast, and the rapid growth of the cruise ship industry, to name but a few examples. Thus, even though international tourist arrivals did not grow as rapidly in the 1980s and 1990s as they did in the 1960s and 1970s, the industry remains a large and growing component of global production and consumption.

The Impact of International Formal-Sector Tourism   IFS tourism has grown rapidly in many Third World countries, radically transforming those regions where it has taken root. Yet despite the rapid growth of tourism to Third World destinations in the 1950s and 1960s, it was not until the mid-1970s that social scientists began systematically to examine the effects of tourism on Third World societies. As late as 1972, Peppelenbosch and Tempelman could claim that "from a social scientific viewpoint—certainly from a human geographical angle—almost no researches [on Third World tourism] have been made" (Peppelenbosch and Tempelman 1972, 52). The lack of studies is surprising, especially in light of the many positive and largely untested claims made about the industry by government officials, international lending agencies, and industry spokespersons. Throughout the 1970s, 1980s, and 1990s, however, numerous critiques of IFS tourism coming from the academy, the church, and citizens of Third World countries themselves point to the many problems associated with mass tourism from First World to Third World countries. The costs and benefits of international tourism in the Third World extend to the environmental, social, economic, and cultural spheres. I will consider the pros and cons of tourism in each of these areas, beginning with the industry's economic impact.

Economic Impact   With few exceptions, most Third World governments initially viewed the rapid growth of IFS tourism through rose-colored glasses, welcoming the influx of First World tourists and their dollars, francs, yen, and other hard currencies. Policy makers saw tourism as a relatively easy way of earning foreign exchange and generating employment. The World Bank and other multilateral institutions encouraged them to develop their international tourism sectors, issuing loans for the construction of airports, roads, hotels, and other parts of the tourism infrastructure (de Kadt 1979; Wood 1979). The development of Cancún, for example, was originally financed with funds from the Inter-American Development Bank (IDB; Hiernaux-Nicolas 1999). The World Bank, the IDB, and other development agencies encouraged the development of the IFS tourism industry largely on the grounds of comparative advantage and free-trade theory because international tourism would allow Third World countries to cash in on their unspoiled environments, natural attractions, and surplus labor force (de Kadt 1979).

In many respects, the expectations of tourism planners were met. Since the 1950s, IFS tourism has become a major Third World export and a staple of many low-income economies, and although tourism is an important industry in both the First and Third Worlds, it is clearly more important in the Third World. By the late 1990s, among the sixty-seven countries in which tourism receipts account for more than 4 percent of GNP, none were major industrialized countries, and only eight were European Union members: Austria, Czech Republic, Greece, Hungary, Ireland, Poland, Portugal, and Spain. Island nations in the Caribbean, South Pacific, and Indian Ocean regions are the most heavily dependent on international tourism spending. In terms of the share of GNP accounted for by international tourist spending, the world's thirty most tourism-dependent countries are all island nations. Low-income countries are also most dependent on tourism as a source of foreign exchange: All countries where tourism represents more than half of all merchandise exports are low-income countries, and in only six high-income countries does tourism account for more than 50 percent of commercial services exports (Austria, Ireland, New Zealand, Poland, Portugal, and Spain).

In other respects, however, the growth of IFS tourism in low-income countries has proven less of an economic boon than its proponents initially claimed. Whereas tourism has indeed enabled Third World countries to earn foreign exchange, it has also led to significant outflows of hard currency in the form of imports and profit repatriation. Among the many problems facing tourism planners in the Third World is, as I have pointed out, the degree to which the international formal tourism sector is dependent on a handful of countries for its major markets. Another is the worldwide geographic concentration of the industry in value-added terms. A third problem concerns the power of the large transnational hotel and airline companies vis-à-vis the low-income countries where they operate. The triple concentration of the industry, in terms of markets, producer-regions, and ownership, has distinct implications for Third World countries that pursue tourism as a development strategy. A second set of issues concerns the ways in which formal-sector tourism firms actually operate: their employment characteristics, leakage of revenues out of the firm in the form of imports and profit repatriation, and the kinds of linkages that exist between formal-sector tourism firms and other firms in the host country's economy. I will consider each group of questions in turn.

First World countries represent both the largest market for and the largest suppliers of tourism goods and services. The United States, Canada, Western Europe, Israel, Japan, Australia, and New Zealand together account for more than 75 percent of the market for international tourism goods and services and produce more than 65 percent of value added in the industry worldwide (World Tourism Organization 1996). The wealthy countries have not only registered increases in the total number of tourist arrivals but have also seen their share of total industry-wide value-added increase over the last forty years. In contrast, Third World countries have also hosted growing numbers of travelers and have even increased their relative share of international arrivals, but they have seen their share of value-added decline during the same period.

The discrepancy between a growing market share in terms of arrivals and a decreasing market share in terms of receipts from tourism is particularly evident in some countries. Mexico, for example, is now one of the world's leading tourism exporters, accounting for more international tourist arrivals than all but six countries (World Tourism Organization 1997). At the same time, Mexico's total tourism revenues have fallen precipitously since the early 1990s, largely the result of the peso crisis and the IMF structural adjustment policies the country's elite has pursued at the behest of the United States, the International Monetary Fund, and the nation's creditors. Indeed, it was not until Mexico first devalued its currency in the mid-1980s that the country's premier tourist attraction, Cancún, began attracting a majority of foreign tourists; prior to 1984 and due largely to Mexico's "overvalued" exchange rate, the resort overwhelmingly attracted wealthy domestic travelers (Hiernaux-Nicolas 1999).[5]

There are, of course, additional structural factors that explain why Third World countries are providing more and more tourism services and receiving relatively less foreign exchange in return. One is the fact that Third World tourism exports are not exempt from the general decline in the terms of trade for Third World exports. As early as the 1950s, Argentine economist Raul Prebisch and the Economic Commission for Latin America (ECLA) found that Third World countries needed to export ever larger quantities of their primary products to the First World in order to receive the same basket of manufactured goods in return. Prebisch identified inflexible labor markets in the North as a major factor behind the declining terms of trade: Whereas productivity increases in northern markets are translated into higher wages,[6] increased productivity in the South results only in lower prices on international markets. What is true of bananas, sisal, cacao, nickel, and textiles is also true of tourism goods and services, which have not proven an exception to this general rule (Wood 1979).

The reason is clear when tourism goods and services, like traditional primary products, are seen as competitively produced exports with markets restricted to just a few countries. Third World countries are structurally dependent on the oligopsonistic transportation and hospitality firms based in the North (Britton 1982; Ioannides 1994). Without access to marketing information and the means to shape consumer demand through advertising and tourist promotion, low-income countries must compete with each other for inclusion on the itineraries of foreign-owned cruise ship lines, travel organizations, and airlines. Because Third World tourism destinations are highly fungible (one beach or island is as good as the next), the large airlines, hotel companies, and tour operators easily play them off against each other, a fact that serves to tilt the terms of trade heavily against destination countries (Pattullo 1996). Increased competition among nations producing similar tourism commodities is essentially no different than the competitive structure of any other Third World industry, along with the problems of declining terms of trade that this creates. The fact that tour operators in the First World countries have literally thousands of similar sun, sand, sea, and sex destinations to choose from, with most of their customers either not knowing or even caring which one they go to, means that Third World resort areas are under pressure to cut prices and provide more subsidies to lure foreign investment. Lower net receipts for tourism goods and services translate into declining terms of trade in international markets.

In addition to the structural effects of declining terms of trade for tourism exports, Third World tourism is also dependent on the metropolitan countries in other ways. Recession in the larger First World countries translates into reduced demand for IFS tourism goods and services because tourism commodities are both income and price elastic: That is, after one loses one's job, the first thing to be put on hold is one's yearly vacation in Barbados or similar tourism destination. The oil price hikes in the 1970s and recession in the early 1980s and early 1990s each resulted in significant drops in tourist expenditure in the Third World (World Tourism Organization 1986; 1996). Additionally, the consumption of tourism goods and services, particularly pleasure tourism, is greatly susceptible to perceived international political developments. When international tourists and the travel firms that organize their tours deem a particular destination or region "unsafe," the tourism industry in that particular region/destination will almost inevitably collapse. Such has been the case in Egypt and India (Kashmir) in the 1990s, in Grenada and Fiji in the 1980s, in Mexico (particularly the state of Chiapas) in 1994, in Northern Ireland since the early 1970s, and in Indonesia and most of Africa today, among other destinations. The phenomenon was particularly acute in the fall of 2001, when one result of the September 11, 2001 terror attacks in New York and Virginia was a precipitous decline in travel bookings worldwide.

The dependence of Third World IFS tourism on a handful of First World countries is not limited to market-based structural factors, such as declining terms of trade for Third World exports or to the vagaries of the business cycle and perceived political instability. In many cases the dependency relationship is much more immediate. For example, much of the tourism infrastructure in the Third World is owned or controlled by resort transnational corporations (TNCs) in the First World. Firms such as Club Méditerranée, Hilton, Sheraton, and Accor control large parts of the upscale, formal-sector tourism market in countries as diverse as Mexico, Indonesia, the Bahamas, and India. As noted earlier, much of the reason for the low multiplier effect of tourism spending in the Third World is the large outflow of hard currency required to sustain the industry. Profit repatriation, particularly evident in countries with a large for-eign-owned sector, makes up a significant part of the outflow. Indeed, countries that seek to attract the hotel and resort TNCs are almost always required to stipulate generous profit repatriation provisions as part of any tourism develop-ment strategy, even in countries that otherwise impose onerous restrictions on the outflow of foreign exchange (Britton 1983; Pattullo 1996).

An increasing trend among resort and hotel TNCs with operations in low-income countries is to forego direct ownership in favor of franchise fees, licensing arrangements, and management contracts. The trend varies accord-ing to the level of perceived risk in specific countries and regions. In Africa, for example, most foreign IFS hotel operators prefer to manage—and not to own—the properties bearing their names (Ankomah 1991). In this way, the risk assumed by the TNC is virtually eliminated and shifted to domestic elites. One implication of this arrangement, of course, is that the flow of foreign ex-change into the Third World in the form of direct foreign investment, one of the supposed benefits of IFS tourism development, ceases. TNCs invest noth-ing, borrow domestically, assume little if any risk, and collect high fees for their management expertise, licensing trademarks, and computerized reserva-tions systems.

Despite the structural factors working against the interests of low-income countries, the World Bank and other international development agencies ini-tially promoted and continue to promote tourism development as a way for the poor countries to exploit their comparative advantage as sea, sun, sand, and sex destinations. It was and still is widely held by industry boosters that tourism development would prove to be a clean industry and an economic boon for Third World societies with few economic or other costs; not only will tourism increase foreign exchange revenue and create employment, it will also generate significant external economies. For example, the construction of roads, water, and electrical supply systems, airports, and other infrastructural development not only furthers the developmental objectives of the tourism industry but also generates growth in the country's other economic sectors. Similarly, arguments in favor of tourism development maintain that employ-ment and management skills not only benefit the tourism industry itself but are also transferable to other sectors of the economy.

When evaluated in light of the available evidence, however, the claims of industry promoters are only partially borne out by the facts and almost always omit serious discussion of the industry's major drawbacks. One example is foreign exchange. Tourism development is often justified solely on the grounds that it generates copious amounts of hard currency. Most Third World governments, including socialist ones such as Cuba and Tanzania, have embarked on tourist development schemes for the sole purpose of acquiring foreign exchange with which to import capital and other goods necessary for their overall industrial development strategies. It is often the case, however, that tourists from the First World demand goods and services with a high import content. The upmarket hotels and resorts in the Caribbean and elsewhere must import large quantities of food, construction materials, and the technical "advice" of expatriate managers in order to vie successfully for the international tourist dollar. Some researchers have found that when the foreign exchange requirements of airports, cruise-ship docking facilities, internal transportation projects, and other infrastructural prerequisites for a successful tourism policy are taken into account, formal-sector tourism development may even result in a net drain of foreign exchange (Britton 1982; 1991; Britton and Clark 1987; Freitag 1994; Rajotte 1987; Tüting and Dixit n.d.).

Directly related to the question of foreign exchange leakage is the concept of the tourism-spending multiplier, a number that reflects the general integration of the tourism industry into a given economy. It measures the amount of employment, income, or other economic magnitude generated in the economy for a given unit of tourism expenditure. The more highly integrated the tourism industry is with the larger economy and the smaller the import leakages, the greater will be the multiplier effect of tourism spending, and the better tourism will be for the country in question, at least economically. Conversely, the less integrated the industry is with other sectors of the economy—the more enclavic it is—the smaller will be the tourism multiplier.

Early studies of the impact of tourism on Third World economies found the tourism multiplier to be quite large, often exceeding a value of two. In other words, for every dollar of tourism expenditure generated in a given economy, a total of two additional dollars of income were generated in the economy (Zinder 1969). Later studies pointing to the large amounts of imported goods and services a successful tourism industry requires have found the earlier accounts grossly inflated and have significantly reduced the estimates of the tourism multiplier (Archer 1989). One study found that in the Bahamas, for each dollar of foreign exchange entering the country in the form of tourist expenditure, more than seventy cents leaves the country to pay for imports (Pattullo 1996). The World Travel and Tourism Council (WTTC), a London-based industry association, estimates total leakages in the Caribbean as a whole at about 50 percent (World Travel and Tourism Council 1996). Of course, the actual multiplier for any particular country depends on the prevailing economic conditions in that country and the structure of its economy. The Cook Islands, Barbados, the Bahamas, and other small island nations with highly developed tourism industries and un(der)developed industrial sectors will generally register much smaller multipliers than India, Thailand, Mexico, and other large countries with highly extensive and diverse industrial structures.[7] Country size, however, does not always correlate with the extent of import leakages and the consequent value of the tourism spending multiplier. The Bahamas, for instance, compares quite favorably in this respect with Indonesia. A major problem with effectively measuring multipliers in low-income countries is a lack of data; input-output tables are notoriously difficult to construct, even for high-income economies.

Apart from the industry's contribution to foreign exchange earnings and a positive balance of payments, tourism firms are also said to provide Third World workers with much-needed employment opportunities. In regions hosting large numbers of tourists, both the absolute number of workers and the percentage of workers in the tourism industry can be very large. In the Caribbean, for example, nearly one in five jobs is found in the tourism sector. According to the WTTC, 22 percent of the Caribbean workforce, or 2.37 million persons, are employed directly or indirectly by hotels, airlines, car rental companies, construction firms, convention centers, airports, and other tourism-related enterprises (World Travel and Tourism Council 1996). In Mexico, 2.2 million workers, over 10 percent of the workforce, is employed in tourism-related enterprises (World Travel and Tourism Council 1996). Of course, the impact of the industry in terms of job provision varies significantly from country to country and regionally. IFS tourism enterprises employ relatively far fewer persons in countries and regions where international tourism is not as important an industry (in India, for example) than they do in places where the industry is one of the leading economic sectors.

Few studies deal with the employment effects of IFS tourism spending in low-income countries, which is surprising, given the economic importance of the industry in many low-income countries and the high rates of un- and underemployment in the Third World. Indeed, one of the major reasons the World Bank and national governments promoted tourism in the first place is because of the industry's supposed employment-generating characteristics. Tourism in particular was singled out as a suitable industry for Third World countries because of its labor intensity and because many of the jobs it creates are low-skilled and present few educational barriers for unskilled individuals entering the workforce. Moreover, the kinds of jobs tourism creates, even those that are low-skilled and menial, such as housekeeping or kitchen positions, are often said to be preferable to employment in agriculture or other traditional industries.

A closer look at employment in IFS tourism establishments bears out some of the claims that proponents of tourism development have made; other claims are seen to be only partially accurate or even misleading. It is, of course, true that tourism generates jobs. According to the WTTC, over 67 million individuals worldwide are directly employed by tourism-related enterprises (World Travel and Tourism Council 1996). The World Bank estimates that each additional IFS hotel room generates between one and two jobs directly or indirectly, depending on conditions prevailing in the subject country (World Bank 1998). We have seen that in the Caribbean and Mexico, IFS tourism employment represents a significant proportion of total employment (22 percent and 10 percent, respectively). Moreover, labor tends to be used more extensively in low-income countries than it does in high-income countries. For each million dollars of additional tourism-related GDP growth in the Caribbean, 113 jobs are created; the comparable figure for Hawaii is 16 (World Travel and Tourism Council 1996; 1998). That tourism is more labor intensive than other industries is revealed, at least in the Caribbean, by the fact that a general increase of 1 million dollars of GDP in the Caribbean creates only ninety-seven jobs (World Travel and Tourism Council 1996).

The real question critics of the tourism industry pose is not whether tourism generates employment; even ardent critics of the industry concede that tourism firms employ relatively large numbers of workers. Rather, the critique of tourism's employment-generating capabilities in both the First and the Third World concerns the quality of jobs created, their relative level of remuneration, the kinds of skills that tourism workers acquire on the job, and the structural changes in labor markets that tourism brings about.

Employment

One place to begin a discussion of tourism-related employment practices is with the economic concept of opportunity cost, or the benefits foregone from engaging in that particular activity. As Alister Mathieson and Geoffrey Wall (1982, 86) point out: "[Tourist] destination areas, in investing their scarce resources in the development of tourism, have seldom considered what the same resources could provide were they to be invested in another industry." Few researchers have sought to measure the opportunity cost of tourism development, largely because of the difficulties involved in measuring foregone benefits. Nonetheless, the concept is useful in evaluating the merits of tourism development and its employment effects, especially because many governments in low-income nations have pursued tourism development strategies.

In the Caribbean, Latin America, and elsewhere in the Third World, the rapid growth of IFS tourism has contributed to structural changes in labor markets as workers are drawn out of agriculture and other traditional industries and into the new tourism enterprises. Many rural workers move readily into the tourism sector, where they find the working conditions, remuneration, and social opportunities of the tourism resorts preferable to those obtained in the countryside. Nonetheless, the shift from an agricultural-based to a service-based economy is not without its costs. Caribbean tourism researcher Polly Pattullo has found that in many Caribbean nations:

> In one generation, the coming of tourism has changed the pattern of employment and the structure of communities forever. Peasant economies have been moulded into service sectors where cane-cutters become bellhops and fisherman are turned into "watersport officers." Where statistics exist, the slide away from agriculture into the service sector over the last 30 years . . . looks dramatic. Traditional life patterns are altered as women become wage-earners, often for the first time, in the hotel sector where the demand for domestic work is high. (Pattullo 1996, 53)

Despite the tourism industry's employment-generating characteristics, numerous critics perceive the shift from raw materials production and cash-crop agriculture to a service-oriented economy producing tourism commodities as only further reinforcing Third World workers' dependence on First World markets. The historical and structural similarities between tourism and cash-crop agriculture are indeed striking. Whereas previously Third World farmers in Africa, Asia, and Latin America were forced to grow cash crops to complement the home industries of their colonizers, today multilateral lending agencies, such as the IMF, the IDB, and the International Finance Corporation—global institutions controlled by the same colonial powers—promote IFS tourism in the Third World as a complement to the industrial economies of the North. The underlying rationale of colonialism, critics of tourism assert, remains the same: the orientation of Third World economies toward the requirements of the metropolitan countries.

The question of the opportunity cost of tourism in employment terms may be stated as follows: Would an alternative deployment of resources result in a greater utilization of labor in the Third World, providing either more employment opportunities or higher quality jobs (or both)? The difficulty in answering the question stems from the problem of quantifying a hypothetical deployment of resources. We can, however, compare employment in tourism with traditional employment in low-income countries, as well as with other important Third World export industries, such as textile production, garment manufacturing, assembly operations, cash-crop agriculture, and electronics. IFS tourism is, for example, relatively labor intensive and compares favorably with other industries in terms of marginal rates of labor absorption. Employment in tourism also compares favorably with employment in cash-crop agriculture and assembly plants, with workers expressing a preference for work in the IFS tourism industry, even those working in low-skilled, low-paying tourism-related occupations.[8]

A persistent critique of IFS tourism is that it tends to create unskilled, lower-paying jobs for local people, whereas the skilled, higher-paying management positions go overwhelmingly to foreign expatriate workers. Moreover, tourism employment is often seasonal in nature, with mass layoffs of workers generally occurring during periods of slack tourism demand in the low season. It is, however, very difficult to generalize about the nature of IFS tourism employment across the Third World because conditions vary greatly from one country to the next. Whereas some countries are overwhelmingly dependent on foreign management consultants for senior management positions, other countries have extensive training programs for resident nationals. Thus, in the Caribbean nation of St. Lucia, close to 90 percent of senior management positions go to expatriate workers, and in much of sub-Saharan Africa, "almost all hotel positions requiring management and technical skills are occupied by Europeans" (Ankomah 1991, 435). In contrast, large Indian-owned tourism firms, such as Oberoi and the Taj Group, recruit and train their own managers, and Indian nationals fill most, if not all, management positions.

Sociocultural Impact

Although tourism has been hailed as "the largest peacetime movement in history" and "a vital force for world peace" (D'Amore 1988, 269; Jafari, Pizam, and Przeclawski 1990, 469), most Third World countries adopt tourism development strategies on the basis of their supposed economic benefits. Indeed, most studies concerned with the social and cultural impacts of tourism in Third World countries note that the income differential between First World "guests" and their Third World "hosts" is usually very large and conclude that the sociocultural exchange is distinctively one-sided. In most Third World countries, the cost of one or two nights' accommodation in a five-star hotel or an enclave resort will routinely exceed the yearly income of most of the country's residents. And despite some claims that tourism leads to greater cultural sensitivity and intercultural awareness, the relationship between host and guest is rarely one of equality but more nearly approximates that between employer and employee, if not master and servant. Whereas tourists are generally interested in relaxing or having fun, hosts are not, because they are there to serve the tourists.

IFS tourism is associated with numerous social ills in Third World tourist destinations. One of the most egregious is the rapid growth of prostitution and pedophilia in Thailand, the Philippines, Cuba, the Dominican Republic, Sri Lanka, Costa Rica, and other Third World countries (Leheny 1995; Seabrook

1996; Srisang 1989; Truong 1990). Although prostitution in the Third World certainly predates mass tourism from the West, the industrialization and rapid growth of prostitution is directly related to the increased demand that mass tourism generates. Specialized tour operators in North America, Western Europe, and Japan have been organizing "sex tours" to Southeast Asia for several decades. The lucrative nature of this type of tourism has led to the enslavement of hundreds of thousands of young girls and boys, usually sold by their desperately poor parents or lured from their villages by brothel agents who transport them to the red-light districts of Bangkok, Manila, and other Third World cities (Human Rights Watch/Asia 1995). The rapid spread of HIV infection and AIDS in the Philippines and Thailand has only recently led to government recognition of the problem (Turshen and Hill n.d.).

Additional social problems associated with mass tourism to the Third World include increasing levels of drug use, rising crime rates, the commodification of culture, and the decline of traditional art forms. The "demonstration effects" of international tourists also play a role in fostering social unrest in the Third World. Tourists' ostentatious displays of wealth and their demand for expensive items results in local elites cultivating similar desires, a phenomenon that may not only result in a drain of foreign exchange to finance the importation of such items but may also create demands on the part of local non-elite groups for a standard of living that the country's limited resources cannot support. Such a situation is socially volatile and can result in rising crime rates, social unrest, and political instability.

In a more general sense, IFS tourism, along with the global media industry, spearheads the consumerist ideology of the West into Third World regions. Under the guise of globalization, consumerism—the belief that increased consumption of nonessential items will lead to happiness and fulfillment—is taking hold everywhere, and in the Third World chiefly among upper-income groups. The implications for income distribution and the preservation of the environment in the Third World—and everywhere else for that matter—are disturbing, as more of the world's resources go into the production of questionably useful items on terms most amenable to the TNCs that propagate consumerism in the first place.

Tourist Enclaves and Spatial Exclusion

One of the more pernicious effects of IFS tourism in the Third World is the way in which its development destroys local communities and displaces long-term residents from their land and traditional ways of life. In the Caribbean, Mexico, South Asia, Southeast Asia, Africa, and South America, indeed, wherever IFS tourism develops, it overwhelmingly tends to benefit outside investors at the expense of the local population. It benefits not only outside investors, however, but outside workers as well, because local people rarely possess the requisite skills and knowledge to labor at any but the most menial occupations in the newly developed resorts. Most of the employment opportunities go to outsiders, many of whom migrate from the national or state capital to take advantage of the new positions. A desk clerk at one of the new five-star resorts in Cancún, for example, is much more likely to be from Mexico City or Guadalajara than from the Yucatán. Only the lowest-paid positions in Cancún and Playa del Carmen go to Quintana Roo's indigenous inhabitants, many of whom claim that they and their families were much better off before the tourism boom hit Mexico's Caribbean coast. Compounding the problem for the local inhabitants is the land and price inflation that tourism inevitably brings in its wake, with higher prices for essential items eroding the purchasing power of their relatively meager wages.

A common refrain voiced by locals at IFS tourist destinations the world over is that the rich people from some other place, usually the state or national capital but also from overseas, displaced the local people from their lands, sometimes violently. Such is the case in Goa, a coastal state in India, where local residents have long protested the development of enclave resorts and the deforestation, pollution, beach erosion, and residential displacement that the poorly planned facilities have brought about. In one display of their adamant opposition to the growth of formal-sector tourism, Goans pelted tourist buses carrying German tourists with rotten tomatoes and carried placards that read: "Our people don't have enough drinking water because it is used by the hotels so that you can swim in their pools" (Informationszentrum Dritte Welt 1990, 12).

The problem is not solely one of local community displacement; it is also one of spatial exclusion, the fencing off of areas reserved exclusively for foreign tourists, national elites, and others who can afford to stay at the newly constructed hotels and holiday "villages," many of which, ironically, are constructed on the sites of what had formerly been real villages. The fencing off of beachfront property and prohibitions against local residents vending to tourists or even *being* on the beach has become widespread in the Caribbean and other Third World regions with large IFS tourism industries.[9] Spatial exclusion is not limited to islands and beachfront property; the practice is common in Third World cities as well, where five-star hotels are often designed as fortresses completely cut off from the surrounding urban space and often not even on the same power grid as the surrounding areas. Although ostensibly undertaken to protect Western tourists from the depredations of the native population, local people view spatially exclusive development as a denial of their birthright and, for the more politically astute among them, as another form of Western imperialism. The cordoning off of affluent spaces from the surrounding villages and, in the case of cities, from surrounding neighborhoods may also resonate with inner-city residents in First World cities, where the exclusive spaces of urban redevelopment are designed to attract the "right" people (whites, yuppies, etc.) while keeping the "wrong" people (persons of color, the homeless, etc.) out.

Environmental Impacts

Despite its image as a clean, smokestack-free industry, mass tourism is associated with numerous environmental ills in both high-income and low-income countries. Environmental impact of mass tourism includes deforestation, coral reef damage, the destruction of flora and fauna, depletion of aquifers, and beach erosion. Much of the environmental damage in tourism regions is the result of uncontrolled development without adequate site monitoring and planning. The likelihood of environmental damage is magnified in peripheral areas of Third World countries, such as the Himalayas, the Belizean Cayes, and the Central American rainforests, because these areas contain extremely delicate and unprotected ecosystems. The indigenous people in such areas, themselves often forming part of the attraction, are overwhelmed by successive waves of tourists and resort developers. Their poverty and lack of political power often preclude the effective implementation of plans designed to protect the environment—assuming, of course, that such plans have been drawn up at all.

The environmental effects of tourism is of particular importance for destinations that have as their chief attraction a pristine natural environment. As Western tourists inundate coastal regions and mountain ranges, the very factors luring tourists to these destinations in the first place are jeopardized. The Thai resort city of Pattaya, which first gained notoriety as a popular R&R destination for U.S. soldiers during the Vietnam war, provides one example of tourism gone awry. The resort, which thirty-five years ago was little more than a fishing village, experienced rapid growth through the 1970s and 1980s as its tourism industry boomed. Due to a lack of proper planning, however, Pattaya went into serious decline in the late 1980s. As the *Economist* notes, "uncontrolled building has ruined its shoreline [and] the sea is coated with a film of raw sewage" (Economist 1991, 72). Pattullo (1996) points to a similar albeit not as dramatic decline in the Caribbean nation of Antigua and Barbuda, where developers have destroyed much of the islands' native mangrove habitat and other wetland areas to construct hotels and other parts of the tourism infrastructure:

> One of the busiest stretches of coast is the sandy sweep of Dickenson Bay and nearby Runaway Bay. There, hotels, including the all-inclusive Sandals (opened in 1993), and restaurants edge the beach, facing seas used by scuba divers and snorkellers, windsurfers and waterskiers. Some locals, however, who are familiar with the recent history of the area have been reluctant to swim in its murky waters, complaining

of itchy skin and, during some months of the year, peculiar smells. (Pattullo 1996, 107)

The cruise-ship industry, one of the fastest-growing categories of IFS travel, has come under attack from governments and environmental groups for dumping garbage, raw sewage, and other waste products at sea and in harbors. (Critics also charge that the industry exploits the Third World workers that it imports from countries outside the regions in which it operates, and that its floating hotels have virtually no linkages with local communities in their "ports of call.") Royal Caribbean Cruises, one of the larger cruise ship companies, pleaded guilty in 1999 to eighteen counts of violating U.S. water pollution laws in areas ranging from the Caribbean to Alaska (Anonymous 1999a). The state of Alaska is suing the company in state court, claiming that it dumped oil and hazardous wastes in Juneau's harbor. It is more difficult for other states and countries to sue the cruise ship companies, particularly small Caribbean microstates with limited resources, because polluting vessels usually discharge their wastes in international waters, outside the legal jurisdiction of any particular country (Klein 2002).

Ecotourism   In recent years, various forms of nature-, culture-, and park-based tourism have become popular with Western travelers. Comprised of two broad categories, "soft" park- and culture-based tourism and "hard" adventure travel, nature- and culture-based tourism (also known as *alternative tourism* and *ecotourism*) feature a pristine environment or traditional culture as a major draw for Western travelers.[10] Although arrivals and expenditure data vary significantly, depending on the definition(s) one employs, ecotourism and other forms of specialty travel to Third World destinations are clearly on the rise. A Canadian government-sponsored survey of seven major North American markets found that 77 percent of respondents indicated that they had recently been on a trip involving "nature, outdoor adventure, or learning about another culture and that was experienced in the countryside or wilderness" (Wight 1996, 9). The World Resources Institute (2005) estimates that nature- and culture-based travel is growing more than twice as rapidly as traditional forms of tourism. According to the Ecotourism Society (Anonymous 1999b), nature-based international travel may be growing up to 7.5 times faster than international tourism overall. As with the international travel and tourism industry generally, some countries have seen their nature-based arrivals grow very rapidly. In Nepal, for example, nature-based arrivals grew by 255 percent from 1980 to 1991. Costa Rica's international visitors, two-thirds of whom visited at least one national park during their stay, increased from 299,000 in 1976 to 924,000 in 1995. In Honduras, nature-related travel is increasing 15 percent annually. Kenya's international tourist arrivals grew 45 percent from 1983 to 1995; 80 percent of all international tourists to Kenya visit a wildlife park, and receipts from nature-based tourism currently represent one-third of the country's foreign exchange receipts (Anonymous 1999b; Honey 1999).

Although they often come with the best of intentions, a rapid influx of eco-tourists and other nature- and culture-oriented travelers may have highly undesirable effects on the places they visit, particularly when they demand the type of luxury accommodation and related tourist facilities common to traditional IFS tourism resort areas. Anyone who has visited Benidorm, Las Palmas, Pattaya, or Acapulco, all traditional mass-tourism destinations, understands that IFS tourism quite often kills the goose that lays the golden egg, and IFS ecotourism destinations have not proven an exception to the general rule. Walter Christaller (1963) was perhaps the first to point out that the initial attractions of a place may have the perverse effect of destroying the very preconditions of its success as a major tourist attraction. The sun, sand, and sea of Spain's Costas, of Caribbean and South Pacific island nations, and of Thailand's resort areas, among other places, attract such large numbers of tourists that once the destinations' carrying capacities are exceeded, filthy water, dying coral reefs, and littered beaches serve to dissuade visitors from making repeat visits. The resorts go into decline as tour operators send their customers elsewhere to enjoy "unspoiled" scenery, only to begin a new cycle of popularity and decline.

Richard Butler's (1980) concept of the resort cycle provides an evolutionary model of IFS tourism destinations that serves to underscore the contentions of ecotourism advocates (and increasingly of IFS ecotourism critics) that without proper planning and continuous monitoring of tourist activity (and even with it), tourism in ecologically sensitive regions is often unsustainable. Predicated on the dynamic nature of formal-sector tourism development, Butler's model traces a series of succeeding stages in the "life" of a typical resort area. From the initial period of exploration and involvement ("discovered," perhaps, by international informal-sector tourists), a resort goes through a developmental stage as growing numbers of tourists seek out its attractions. Investors and tourism entrepreneurs recognize the profit potential of the new resort area and invest in hotels, restaurants, travel agencies, and other tourism-related businesses. Eventually, the growth in tourist arrivals begins to exceed the carrying capacity of the destination. The resort languishes as tourist arrivals decrease and investment in tourism-related infrastructure declines. At this point, the resort will either continue to decline as tourists begin to go elsewhere or it will rejuvenate, although as Butler points out (1980, 9), "it is almost certain that this stage will never be reached without a complete change in the attractions on which tourism is based."

One of the major drawbacks of ecotourism and other forms of nature- and culture-based travel, their critics charge, is that it may prove difficult for planners to prevent an ecotourism destination from developing into a mass-tourism destination. Particularly in the Third World, the careful planning and monitoring that a genuine IFS ecotourism industry requires may not be feasible due to a lack of skilled personnel and the requisite governmental resources. Moreover, the concept of tourism carrying capacity is a relative one; even a small number of tourists may negatively impact a delicate ecosystem or adversely affect the local cultural life of a place, particularly because First World ecotourists demand many of the same capital-intensive accommodation and tourism-related facilities (luxury hotels, golf courses, swimming pools) as more traditional IFS tourists.

Third World Tourism and Western Imperialism

At the most general level, critics of Third World IFS tourism have long claimed that the industry is neocolonial and serves to reinforce and perpetuate the dependence of peripheral countries (former colonies) on the core metropolitan countries (former colonizers). There are at least four dimensions of dependence as it relates to the tourism industry in low-income countries. First, there are the economic dimensions. As we have seen, the IFS tourism industry exhibits a high degree of concentration. Just a handful of airlines, hotels, cruise lines, car-rental agencies, and tour operators dominate their respective branches of the travel industry. The ability of these firms to direct international travel flows and market travel products in First World countries gives them a distinct advantage relative to the Third World countries their customers visit, perhaps most evident in small island nations in the Caribbean, Pacific, and Indian Ocean regions that lack large domestic markets and are thus completely dependent on overseas suppliers. In Third World nations with extensive foreign corporate investment in their tourism industries, the dependence relation is more immediate; tourism firms' decisions to invest or disinvest in their overseas holdings may be completely unrelated to the development needs of the particular countries in which they operate, a dilemma that is not unique to the tourism industry but extends to foreign direct investment in general. TNCs seek to maximize their profits overall, a goal that may entail investment strategies that at times diverge from the interests of any one country in which a particular TNC operates.

A second dimension of dependence is political in nature. Because many Third World tourist destinations and their tourism industries are heavily dependent on overseas markets, the perceptions of foreign investors and potential travelers regarding particular countries are crucial to the long-term viability of development strategies based on tourism. Untoward political events in Third World countries may have disastrous consequences for their tourism industries. Moreover, recession or terrorist attacks in the metropolitan countries will likely cause a decline in tourist departures and a drop-off in tourism earnings. The experience of Southeast Asian countries with respect to the current

Japanese recession is just one example of how adverse economic conditions in the First World may involve high costs for Third World industries dependent on those markets. Politics takes a much more direct role in influencing travel to Third World destinations when First World governments, for avowedly political reasons, seek to prevent their nationals from traveling to particular countries. The U.S. ban on travel to Cuba is perhaps the most notable example of politics affecting tourist flows to low-income countries, as was the U.N.-imposed seven-year ban on air travel to Libya that has only recently been lifted. Other, less extreme examples include the many travel advisories First World governments routinely announce warning their nationals about potentially dangerous situations in particular countries and regions in the Third World.

Critics' arguments that IFS tourism is exploitative of Third World societies and perpetuates relations of dependence are usually made in economic terms. There is, however, a distinct social dimension to charges that tourism fosters dependence and neocolonialism, a feature of the industry not lost on observers of IFS tourism and those working in the industry. The common sight of "native" Third World workers serving mostly white tourists has led some to question the underlying power relations embedded in the "host-guest" relationship, which some have compared to slavery. Among the latter is the Trinidadian author V. S. Naipaul, who equates IFS tourism in the Caribbean with a new form of bondage: "Every poor country accepts tourism as an unavoidable degradation. None has gone as far as some of these West Indian islands, which, in the name of tourism, are selling themselves into a new slavery" (Naipaul 1962, 210). Restaurant and hotel workers in the Mexican resort of Cancún also express misgivings about serving tourists from the United States, with one hotel worker asserting, "The gringos expect to be treated like kings and queens when they travel to Mexico on vacation, but we are not their subjects."[11]

IFS tourism development in low-income countries is dependent on the First World countries, their markets, and their corporations in the most general sense: It is dependent for its growth on conditions prevailing elsewhere, in the core capitalist countries. Recession in the metropolitan countries often translates into the curtailment of tourism-related activities in the Third World. So too does any form of political instability in destination countries. Airline, travel services, and hospitality TNCs, through their control of markets, capital, and management resources, influence the shape and magnitude of tourism flows to Third World countries. For all of these reasons, a number of critics have claimed that international tourism is a form of imperialism, citing strong similarities between the structure of IFS tourism and traditional export industries dominated by foreign interests (Britton 1982; Nash 1989). Although tourism may have some advantages as a development strategy when compared with traditional raw materials exports, assembly operations, and garment manufacturing, it still locks Third World countries into an international division of labor that continues to perpetuate gross inequality and underdevelopment both among and within nations. A major difference between tourism and other export-based development options lies in the sociocultural realm because it is the only Third World export in which the unabashed affluence of First World consumers (for instance, the gluttony of cruise-ship passengers) and the stark poverty of Third World peoples literally exist side by side.

Mexico's International Formal-Sector Tourism Industry

Even though Mexico is among the most popular tourist destinations in the world, the structure of its tourism industry is similar to that of many other Third World countries: Domestic tourists greatly outnumber international travelers, and there is a clear division between formal- and informal-sector tourist facilities (figure 3.1). In 1997, Mexico hosted over 19 million international overnight visitors who spent more than U.S.$6.9 billion on lodging, food, transportation, and other goods and services.[12] The vast majority of Mexico's foreign visitors are from the United States (87.5 percent), followed by Canada (4.6 percent), South America (4.3 percent), Europe (3.0 percent), and the rest of the world (0.6 percent). In comparison, the country's domestic arrivals exceeded an estimated 138 million in 1994, more than seven times the magnitude of international arrivals (Secretaría de Turismo [SECTUR] 1996).

Figure 3.1 Zipolite, Mexico

As in other low-income countries, Mexico's tourism industry is characterized by distinct formal and informal sectors, with a relatively small number of
highly capital-intensive five- and four-star hotels and international-class restaurants at one end of the spectrum and a much larger number of small-scale
accommodation facilities and food stalls at the other. Nearly 40 percent of the
country's lodging establishments are *posadas*, *casas de huéspedes*, bungalows,
furnished rooms, camping sites, *cabañas*, and other typically small-scale, family-owned and -operated, and often unlicensed facilities. That such facilities
are relatively small is indicated by the fact that even though they make up
40 percent of lodging establishments, *posadas*, *casas de huéspedes*, and similar
establishments account for just 20 percent of the total number of rooms in
the country. At the other end of the scale, five- and four-star hotels represent
just over 12.5 percent of total lodging establishments but account for 38.5 percent of the total number of rooms. The average five-star hotel in Mexico has
over ten times the total number of rooms as the average unclassified lodging
establishment. What is true of lodging is also true of restaurants and eating
establishments: Tourist resorts and major cities feature thousands of upscale
and franchised restaurant chains but the vast majority of eating establishments
in Mexico are street stalls and food carts serving tacos, *tortas*, salads, and other
typical Mexican fare. *Ambulantes* (traveling salespersons) also provide tourism-related goods and services in Mexico, ranging from tacos and T-shirts to
musical instruments and *mota* (marijuana), and sell their wares in both formal
and informal tourism destinations.

Mexico's major tourist destinations fall into four broad categories, as I out-
lined in the previous chapter: the IFS, the international informal sector (IIS),
the domestic formal sector (DFS), and the domestic informal sector (DIS).
Cancún, Ixtapa-Zihuatenejo, and Cozumel are examples of destinations in
Mexico with a large supply of capital-intensive, five- and four-star tourism
facilities where international travelers greatly outnumber domestic tourists.
Beach resorts such as Acapulco and Huatulco, as well as large cities such as
Mexico City and Monterrey are examples of DFS destinations: Mexican nationals greatly outnumber international travelers but the supply of international-standard, formal-sector accommodation and related tourist facilities is
still very large. IIS destinations include such places as Zipolite, Tulum, and San
Cristobal de las Casas, and DIS destinations are found in the country's urban,
rural, and coastal areas. In this chapter, I will focus exclusively on Mexico's IFS
tourism destinations.

There are six tourist destinations in Mexico where international tourists
outnumber domestic travelers and where the supply of five- and four-star
accommodation facilities exceeds that of other lodging categories: Cancún,
Cozumel, Ixtapa-Zihuatenejo, Loreto, Los Cabos, and Puerto Vallarta. Each of
these destinations differs with respect to the magnitude of international tourist

arrivals and degree of formality. Los Cabos is the most internationalized of Mexico's tourist resorts: International tourists outnumber domestic travelers eight to one, and the supply of luxury accommodation is 1,900 percent higher than the supply of lower-class accommodation. Although the six destinations are geographically dispersed throughout the country, they all share a number of important characteristics in addition to a preponderance of luxury accommodation and an international orientation (figure 3.2).

To begin with, each is a coastal, "sun, sand, and sea" tourist destination (figure 3.3).[13] In this respect, Mexico bears a striking similarity to the Dominican Republic, Jamaica, the Cook Islands, and other Third World countries with relatively large international formal sectors: Worldwide, IFS destinations in low-income countries are almost always beach or island resorts. Second, each destination has an international airport and docking facilities for oceangoing cruise ships. IFS tourism destinations almost always feature international airports within close proximity of the resort areas because IFS tourists travel for relatively short periods of time and usually for specific purposes. For most IFS travelers, getting there is *not* half the fun, particularly when land-based travel is uncomfortable and unreliable, as is often the case in the Third World. Docking facilities for passenger liners are also important because many package tours combine land-based travel with a cruise. Third, four of the six destinations are *integralmente planeados* (planned resorts), with only the resorts of Cozumel and Puerto Vallarta not the result of deliberate national tourism planning.

Figure 3.2 Mexico's tourism megaprojects.

Figure 3.3   Cancún, Mexico

The Impact of International Formal-Sector Tourism in Mexico

Prior to the early 1970s, Mexico did not have a large formal tourism sector. Aside from the U.S.–Mexico border region and major cities, only the coastal resort of Acapulco attracted sizable numbers of foreign visitors. The country's politicians and planners did not consider tourism a viable development option because the Mexican economy was relatively closed; the import substitution policies pursued by successive national governments and the relative value of the peso made Mexico expensive for international travelers. Border tourism predominated during this period, and most international visitors to Mexico drove there from the United States. In 1970, 61.1 percent of international tourists to Mexico reached their destinations in buses, trains, or automobiles, and only 38.9 percent traveled via air (Jimenez 1993).

The nature of Mexican tourism and the structure of the Mexican tourism industry changed considerably during the 1970s. Prior to that time, the state had devoted relatively few resources to developing the nation's tourism industry, and the industry was overwhelmingly dependent on market forces for its continued growth. In the late 1960s, however, state planners slated tourism as a major export industry and embarked on an "export push" designed to increase the flow of international travelers to Mexico (Clancy 1996). The reasons for the change of policy were rooted in Mexico's political economy and in particular the country's thirty years of import substitution industrialization (ISI). Like other

Third World countries that had adopted ISI development policies, Mexican officials discovered that continued growth depended on the importation of capital goods produced in the First World countries. ISI had not resulted in fewer imports but rather in a different composition of imports. Whereas the country was producing most of its consumer goods, Mexican firms found that they needed to import increasing quantities of intermediate capital producer goods. State officials recognized that the necessary foreign exchange could be acquired through the promotion of certain export industries, and they seized on tourism as a viable option and as a way of lessening the country's dependence on petroleum exports.

Politicians and planners envisioned the creation of several growth poles, or what they called *mega-proyectos* (megaprojects), based entirely on international tourism. The project was administered by the Mexican national bank (Banco de México), or more particularly by an agency set up within the national bank, the *Fondo de Promoción de Infraestructura Turística* (National Trust Fund for Tourist Infrastructure [INFRATUR]), which later came to be known as the *Fondo Nacional de Fomento al Turismo de México* (National Fund for the Promotion of Tourism in Mexico [FONATUR]). After an exhaustive computer-aided analysis of potential sites that took such factors as climate, topography, and flight times from major U.S. cities into consideration, four sites were chosen: Cancún, Ixtapa-Zihuatenejo, Loreto, and Los Cabos. A fifth site, Bahías de Huatulco, was added in the mid-1980s. The five resorts are geographically dispersed throughout the country; Bahías de Huatulco is in the southern state of Oaxaca, Cancún is in the eastern state of Quintana Roo on the Yucatán Peninsula, Ixtapa-Zihuatenejo is in the south central state of Guerrero (near Acapulco), and Loreto and Los Cabos are both in the western state of Baja California Sur. The resorts were not to be developed simultaneously: Cancún and Ixtapa-Zihuatenejo were to be developed first, followed by Bahías de Huatulco, Los Cabos, and Loreto (Clancy 1996).

Tourism Development and Employment Growth

The state agencies responsible for developing the five tourist poles were granted broad powers over the entire development process, including site planning, infrastructure provision, real estate development, and marketing (Clancy 1996, 127). State control over the development process, particularly the land, was very important to the success of the project, not least because of the rising land values that the massive development projects would bring about. The state not only developed the resorts but also owned and operated the hotel properties, at least in the early project stages. In both Cancún and Bahías de Huatulco, either FONATUR itself or other government-owned hotel chains, such as Hotel Nacionalera, accounted for a large share of hotel rooms. INFRATUR received substantial infusions of capital from the Mexican State, mostly in the form of loans with concessional rates of interest. IFS tourism development in Mexico was also very much an international affair. Multilateral lending agencies, such as the IDB and the World Bank, participated in the financing of Mexico's tourism poles; both the IDB and the World Bank made loans to the Mexican government of over U.S.$20 million in the early 1970s for the development of Cancún and Ixtapa-Zihuatenejo, respectively (Clancy 1996; Hiernaux-Nicolas 1999).

Although the government's primary motivation for developing the five tourist poles was to generate foreign exchange, state planners also recognized that the intensive development of the tourist poles, all located in historically underdeveloped regions, would bring social and economic benefits to the areas in which the resorts were situated. Providing employment and countering historic regional inequalities were particularly important factors influencing state action: Government officials were concerned with the potential for violent uprisings in the Yucatán and Baja California, and by the 1960s, guerilla armies were already operating in Guerrero (Hiernaux-Nicolas 1999). An additional factor underlying the choice of developing the new tourist resorts was, at least in the case of Ixtapa-Zihuatenejo, to relieve the pressure on the older resort area of Acapulco, which by the late 1960s was showing signs of severe environmental and social strain.

IFS tourism in Mexico has had a tremendous impact on the localities and regions where it is found. Perhaps the most dramatic example is Cancún. A Mayan fishing village of 500 inhabitants only thirty-five years ago, Cancún is today the largest city in Quintana Roo and one of the leading tourist destinations in Mexico. In 1994, the resort city accounted for 20 percent of all international tourists to Mexico and more than 30 percent of the country's total foreign exchange earned through tourism (Hiernaux-Nicolas 1999). Similarly, the rapid growth of Ixtapa-Zihuatenejo, Puerto Vallarta, Loreto, and Los Cabos has completely transformed these once isolated fishing and farming communities into centers of international tourism. Populations have grown rapidly as migrants from the region and from the country's urban centers gravitate to the tourist poles in search of employment. During the initial construction phase of Ixtapa, the 4,000 construction workers alone exceeded the entire population of what had been the small fishing village of Zihuatenejo (Reynoso y Valle and de Regt 1979). In each of Mexico's tourist cities, landscapes of high-rise hotels, golf courses, and Hard Rock Cafés, as well as the millions of foreign tourists for whom they were built, contrast sharply with the older vistas of farms, fishing boats, and the people who had worked on them. Clearly, a lot of eggs were broken to make the omelet of IFS tourism in Mexico.

In a study of Mexico's tourism industry prepared for the U.S. Congress, Daniel Hiernaux-Nicolas and Manuel Woog (1990) provide estimates of employment in hotels based on class of accommodation. They found that, on average, larger hotels employ more people per room than do smaller hotels. Whereas "Gran Turismo," five-star, and four-star hotels employ, on average, 1.55, 0.99, and 0.83 people per room, respectively, three-star, two-star, and one-star hotels employ only 0.68, 0.63, and 0.23 people per room. Hiernaux-Nicolas and Woog also found that hotel employment represents a relatively small share of total tourism-related employment in Mexico's major tourism destinations: Employment in travel agencies, airlines, car rental agencies, taxis, handicraft and boutiques, miscellaneous businesses, restaurants and bars, and related miscellaneous services accounts for more than eight in ten jobs.

Based on Hiernaux-Nicolas and Woog's figures, it is possible to estimate total tourism employment in each of Mexico's six IFS tourism destinations and for the country as a whole. In 1997, there were 953,106 individuals employed in Mexico's major tourist centers.[14] Of these, more than 300,000 people are directly employed in tourism-related activities in the country's international formal sector.[15] Of Mexico's IFS resorts, Cancún is clearly the most significant in employment terms, accounting for more than half the total number of workers employed in Mexico's IFS resort areas (160,195). Puerto Vallarta is the second most important IFS tourism resort with 62,479 tourism workers, followed by Ixtapa (31,785), Los Cabos (28,309), Cozumel (20,421), and Loreto (1,299). Employment in Mexico's IFS tourism resorts represents a sizable percentage of the country's employment in tourism production, and about one-third of the total employment in Mexico's major tourist centers.

Despite the methodological problems involved in measuring total IFS tourism employment in Mexico, there is no question that sizable numbers of people find employment in Mexico's resort cities and other IFS tourism destinations. The importance of the employment opportunities generated by IFS tourism is magnified by the fact that all of the country's IFS tourism destinations are in historically underdeveloped regions.

Employment in Mexico's International Formal-Sector Tourism Resorts

The question remains, however, as to the quality of the employment opportunities created in IFS tourism destinations. As we have seen, critics have characterized tourism employment in both the First and the Third Worlds as low-paying, seasonal, and insecure, and have gone so far as to equate tourism employment with slavery (Fanon 1963; Naipaul 1962). They claim that the best jobs in the large hotels and resorts go to expatriates and other outsiders while the local population is relegated to cleaning up after foreign tourists for meager wages on land that once belonged to the community as a whole. Critics also claim that IFS tourism development has few linkages to the regional economy. The resulting "tourist bubble" effectively limits the types of employment to those found in the large hotels and other tourism-related enterprises. Moreover, in most IFS tourism resorts, the state actively discourages the growth of small-scale and informal-sector activities that could conceivably benefit the local population. The distribution of income resulting from IFS tourism activity is thus skewed toward the owners and managers of hotels and other parts of the IFS tourism infrastructure, which in most cases are large national firms or TNCs.

In the case of Mexico's IFS tourism resorts, almost all these contentions are true. Although detailed employment data for Mexico's IFS tourism destinations are scarce, what data there are suggests that most workers earn low pay; that IFS tourism employment is highly seasonal in nature; that many local people feel cheated by the government and large tourism firms, particularly in the land regularization and expropriation process but also in the employment opportunities open to them; and that the best jobs go to outsiders and not locals. In addition, IFS tourism development in Mexico lacks extensive linkages to the regional economy. The evidence also suggests that the benefits of IFS tourism in Mexico are highly skewed toward transnational hotel chains and national elites, with local and even regional participation in ownership and control virtually nonexistent in most cases.

In a study of labor markets in Cancún and Ixtapa, Adrian Aguilar (1994) found that over 40 percent of hotel workers in Cancún and over 50 percent of hotel workers in Ixtapa earn less than two minimum wages. Although these figures compare favorably with the national average (56 percent of the Mexican workforce earns less than two minimum wages), the highly seasonal nature of hotel employment in the two resorts means that many workers must stretch their earnings over long periods of un/underemployment. The number of people working only part of the year is significant, given that hotels in Ixtapa lay off up to 40 percent of their workers during the five-month low season. Aguilar also found that most occupations in the two tourist centers require only minimal educational qualifications and provide few avenues for advancement. Moreover, IFS hotel employment is characterized by a high degree of occupational and income polarization; relatively few positions in Cancún and Ixtapa are professional-managerial and well paid, and a much larger number of positions are unskilled and poorly paid. Like the tourism industry everywhere, there are few "middle-class" positions in either Cancún's or Ixtapa's IFS hotels.

The ownership and control structure of tourism enterprises in Mexico's IFS tourism resorts is highly concentrated in the hands of TNCs and big national capital. In Mexico, as in other countries, most luxury hotels are owned by a relatively small number of firms. Whereas the largest fifteen hotel firms operating in Mexico make up just 1 percent of hotel establishments, they represent 43 percent of all hotels in the top categories (Clancy 1996). In the "Gran Turismo" category, 100 percent of hotels were associated with TNCs in 1988 (Schédler 1988). Because a defining characteristic of Mexico's IFS tourism resorts is a high percentage of five- and four-star hotels, relative to small-scale accommodation facilities, it should come as no surprise that Cancún, Ixtapa, and the other IFS tourist destinations in Mexico are characterized by high levels of TNC participation.

Ownership and control of tourism enterprises are, however, not always synonymous; many transnational hotel firms prefer management contracts and licensing fees to direct equity participation, particularly in low-income countries where they perceive investment risks as high. Mexico is no exception, with little equity participation by resort TNCs in the properties that bear their names. Instead, national industrial and financial groups based in Mexico City are the actual owners of the hotel properties in Mexico's IFS tourism resorts. Local residents own very few hotels and none of the five- and four-star properties in Mexico's IFS tourism resorts; the benefits of owning and controlling tourism properties in the country's IFS resorts flow not to local residents but to powerful interests external to the community. As political scientist Michael Clancy (1996, 209) observes, "class is more useful than nationality in order to understand who are the primary beneficiaries within the Mexican hotel industry."

The ownership structure of Mexico's IFS tourism resorts is hardly surprising, given the original impetus and rationale for developing the tourist poles in the first place. From the beginning, Mexico's tourism planners viewed the country's tourist cities in national terms, primarily as a means of generating foreign exchange and diversifying the country's exports. Regional development, although certainly a consideration of government planners, was never the motivating rationale. National bureaucrats planned the five tourist poles from their drafting tables in Mexico City, and local input into the planning process was virtually nonexistent. Planners, as well as the international lending agencies with whom they worked, viewed the local population more as a problem to be managed than as a group to be consulted about the course of local and regional development. Federal authorities considered the lands expropriated from peasants as "national" land to be used to further "national" objectives. Thus, it is not surprising that national firms are the ones that benefit overwhelmingly from development of the new tourist centers.

Indeed, local residents almost always occupy the lowest and the most poorly paid positions in Cancún, Ixtapa, and the country's other IFS tourist destinations. In the Cancún region, for example, the indigenous Maya of Quintana Roo are often unable to speak English (and often unable to speak Spanish well, for that matter) and thus cannot obtain employment in the large hotels along the coastal Cancún-Tulum tourist corridor. Most mid- and upper-level management positions at the city's hotels and other large-scale tourism establishments go to outsiders, many from Mexico City and other large urban areas in Mexico (Camacho 1996; Daltabuit and Pi-Sunyer 1990; Long 1989).

Although prior to 1965 fewer than 500 people lived on the site of the present-day city and resort of Cancún, with several hundred more people living in small fishing communities on nearby Isla Mujeres, the regional effects of the city's development extend throughout the Yucatán Peninsula. What is particularly disturbing is the way in which the Maya, often without any choice in the matter, are becoming integrated into a tourist complex that includes not only Cancún but also the entire Yucatán region. The establishment of "La Ruta Maya" is a case in point. In the late 1980s, the governments of Mexico, Guatemala, El Salvador, Belize, and Honduras embarked on a joint venture to market the entire Maya region to international tourists. Supported by international organizations, such as the U.S.-based National Geographic Society, the tourist complex is to include both archaeological sites and environmental "biospheres" on land expropriated from the indigenous Maya. Today, many international tours to Cancún include an overnight stay in one or another of the archaeological sites or nature preserves, areas often adjacent to indigenous Mayan villages inhabited by the descendants of the people who built the archaeological sites in the first place. The world of these hotels and package tours, populated by upper-middle-class tourists from the wealthy countries, stands in stark contrast to the realities of the often poverty-stricken Yucatecan communities. As anthropologists Magali Daltabuit and Oriol Pi-Sunyer observe of Cobá, one such site: "Outside the hotel compound is a life where poverty remains the norm and the future, in all its dimensions, is far from secure; inside is a world of plenty—of tennis courts and swimming pools, bathrooms with unlimited water, and self-contained electrical systems" (Daltabuit and Pi-Sunyer 1990, 12). The ideology of Western environmentalism underlying the growth of La Ruta Maya and other forms of alternative tourism, one that is increasingly coming to define North-South relations, is very similar to developmentalism in its underlying dynamics: Both provide justification for Western intervention in Third World societies that must now be "saved" for the benefit of all humankind. The problem with this type of environmentalism is that the resources of Third World peoples become "our" resources, the common heritage of humanity, while the poverty of those who live in the Third World persists.

There are relatively few scholarly studies that deal with the environmental dimensions of Mexico's IFS tourism resorts. Clearly, the environmental impact of Cancún, Ixtapa, Los Cabos, and Puerto Vallarta has been immense. As we have seen, Cancún grew from a small village of 500 people into a city of several hundred thousand inhabitants over the course of three decades. Indeed, the entire population of Quintana Roo was only 50,000 in 1960. The population of Ixtapa-Zihuatenejo increased from 5,000 to over 80,000 in just twenty-five years. Puerto Vallarta, a city of over 300,000 people, did not have paved-road access to the rest of the country until the 1960s. Such rapid growth does not occur without exacting an environmental toll, either from the immediate locality or from the surrounding region. In Mexico's planned IFS tourism resorts, however, the environmental impact is arguably more benign than in unplanned resort areas.

Indeed, government planners had the resort of Acapulco very much in mind when drafting their plans for Cancún, Ixtapa, and the country's other IFS tourism resorts. Today a city of 1.5 million people, Acapulco had grown rapidly but in an unplanned and haphazard manner. As Hiernaux-Nicolas (1999, 128) points out, by the early 1970s, "urban growth [in Acapulco] took place without control and planning, poverty was rising, and the city and touristic zones had inadequate infrastructure." The results of the city's lack of planning is evident today in the polluted waters, eroded hillsides, and overcrowded *colonias* that have grown up only a short distance away from the tourist strip. International tourists have stayed away from Acapulco in large numbers; whereas once a majority of visitors to the resort were foreigners, today most of the city's visitors are Mexican nationals (Jimenez 1993). Because the government's primary rationale for constructing IFS tourism resorts was to earn foreign exchange, it was essential that the new tourist areas not suffer a similar fate.

The planning and design of the new tourist cities clearly reflects planners' concerns about avoiding the kinds of problems that beset Acapulco. The government granted the planning agencies responsible for the development of the resorts broad powers over land acquisition and real estate development. Planners at INFRATUR (later FONATUR), the lead planning agency overseeing development of the poles, regularized and expropriated land before construction began so as to control the entire site and prevent unplanned and haphazard real estate development. They sought to install the required infrastructure prior to the construction of hotels and other tourism facilities. To avoid the construction of shantytowns close to the hotel area, the planners designed two distinct zones in the IFS resorts: a tourist zone for the luxury hotels, golf courses, convention centers, and shopping malls; and a separate city to house the workers. In Cancún, for instance, the tourist zone is a barrier island connected to the mainland by two causeways, and the worker zone is on the mainland in Ciudad de Cancún (the City of Cancún). In Ixtapa, the planners designed the luxury hotel area a short distance away from Zihuatenejo, the town that would house the resort's workforce. In the case of Ixtapa-Zihuatenejo, not only did the state planners expropriate land in the hotel area, they also regularized and expropriated *ejido* (communal) land in Zihuatenejo as well (Reynoso y Valle and de Regt 1979).

Conclusion

IFS tourism may or may not prove beneficial to a country's national economy and its general level of economic development. Although some researchers have concluded that it is not primarily because of import leakages, low spending and employment multipliers, and dependence on overseas markets and the TNCs that control them, some countries' tourism industries are major foreign exchange earners and provide employment for millions of people. Workers in tourist resorts often work long hours under difficult conditions, but for many people, employment in an IFS tourism enterprise is preferable to agricultural labor, informal employment, or wage work in free-export zones and foreign-owned assembly plants. Working conditions are generally better, and the pay, particularly in tipping positions, is usually higher—and in some cases much higher—than in most other export industries. Whether IFS tourism proves advantageous in foreign exchange and employment terms is, in the final analysis, dependent on a host of country-specific factors, not least of which is how well integrated the country's IFS tourism industry is with other industries and the degree to which the country has embraced IMF-dictated structural adjustment policies, particularly with respect to currency devaluation and wage reduction—in other words, the degree to which the country has become "internationally competitive." Another factor is the proximity of a country to major sending regions because international tourism flows are clearly characterized by a distance decay function.

A key determinant of a successful IFS tourism industry is the nature and level of state planning involved in developing a country's tourism potential. The available evidence clearly indicates that the greater the planning effort, the more likely the sites chosen for tourism development will prove economically viable for the nation as a whole and environmentally sustainable over the long term. In this respect, Mexico's integrated tourism resorts of Cancún, Ixtapa-Zihuatenejo, Loreto, Los Cabos, and Las Bahías de Huatulco compare quite favorably with unplanned IFS tourism resorts in the Caribbean, Southeast Asia, South Asia, and even Mexico itself. A major factor in the success of Mexico's system of *integralmente planeados* (planned tourist resorts) was the ability of a central planning agency to control all aspects of the development process, from the original land acquisition to the provision of infrastructure, supervision of building construction, and joint venturing of the resort's first hotels.

As to the question of economic dependence of IFS on overseas markets and foreign control of the industry, it is often the case that five-star hotels and enclave resorts bear the logos of major hospitality TNCs and may even be managed by foreign nationals. Indeed, IFS tourism development without the hotel TNCs, their brand name recognition, and their computerized, worldwide reservations systems is nearly impossible. The trend in the Third World, however, has been away from foreign ownership and control and toward increasing ownership and management of hospitality enterprises by residents of the countries in which they are located. In fact, several Third World-based hospitality TNCs, including Mexico's Grupo Posadas, India's Oberoi Group, and Jamaica's Sandals Resorts, have become hospitality TNCs in their own right.

Furthermore, IFS tourism does not appear any more dependent on overseas suppliers and TNCs than do apparel, petroleum products, assembly operations, raw materials, cash-crop agriculture, and other major Third World export industries. The spending multipliers of IFS tourism, particularly in large low-income countries, probably exceed that of other export industries because tourism is both a labor-intensive industry and one in which many of the intermediate inputs are produced nationally. Although radical change in the nature and scope of North-South relations may certainly be in the best interests of most people in the Third World, particularly in light of the rapid growth of worldwide inequality and the growing domination of the international political economy by TNCs accountable to no one but their shareholders, IFS tourism does not appear to exacerbate North–South inequality any more than do other large, global industries. It may even reduce economic inequality, if not in class then in national terms, because many low-income countries maintain tourism trading surpluses with First World countries.

Whatever benefits IFS tourism may bestow nationally in terms of employment and foreign exchange earnings, however, it is almost always destructive of local communities in the places where it develops. Throughout the world, in localities as different as Goa (India), Kovalam Beach (India), Phuket (Thailand), Koh Samui (Thailand), Nusa Dua (Indonesia), Hawaii (United States), and Sosúa (Dominican Republic), IFS tourism displaces local residents and often excludes them from whatever benefits the industry may generate nationally. Because local residents lack the economic resources and political clout to compete successfully with national elites and the managers of TNCs, they are often pushed aside in favor of outsiders and watch as the best jobs and most lucrative contracts go to people from the national capital or overseas. Scarce local resources are diverted to the luxury resorts, often at the expense of the surrounding communities. It is not uncommon for golf courses to appear lush and green even as water is rationed to surrounding communities. Even the informal enterprises formed by local people in an effort to reap a miniscule share of the tourist dollar are often discouraged and at times even outright banned by the governing authorities on the grounds that hawkers and other vendors disturb the foreign tourists and discourage them from returning.

Mexico's planned tourist resorts are no different in this regard than other IFS tourism destinations. Despite a myth that Cancún, Ixtapa-Zihuatenejo, Huatulco, and other tourist cities were built on sites devoid of people, entire communities of poor Mayan, Zapotec, and other indigenous groups were at times forcibly uprooted to make room for the new luxury hotels, enclave resorts, yacht clubs, time-share developments, and golf courses, a process that continues along the *Cancún-Tulum Corredor* (Cancún-Tulum tourist corridor) taking shape along Mexico's Caribbean coastline and in the rainforests of Chiapas and the Yucatán. Ironically, it is the Maya themselves who stand to benefit the least from tourism development along the National Geographic-backed La Ruta Maya, a fact not lost on Zapatista rebels and rebel sympathizers who believe that formal-sector tourist development in the Lacandón rainforest and other ecologically sensitive areas by the Mexican state and its corporate and overseas backers will lead to the expropriation of local communities so that rich gringos and ecotourists can enjoy the "unspoiled" scenery in peace. For the Zapatistas and other rebel groups, expropriation of local residents by rancheros producing bananas and coffee for export or displacement of *campesinos* (peasants) by transnational hotel chains serving foreign tourists amounts to pretty much the same thing, at least with regard to the indigenous population.

As we will see in the next chapter, international tourism in the Third World is not restricted to five-star resorts and formal-sector enclaves that destroy local communities and turn self-sufficient farmers and fisherfolk into bellhops and maids who clean toilets for package tourists from rich countries. In many cases, local communities are able to mediate a growing international tourist trade on their own terms. And as chapter 5 will make clear, formal-sector tourism is not restricted to international travelers; in many Third World resort areas, the farmers and fisherfolk end up either scrubbing toilets for elite groups from their own countries or becoming marginalized from both their traditional and preferred ways of life and the tourist economy altogether.

CHAPTER 4

The International Informal Sector

Drifter Tourists in India and Mexico

Scene One

In a remote mountain valley in the Indian Himalaya, about twenty Western tourists are gathered around a fire, chanting hymns. Some play *dijeradoos*, an Australian aboriginal instrument made from a hollowed-out piece of bamboo. As one dijeradoo player puts it (in heavily German-accented English), "good vibration, man, the dijeradoo makes an excellent vibration." One of the tourists clangs a cymbal in concert with the dijeradoo player, and a third strums the same chord over and over again on a guitar. Meanwhile, a Spanish woman dressed in medieval minstrel clothing juggles fire on a rocky outcropping. A few European children are running around playing with a dog. The tourists and some local men are passing around a *chillum* (clay pipe), and the air is thick with the smell of *charas* (hashish). Some local people sell *chai* (tea) to the tourists while others look on in amusement. The smoke from the fire rises up into the morning sky and hangs over the valley. The event is a Rainbow Gathering, or "gathering of the tribes," as one of the organizers described it.

I learned of this particular Gathering from a man I met in a cheap hotel in Delhi's Pahar Ganj district, an Australian who calls himself Vishnu Das (literally, Vishnu's servant). Vishnu Das had been living in India for three years and told me that he goes days at a time without spending any money whatsoever. He said he sleeps outside or stays in Hindu temples. He smokes charas and *bidis* (leaf cigarettes) but avoids harder drugs such as opium, heroin, or alcohol. He believes that Western society is morally and socially bankrupt, and that people in India and other Third World countries lead more honest lives and are certainly less destructive of the environment than their counterparts in First World countries. Before coming to India, he had worked for the Australian postal service in Melbourne but decided to leave and search for Absolute Truth. When I last saw him, he was in the process of being deported by the Indian authorities for overstaying his visa. He told me that one of the officers at the immigration office in Delhi thought he was a sincere person and took a liking to him. "He was just asking me to leave for awhile, that's all." He could have been jailed for many months—even years. His current whereabouts are unknown.

Scene Two

Playa de Zipolite, or "beach of the dead," is a mile-long stretch of white sand beach, located on Mexico's southern Pacific coast about ten hours by road from Acapulco and fourteen hours from Mexico City (figure 4.1). Bungalows, cafés, tents, and *palapas* (lean-tos) line the beach. Many *ambulantes* (traveling salespersons) ply their trade up and down the sandy strip from morning to evening, selling donuts, tamales, enchiladas, tacos, jewelry, clothing, marijuana, fruit, nuts, sandals, hammocks, hats, blankets, and postcards to tourists lying naked on the sand or lounging in their hammocks. In a small café at the north end of the beach, several Italian tourists are comparing travel notes. A Bob Marley flag flutters from a flagpole alongside the café. The Italians have been touring Mexico for nearly six weeks and still have another three weeks to go before they have to return to Italy, a prospect they find rather daunting. One says

Figure 4.1 Zipolite, Mexico

that he learns "more about the world in places like this than in the University." Another concurs and says that she much prefers Zipolite to "other beaches in Thailand and India" because "it is just as nice here, and I can understand the local people much better." She lights a cigarette and orders a beer. "And yes," she adds, "the beer in Mexico is much better." A group of young Argentine tourists joins the Italians (the Italians and Argentines had met earlier in the day), and they all decide to go to an open-air discotheque that evening.

Scene Three

Pahar Ganj, New Delhi's main bazaar, is a part of New Delhi's tourist geography that is rarely, if ever, included on the itineraries of international formal-sector (IFS) tour operators. (*Pahar Ganj* means "mountain settlement" in Hindi and probably got its name from the area's original settlers.) Just a ten-minute walk from Connaught Place, New Delhi's commercial center, Pahar Ganj is a popular tourist destination and has attracted large numbers of international travelers since the 1970s. This particular winter day is no exception: The cafés catering to Western palates are crowded with travelers, and some restaurants have set up tables outside under awnings. The dozen or so hotels popular with European, African, Middle Eastern, and Central Asian tourists are full. Getting a room in Pahar Ganj is not always easy because the more popular hotels fill up quickly. The streets are literally choked with pedestrian and rickshaw traffic, and the shops are full of Indian, African, European, and Central Asian shoppers. Pahar Ganj is a major wholesale shopping district, with hundreds of clothing and handicraft shops, moneychangers, sari shops, travel agencies, jewelers, shipping agents, and communications offices. Many of the tourists staying in Pahar Ganj's budget hotels also purchase large quantities of merchandise, mainly clothing and jewelry, to sell in their home countries, one way they finance their travels to India and other low-income countries (figure 4.2).

Scene Four

The temple complex is buzzing with activity, just as it always is this time of the evening during *darshan* (the unveiling of the deity). Men with long *dhotis* (traditional, loose-fitting clothing) play drums and chant while women in saris look after their children and discuss the day's events. The marble temple complex is immense, with an attached *gurukula* (religious school), guesthouse, restaurant, and snack bar. Opposite the gated compound, a new shopping center with *chai* (tea) stalls, gift shops, travel agencies, grocery stores, and communications offices does a brisk business. Tourists drinking chai and eating snacks sit at tables set up in front of the shopping center. The large crowd is a mix of both Western and Indian tourists, most of whom are pilgrims who

Figure 4.2 Pahar Ganj (Main Bazaar), New Delhi, India

have come to Vrindavan to pay their respects to Krishna, one of the more popular Indian deities. The temple, one of the thousands in Vrindavan dedicated to Lord Krishna or to one of the many other Indian deities, was built by the International Society of Krishna Consciousness (ISKCON), a religious sect with millions of followers in India and abroad. Although Vrindavan, a town of 50,000 people located in a poor northern Indian agricultural region, attracts many more domestic tourists than international travelers, certain areas of the town contain high concentrations of Western tourists. Most are affiliated with ISKCON but others come to observe the Hare Krishnas or to visit the area's many temples. Vrindavan offers little in the way of formal-sector accommodation, restaurant, or transportation facilities. The town lacks any international-standard hotels, no restaurants with the exception of the one operated by ISKCON offer Western-style cuisine, and local transport consists of rickshaws, *tongas* (horse drawn carriages), and *tempos* (three-wheeled tractors).

Scenes like these are common in India, Mexico, Guatemala, Thailand, Morocco, Indonesia, Peru, and other low-income countries, where large numbers of young (and some not-so-young) tourists from the wealthy First World countries have beaten a well-worn path since the 1960s. As a group, these First World tourists share an aversion to formal-sector accommodation and transportation facilities,[1] travel for longer periods, and spend less money per day than the average international tourist. They are overwhelmingly young, white, and male. Most are Western European, North American, Israeli, Japanese, and Australian. Although their socioeconomic characteristics vary considerably, they all share a distinct preference for informal-sector tourism establishments and the informal tourist spaces where such establishments proliferate. And from all available evidence, their numbers and cultural influence are growing.

As we will see, however, many international informal-sector (IIS) tourists in low-income countries are not from Western countries at all but from other low-income nations. We know very little about the travel patterns of non-Western international tourists in other low-income countries, but what evidence there is suggests that they represent a sizable share of total international arrivals in low-income countries and that many frequent informal-sector tourism establishments. Moreover, non-Western IIS tourists are more likely to come from neighboring countries and often share the same language and cultural characteristics as their hosts, an important factor in light of recurring critiques of international tourism as a form of cultural imperialism.

In contrast to the IFS tourists described in chapter 3, I refer to the group of both Western and non-Western international travelers as IIS tourists. IIS tourists and the establishments that sell them goods and services comprise the international informal tourism sector. International informal tourism destinations are those frequented by relatively large numbers of international travelers where informal-sector enterprises predominate.

The Extent of International Informal-Sector Tourism

Although researchers have recognized the "mass" nature of IIS tourism since at least the early 1970s, its magnitude is unknown, either on a countrywide basis or overall. There are, however, some limited arrivals and expenditure data. The Federation of International Youth Travel Organizations (FIYTO), for example, reports that its 330 members from 60 countries arrange for the travel and tourism experiences of 14 million young travelers every year, which together account for U.S.$6 billion in travel-related sales and $6 million air and surface transportation tickets (FIYTO Web site). FIYTO estimates that student travel accounts for 20 percent of all international travel, about 140 million travelers in 2004, and the International Youth Hostel Federation reported that its members provided more than 10 million bed nights in 1991 (Bywater 1993; Chadee and Cutler 1996). Of course, not all student travelers visit low-income countries, and those who do may not patronize informal-sector hotels, guesthouses, and other tourism-related enterprises. Conversely, students are by no means the only IIS tourists who travel in low-income countries. In fact, they probably make up a minority of IIS travelers when non-Western IIS tourists are taken into account.

Estimating total IIS visitor arrivals in individual countries is therefore fraught with difficulties. Surveys are costly, and in most low-income countries, funds to carry out tourism research are scarce. Consequently, little statistical information is available pertaining to the social characteristics of international tourists who travel to Third World destinations. The World Tourism Organization supplies tourist statistics for member countries, but the data are highly aggregated, usually on a national basis, and do not reveal much about the social attributes of travelers, apart from very broad classifications such as the share of tourists who travel for leisure or business purposes. Third World governments that undertake detailed marketing surveys of foreign tourists, such as some Caribbean nations, have relatively large, well-developed IFS tourism industries and are not representative of countries that attract many IIS tourists.

Enough data is available for some countries, however, to approximate annual IIS tourist arrivals. A 1989 survey of international tourists to India reveals that close to one-third are between the ages of seventeen and thirty, 38 percent earn less than U.S.$15,000 per year, and about 10 percent identify themselves as students. In addition, more than 35 percent of India's international visitors remain in the country for more than four months, 40 percent report spending less than U.S.$20 per day, and 20 percent report spending less than U.S.$10 per day (Government of India Ministry of Tourism 1989; table 4.1).[2] Thus, even if we assume that only 20 percent of India's international visitors share only some of these characteristics, particularly length of stay and average daily expenditure, and extrapolate the 1989 survey findings to the mid 2000s, we can say that at least 600,000 IIS tourists traveled to India in 2004.

Table 4.1

India's International Informal-Sector (IIS) Tourist Arrivals 1989 (%)

	Arrivals	Indian Origin	Male	Female	17–30 years old	Annual income < $15,000[a]	Student	Business	Pleasure	Daily Expenditure < $20	Daily Expenditure < $10
United Kingdom	17.1	13.0	11.5	5.6	28.7	38.6	8.8	24.8	63.4	34.6	21.7
France	6.5	0.3	4.0	2.5	32.0	36.5	7.3	17.2	74.0	30.5	17.3
Germany	6.0	1.7	4.3	1.7	37.1	34.5	9.0	23.5	63.9	28.5	17.3
Rest of Western Europe	15.4	1.7	10.1	5.4	34.2	34.6	9.3	18.7	67.4	31.0	15.4
Japan	4.0	0.0	3.2	0.7	21.4	36.9	9.8	32.8	48.3	14.5	11.1
United States	10.0	5.9	6.9	3.1	42.4	35.1	12.5	17.8	59.9	33.8	14.5
Canada	3.2	7.7	2.0	1.1	27.6	35.4	9.5	21.8	64.9	34.4	16.9
Australia	2.4	1.1	2.0	0.3	20.0	39.6	2.1	24.0	67.5	29.5	16.9
Eastern Europe	5.3	1.5	4.2	1.1	26.1	29.2	9.2	17.1	71.6	49.1	30.4
West Asia	7.7	12.9	6.2	1.5	28.2	40.4	9.1	27.5	40.7	17.2	6.8
Southeast Asia	6.3	27.5	5.4	0.9	32.5	36.9	8.0	27.9	44.1	45.6	23.7
Rest of the world	16.2	10.8	12.8	3.4	34.1	49.0	11.3	25.0	41.7	41.0	23.5

[a] All currency figures in U.S. dollars.

Source: Government of India Ministry of Tourism (1989).

Other studies suggest, however, that India's annual IIS tourist arrivals are significantly higher. For example, more than 50 percent of India's international visitors stay in guesthouses, youth hostels, and other informal accommodation facilities. Although a higher percentage of foreign visitors (about 25 percent) in the country's largest cities report staying in a star category hotel, in most tourist centers the vast majority of tourist nights are spent in small-scale, informal-sector accommodation. In a number of the country's tourism destinations (e.g., Ajmer, Kanyikumari, Bharatpur, Dharamshala), over three-fourths of tourists stay in informal lodging facilities (Government of India Ministry of Tourism 1989). Thus, even though the exact number of India's IIS tourist arrivals is difficult to ascertain, it is incontrovertible that IIS tourist arrivals represent a sizable share of India's international tourism market.

Countries as otherwise diverse as Mexico, China, Thailand, Indonesia, Brazil, Guatemala, Peru, Nepal, and Morocco also host large numbers of IIS tourists, although the exact number is even more difficult to establish than in India. For example, in Pokhara, Nepal's second largest city and one of the country's leading foreign tourist destinations, over 90 percent of accommodation facilities fall into the informal category (Pagdin 1996). Indonesia's accommodation establishments are overwhelmingly small-scale and informal; 7 percent of the country's hotel sector consists of "classified" accommodation establishments but more than 90 percent of Indonesia's lodging facilities are *losmen* (simple guesthouses) and similar small-scale establishments (EIU 1991). As we saw in chapter 3, nearly half of Mexico's lodging establishments are similarly "unclassified," despite the fact that Mexico is one of the leading IFS tourism destinations in the world. Whereas in most cases we do not know the number of international visitors, as a proportion of all visitors, who utilize informal-sector accommodation, it is clearly the case that some foreign tourists do so. On the basis of what evidence there is, therefore, I think we can safely say that 20 percent of all international tourist arrivals in Third World countries are IIS tourists, a number that probably underestimates the total number of IIS tourist arrivals by a sizable margin.

IIS Tourist Types

From On the Road *to* Karma Cola: *Western Drifting from a Literary and Cultural Perspective*

Western IIS tourism is a mass phenomenon, with cultural roots extending back at least 200 years. Louis Turner and John Ash (1976, 260) trace the origins of what they call "hippie-drifter" travel to the Romantic Movement of the nineteenth century and specifically its rejection of progress and the enlightenment project: "Disillusioned with the now all too apparent environmental and spiritual effects of 'scientific progress' (pollution and alienation) and tacitly challenging the hegemony of bourgeois values, they travel, they adopt distinctive styles of dress, they experiment with drugs . . . Their 'drifting' is implicitly a rejection of 'straight politics' of whatever colour." Turner and Ash liken hippie-drifter travelers to the Bohemians of early nineteenth-century Paris and to Rimbaud in particular. The Bohemians, like the hippies, were interested in expanding their consciousness and "hashish, opium, and voyages to the Orient or Africa became the most favoured means of 'heightening' experience" (1976, 264). Their similarity to young, Western, twentieth-century travelers searching for Arcadia in Morocco, Nepal, and other Third World countries is, for Turner and Ash, all too apparent.

Others point to tramping as a precursor of modern-day IIS tourists (Adler 1985). Originally a part of European working-class culture, tramping involved a formal organization of skilled laborers that facilitated the movement of workers from areas of high unemployment to areas where their skills were more in demand. As young workers moved around Europe and North America seeking employment, they were able to take advantage of a system of accommodation and employment assistance provided to them by their particular craft guilds or professional societies. These included bookbinders, carpenters, coopers, mechanics, printers, plumbers, and other skilled professions.

By the late nineteenth century, however, the growth of large urban centers and the development of railways significantly reduced the role of tramping for crafts-related purposes. Over the course of a few decades, the tramp was transformed in the popular imagination—and in point of fact—from a skilled craftsperson to an unskilled laborer living on the road or in hobo camps. It was at this time that the public came to associate tramping with the marginalized elements of society, with the vagrant, the hobo, the unemployed drifter. When undertaken by youth, tramping was often associated with juvenile delinquency. As one early twentieth-century writer put it, "hoboland is filled with youngsters who have gotten there on the railroads" (Flint 1898, 113).

As sociologist Judith Adler (1985, 346) points out, however, "the decline of the tramping tradition as a labor institution is matched, step by step, with its romaniticization and adaptation for purely touristic purposes; deprived of its earlier necessity, tramping becomes aestheticized as a form of play." Numerous literary works and guidebooks from the early twentieth century authored by members of the middle and upper classes purport to describe life on the road, life as a hobo, or life as a tramp. George Orwell's *Down and Out in Paris and London* and Jack London's *The Road* are two better-known examples. One guidebook entitled, *A Tramp Trip: How to See Europe on Fifty Cents a Day*, foreshadows the many student and budget travel guides published today (Kerouac 1991; London 1907; Meriwether 1887; Orwell 1999).

The idea and practice of drifting took on new cultural meaning in postwar America with the publication of Jack Kerouac's *On the Road*. A loosely autobiographical novel, *On the Road* chronicles Kerouac's odyssey across the North

American continent in the late 1940s and early 1950s. The hero of the novel is Dean Moriarty (Neal Cassady) who, we learn, was "actually born on the road, when his parents were passing through Salt Lake City in 1926, in a jalopy, on their way to Los Angeles." Kerouac creates in Dean Moriarty a character who is simply "Beat—the Road, the Soul of Beatific." In his later novels, Kerouac tailors his vision of soulful travel to Eastern concepts of enlightenment and in particular to Zen satori, or instantaneous awakening. He finds a fellow drifter-wanderer-hobo in Han Shan, an eighth-century Chinese mystic poet. He identifies travel with soul searching and sees the road as salvation, a new beginning—the idea that out on the road (or down the road) lay the means to one's redemption. In this, Kerouac's work reflects broad themes in American literature: mobility, transience, the never-ending frontier.

An idealized vision of Third World cultures figures into the works of Kerouac and other Beat writers of the 1950s and 1960s. A large part of *On the Road* is set in Mexico, and Kerouac rhapsodizes about Mexico City, "the great and final wild uninhibited Fellahin—childlike city that we knew we would find at the end of the road." Kerouac traveled to Morocco, where he found his friend William Burroughs addicted to morphine and living in a cheap Tangier hotel. The Beat poet Allen Ginsberg spent two years in India in the early 1960s, a trip that culminated in the publication of his *Indian Journals*. Here again we find that mixture of drifter travel, drugs, and an interest in non-European civilizations that Turner and Ash trace back to the Bohemians of 1830s Paris. Ginsberg, who admired Rimbaud, recorded numerous entries in his journal dealing with his visits to Indian "O dens" (opium dens).

On the Road and Kerouac's other novels have inspired generations of Western youth to hit the road in search of a good time. Although Kerouac distanced himself and his generation from the hippies (Kerouac was a Republican and supported the U.S. invasion of Vietnam), the "hippy trail" that emerged in the 1960s, a series of travel circuits around North America, Europe, and Asia, owes much to the influence of Kerouac, Cassady, and other Beats who covered the same ground nearly two decades before.

Indeed, by the late 1960s, thousands of American and European youth were tramping their way across North America, Europe, and Asia. San Francisco's Haight Ashbury, New York's East Village, and Amsterdam's Dam Square became international centers for hippies and others representative of that era's "counter-culture." The overland route to South Asia took on almost mythical proportions (Zurick 1995). The Beatles had traveled to India to meet with Maharishi Mahesh Yogi; hashish was not only legal but sold in government shops; and many who dropped out of Western society found a new home in the many informal communities of travelers springing up in Goa, Marrakesh, Kathmandu, Varanasi, and numerous other places. No doubt influenced by increasing numbers of youthful travelers, James Michener published *The Drifters* in 1971, a novel about a group of young people set in Morocco, Spain, and Mozambique, among other places. Gita Mehta published *Karma Cola* in 1977, a parody of the thousands of Westerners who travel to India seeking spiritual enlightenment.

The popular press was quick to pick up on the growing numbers of young Americans traveling to Europe, Asia, and Africa on cheap economy flights, sleeping in youth hostels or in parks, and basically getting by on as little money as possible. *Time Magazine* (Anonymous 1971) referred to them as "knapsack nomads" and reports that more than 800,000 under-thirty Americans had decided to summer in Europe that year, a cultural phenomenon the article's authors describe as "the Woodstock of the '70s." In 1972, Kenneth Alsop, writing in the British magazine *Punch*, referred to the youthful American and European tourists as "Eurofreaks," the "*wandervoegel* of the new creed of international drop-outism, the waifs and strays of the mass-cult state, overlanders in an underground community, global villagers who scorn TV, the travellers whom the tourist industry doesn't want" (Alsop 1972, 131).

On this last point, however, Alsop was mistaken. The travel industry did want them. The airlines certainly wanted them, with Sabena (Belgium's national carrier), Pan Am, and TWA offering special student discount fares to anyone under thirty. *Time Magazine* reported that budget tourism was big business, with small hotels, greengrocers, car- and bicycle-rental companies, and other "vendors of the goods and services that economy-class tourists want" Europe's primary beneficiaries. Simple arithmetic gets to the heart of the economic impact of "international drop-outism" in the early 1970s: 1 million American travelers spending only U.S.$500 each means that U.S.$500 million flowed from the United States to Europe over a three-month period, not a small amount when one considers that in 1971, total international tourist spending was U.S.$20.8 billion.[3] In the early 1970s, an export industry generating upward of half a billion dollars over a three-month period was big business indeed.

And the travel industry still wants them in the early 2000s. Judging from the number of budget travel guides found in the local bookstore, youth travel represents a large share of the international tourism market. Most of these guides are written expressly for students and the under-thirty crowd: The *Let's Go* series is published by the Harvard Student Agencies, and *Berkeley Budget Guides* were written by University of California students and published by Fodor's Travel Publications. Whereas the *Berkeley Budget Guides* were first published in the early 1990s and discontinued later in the decade, the Harvard Student Cooperative published its first *Let's Go* edition in the mid-1960s and continues to publish guides to an ever-growing number of destinations. The budget guides are fairly conventional in terms of their listings of sights and attractions; they differ from more upscale guides mainly in their focus on low-cost accommodation and eating establishments and on the listing of activities of interest to students. The areas of the world they cover has expanded considerably since the early 1980s: The *Berkeley Budget Guides* covered dozens of countries in Europe and North America, and the *Let's Go* series publishes twenty-eight different guidebooks that provide information on more than fifty countries. European budget guides include the *Guide de Routard* series (France) and the *Rough Guides* (United Kingdom).

The most famous and one of the earliest of the low-budget travel guides is Lonely Planet's *Travel Survival Kit* series. Lonely Planet's first travel guide, *Across Asia on the Cheap*, was written in the early 1970s, "at a kitchen table and hand collated, trimmed, and stapled" by Tony and Maureen Wheeler, an English couple who still own the company. Today, Lonely Planet publishes over 160 travel guides that cover nearly every country, and "the emphasis continues to be on travel for independent travelers" (Rachowiecki 1995). Lonely Planet is the guide of choice for many Western IIS tourists, many of whom refer to it as the Bible. As Wise (1994, 58) points out with reference to the growth of IIS tourism worldwide, "like all historical moments, this one has a text: the Lonely Planet travel guides, a series of low-budget books that do for the modern hippie what the 'Official Preppy Handbook' once did for Izod shoppers." Lonely Planet provides information on both formal and informal-sector tourist establishments, but the emphasis is overwhelmingly placed on the "rock-bottom" category, particularly in the Third World countries that Lonely Planet covers.

Lonely Planet and other Western travel guides to non-Western societies are not without their critics. Many seasoned IIS tourists decry using travel guides of any kind as needlessly restricting one's travel options to what the authors and editors feel is important. Literary and cultural critics are concerned with the meaning and symbolic construction of tourist spaces; they stress the role travel guides play in creating mental maps in the minds of the Western tourists, tourists who subsequently experience a particular destination in scripted ways.[4] Whereas many business owners are happy to have their businesses listed in popular travel guides, others do not seek the publicity; one campground owner in Chiapas, Mexico refused a listing in Lonely Planet because he felt inclusion in the guide would over-commercialize and de-sacralize his property and surrounding areas.[5]

If a growing low-budget travel publishing industry provides evidence of the economic importance of IIS tourism, then changing public and institutional perceptions of backpackers, drifters, and other IIS travelers imparts a certain cultural credence to low-budget travel. Indeed, there has always been a mythical undercurrent to public perceptions of life on the road, particularly in the United States. But whereas Jack Kerouac-types are people one may have enjoyed reading about, they are rarely the people we want our sons and daughters to marry. *On the Road* may have been a bestseller, but real beatniks and hippies have traditionally met with public scorn and social disapprobation.

More recently, however, and perhaps in large part due to the changing social characteristics of drifter travelers themselves (see below), the cultural descendants of traveling beatniks and hippies have gained a certain social and cultural cachet. *The New York Times*, for instance, features a semiweekly, low-budget travel column, "The Frugal Traveler," that dispenses information on the many travel bargains found throughout the world. Commenting on the passing of Asia's "hippie circuit," one reporter notes that the travel counterculture of previous years has given way to a new 1990s rave scene, the beaches pioneered by older generations now "overrun by teenagers hot for a buzz" (Wise 1994, 58). Another views the legions of young backpackers as a travel avant-garde: "Call them budgeteers or independent travelers or plain old backpackers, but those who travel light and cheap are often the trailblazers of the tourist set" (McKinley 1999, 16).

Research on the Social Characteristics of Western International Informal-Sector Tourists

As I pointed out earlier, prior to 1970, very little tourism research of any kind was carried out, let alone research on the travel habits of young, low-budget tourists from Europe, North America, and Australasia. Erik Cohen's work is an important exception. Because he has written several articles on international low-budget travel, he is one of the few authors who incorporate drifter travel into a broader theory of tourism development; his tourist typology is widely adopted by tourism researchers and forms the basis of a number of subsequent studies (Oppermann 1993; Smith 1989). He was one of the first tourism researchers to take note of the growing numbers of youthful American and European travelers moving around Europe and Asia in the late 1960s and early 1970s. Perhaps in accordance with Michener's novel of the same name, he dubbed them *drifters* and defines a drifter as a type of tourist who:

> ventures furthest away from the beaten track and from the accustomed ways of life of his home country. He [*sic*] shuns any kind of connection with the tourist establishment, and considers the ordinary tourist experience phony. He tends to make it wholly on his own, living with the people and often taking odd-jobs to keep himself going. He tries to live the way the people he visits live, and to share their shelter, foods, and habits, keeping only the most basic and essential of his old customs. The drifter has no fixed itinerary or timetable and no well-defined goals of travel. He is almost wholly immersed in his host culture. Novelty is here at its highest, familiarity disappears almost entirely. (Cohen 1972, 168)

Drifters figure into Cohen's tourist typology, an early attempt to categorize international (Western) tourists on the basis of personality traits that the tourists manifest in their choice of destination, accommodation, cuisine, and so forth. The drifter forms one end of a spectrum of four tourist types defined on the basis of how familiar—or strange—the tourists' environment appears to them. *Mass tourists* move from one air-conditioned environment to the next, eat Western-style food, and often travel in groups where they are surrounded by people with the same language and culture. An "environmental bubble" insulates them from any meaningful contact with the local population. Mass tourists are the "ugly Americans," the First World pleasure seekers whom Turner and Ash have dubbed "the golden hordes," a vulgar mob that prefers the decontextualized image to the underlying reality of the places they visit (Boorstin 1992). Theirs is a completely inauthentic and superficial tourist experience. As Cohen points out, "though the desire for variety, novelty, and strangeness are the primary motives of tourism, these qualities have decreased as tourism has become institutionalized" (Cohen 1972, 172).

Independent tourists avoid group travel but retain a familiar environment through their choice of upscale accommodation and Western cuisine. They almost always make their bookings through travel agencies and consume upscale, formal-sector tourism commodities. Independent tourists differ from mass tourists in their greater propensity to travel "off the beaten path" but only to places with established tourism facilities. As Cohen observes, "familiarity is still dominant, but somewhat less so than in the preceding type; the experience of novelty is somewhat greater, though it is often of the routine kind" (Cohen 1972, 168). Taken together, mass and independent travelers are what Cohen refers to as *mass institutional tourists*, which nearly approximates what I have been calling IFS tourists.

Unlike mass institutional tourists, *explorers* and *drifters* involve themselves more in the social and cultural life of the societies they visit. Explorers tend not to deal with travel agents and prefer to make their own arrangements as they go along. Although they often seek out novel travel experiences, they "retain some of the basic routines and comforts of their native way of life." Explorers are, for Cohen, the contemporary equivalent of the "traveler" of previous years and serve as a spearhead for mass tourism in previously untouristed regions and places.

Even more so than explorers, drifter tourists shun their former ways of life, attempt to immerse themselves in the host culture, and have no fixed itinerary. They dispense with the normal comforts of their own cultures and often learn or attempt to learn the local language. The drifter is, for Cohen, "the true rebel of the tourist establishment and the complete opposite of the mass tourist." In Israel, the Netherlands, and other parts of the world, Cohen documents a number of "permanently temporary" drifter tourist centers, what he takes to be evidence of a distinct and growing "drifter tourist subculture." In Cohen's schema, explorers and drifters are noninstitutional tourists and roughly correspond to what I have been calling Western IIS tourists.

On closer inspection, however, Cohen's original definition of the drifter left much to be desired. In a later article (Cohen 1973), he found that drifter tourists do not always exhibit the characteristics that he had attributed to them. In many ways, they have more in common with traditional mass tourists than they do with the idealized drifter tourists of his earlier work. Cohen found that the majority of drifters seek out like-minded travelers and move from place to place in an environmental bubble, much like traditional mass tourists.[6] They are more interested in having a good time than they are in understanding different cultures and experiencing new things. He still recognizes a select group of drifters who forsake the comforts of their traditional lifestyles in order to immerse themselves in the culture of other, and often more "primitive," peoples. But whereas he finds that "the drug-oriented hippie is indeed the most conspicuous type of drifter," most drifters now, Cohen declares (in 1973), are "mass drifters." He defines this category of tourist as "usually the college youth, who spends a limited amount of time to see the world, meet people and 'have experiences,' but tends to stick to the drifter-tourist establishment of cheap lodgings and eating places and cut-rate fares" (Cohen 1973, 100). He documents the growth of "drifter communities" in Europe, Africa, and Asia, permanently temporary homes for international drifter tourists, a trend that continues into the 2000s.

Like other accounts of youth tourism and the youth counterculture more generally in the 1960s and 1970s, Cohen's description of drifters at times assumes a moralistic tone. He claims that mass drifters are usually from affluent backgrounds, "tramps by choice," and that they are unpatriotic, individualistic, and aimless escapists. More recent accounts of Western IIS tourists, however, have sought to present them in less stereotypical terms (Edensor 1998; Hampton 1998; Hutnyk 1996). For example, in a study of Agra's tourism spaces, tourism researcher Tim Edensor (1998) contrasts what he calls the "enclavic" space of five-star hotels and other carefully controlled environments with the "heterogeneous" space of the bazaar. Echoing critics who claim that modern-day tourism is inauthentic, Edensor claims, "the very commodity promised to tourists in the promotional literature of the holiday-makers is that they will undergo a memorable, sensual experience . . . but rather than the multi-sensual, complex, and more immediate sensation of the 'outside world' this is a mediated and simulated experience." In contrast, the heterogeneous spaces of the bazaar-frequenting Western backpackers are conducive to the "formation of a gregarious environment which privileges speech and removes barriers between backstage and frontstage so that visual and verbal enquiry is facilitated" (Edensor 1998, 55).

For Edensor, not only is backpacker travel more authentic, its practitioners are less likely to harbor or maintain the same attitudes of superiority characteristic of tourists who inhabit enclavic space. He observes that:

The power-laden processes of classifying, spectacularising and com-
modifying difference in the disciplined space of tourist enclaves
contrast with the changing juxtapositions of difference found in the
heterogeneous tourist space. Rather than being a distanced spectator
of manufactured spectacle, the pedestrian is part of this heteroglossia
of "otherness." Enmeshed in its sensuality it may be difficult to maintain an imperialist subjectivity. (Edensor 1998, 59)

He concludes by claiming, "the spatial distinctiveness of heterogeneous tourist
space, its material and social form, offers at least the potential to engage with
[an] unrepresentable form of 'otherness,' an other that cannot be drawn back
into colonial discourse" (Edensor 1998, 180).

The evidence Edensor presents, mostly interviews conducted with backpackers and package tourists, does indeed suggest that backpackers are very
interested in embracing what they take to be the "real" India, whereas package
tourists are more critical of what they see, more likely to harbor resentments
against Indian society, and generally welcome the enclavic spaces that distance
them from Indian culture and society. However, like other analyses of tourism based on the behavioral characteristics of tourists, Edensor's claims are
highly problematic when examined more closely. For instance, the heterogeneous space of the bazaar undoubtedly affords a better glimpse of the world
most Indians inhabit than does the enclavic space of five-star hotels. Are we
to assume, then, that a wealthy domestic tourist staying in a five-star hotel has
a less authentic experience of India than a German or North American backpacker in "heterogeneous space" with no in-depth knowledge of either India's
customs or its languages? Moreover, although Edensor's findings may suggest
otherwise, many IIS tourists express disdain for Indian society and associate
mostly with other IIS tourists. In New Delhi's Pahar Ganj district, for example,
an area very similar to the heterogeneous space of Agra that formed the basis
of Edensor's investigation, a significant number of hotel owners refuse to rent
to Indians or serve Indians food in the restaurants attached to their hotels,
a practice that many backpacker tourists welcome. In other words, heterogeneous tourist space can also be enclavic. The removal of barriers between
backstage and frontstage that Edensor associates with heterogeneous space
may not be as common as his analysis suggests.

Non-Western International Informal-Sector Tourists

Perhaps the most glaring omission from Western researchers' accounts of international tourism is the millions of non-Western tourists who travel to other
non-Western countries (figure 4.3). In most cases, neighboring countries supply the largest share of international arrivals. For example, more than 35 percent of international travelers to India are from other low-income countries

Figure 4.3 Pahar Ganj, New Delhi, India

in West and Southeast Asia (Government of India Ministry of Tourism 1989). Nepal, Pakistan, Bangladesh, and Sri Lanka represent more international arrivals in India than all Western European countries combined (World Tourism Organization 2001). Indonesia receives 77.5 percent of its total international arrivals from other Asian countries and close to 40 percent from Southeast Asia alone (World Tourism Organization 2001). Over one-third of all international travel to both Namibia and Tanzania originates in other African countries. Indeed, with very few exceptions, the single largest source of international arrivals for most Third World countries is neighboring low-income countries.

Of course, as with First World travelers, not all Third World tourists visiting other Third World countries frequent IIS tourism establishments and visit IIS tourist destinations. In fact, in some countries, travelers from other low-income countries are more likely to patronize formal-sector tourism establishments, particularly in the major cities. In India, for example, travelers from the Middle East and particularly the Gulf States are less likely to stay in informal-sector accommodation facilities than their counterparts from Germany, France, and the United Kingdom (Government of India Ministry of Tourism 1989). Generally speaking, however, East European, West Asian, Southeast Asian, and African tourists to India, which together comprise one-third of India's annual arrivals, are more likely to patronize informal-sector tourist establishments than are tourists from Western Europe, the United States,

Canada, Australia, New Zealand, and Japan. In 1989, nearly 40 percent of all Third World tourists in India spent less than U.S.$20 per day, and 25 percent spent less than U.S.$10 per day, a significantly higher share than their First World counterparts.

For most accounts of IIS tourism in the Third World, the implications of so many non-Western international tourist arrivals are significant. Even though Cohen's oft-referenced typology, for example, is supposedly a typology of *international* tourists, into which of his categories do non-Western international travelers fit? Presumably, a Bangladeshi or Sri Lankan traveler to India or a Kenyan visiting Tanzania is neither experiencing a completely new environment nor traveling in an environmental bubble. Because the society they have traveled to has much in common with their own, they need not, like Cohen's drifters, reject their own culture in order to embrace the new one. In short, Cohen's international tourist types have almost no applicability to one of the largest groups of international travelers to Third World countries today.

Research on the Impact of Low-Budget Tourism

Despite its growing importance, there are relatively few studies that survey the impact of IIS tourists on particular places and communities. Theories of spatiotemporal tourism development neglect this type of tourist and focus instead on the upscale, formal-sector tourism markets. As geographer Martin Oppermann points out, "although its existence has been accepted by the disciplines of the diffusionist paradigm, even as a major element in the early phases of tourism development, drifters are generally ignored in the tourism research" (Oppermann 1993, 541). The oversight probably has to do with a lack of statistics and the prominence—and particularly the economic importance—of high-end tourism. Some studies have shown, however, that IIS tourists stay longer in the host country and spend as much money per visit as do high-end tourists, who generally stay for much shorter periods (Meijers 1991).

A lack of evidence on the impact of IIS tourism has not precluded tourism researchers from making general claims regarding the specific costs and benefits of this type of travel. In an early article, Cohen claims that "drifters are more of an economic liability than a source of income for the economy of the host country." Several years later, Turner and Ash (1976, 279) conclude that drifters "could not provide the basis for a tourism which was genuinely sensitive to Third World problems and supportive of development." Anthropologist Valene Smith (1990, 34) likens the growing number of youthful travelers to a "virus" that "moves from one beach to the next—Ceylon, Pattaya, Mombasa, Boracay—leaving behind prostitution, alcoholism, juvenile crime, and narcotics." She goes on to say, "unless politically controlled, it is predictable these

Figure 4.4   Sadhus, Parvati Valley, India

'drifters', having ruined one island, will move on to another, perpetuating future land use problems" (figure 4.4).

The surprising thing about such statements is that either they are made without any evidence to back them up (Turner and Ash) or the evidence the researcher herself presents contradicts the claims made. For example, Smith (1989, 35) claims that drifters cause drug abuse among the local population on Boracay (an island in the Philippines), even though she reports, "no Filipino had as yet been proved to be addicted." Her claim that drifter tourism is bad for the local population is lost on the people themselves, who she reports "are delighted with their sudden new riches." Her assertion that drifter tourism has "ruined" Ceylon, Pattaya, and Mombasa is at best an overgeneralization and at worst ridiculous. A vicious ethnic war has raged in Sri Lanka for two decades (could drifter tourists have "ruined" an entire country?); Mombasa is a major city in Kenya where the annual number of international tourist arrivals represents a tiny percentage of the city's total population; and Pattaya has been a mass tourist destination since the United States military began sending its troops there on R&R during the Vietnam War, when it also picked up its reputation as a center for prostitution. Finally, her claim that traditional mass tourists are "seldom a social problem" because "the chosen areas have adequate infrastructure to support the influx" and because "their personal interests are primarily sun-oriented" is clearly mistaken: The vast majority of studies dealing with the negative social and environmental impact of tourism deal with exactly the type of tourist she feels is "seldom a social problem."

As noted earlier, the problem with such analyses of IIS tourism is primarily methodological and common to many studies of tourism destinations: the inadequacy of any attempt to explain specific social outcomes on the basis of the supposed attitudes and psychological characteristics of tourists. This is particularly the case in Third World countries, where most tourism development theory explains the growth of tourism largely in terms of Western travel patterns and completely neglects non-Western international travelers and domestic tourists. Precisely because tourism researchers tautologically define IIS tourist communities as places where (Western) IIS tourists go, they often ignore the larger socioeconomic milieu in which much IIS tourism occurs and its many links with domestic tourism and the informal economy.

Thus, Smith incorrectly argues that because the international long-term budget traveler "is increasingly orientated towards alcohol, drug abuse, sexual freedom and prostitution,"[7] IIS tourism development is always bad and corrupting of host communities. The growth of unregulated, informal-sector enterprises— the substandard accommodation that would "not meet U.S. codes for electrical wiring, fire escapes, or sanitation," as Smith puts it—caused by the demands of low-budget tourists for inexpensive lodging "raises doubts that increased tourism will bring significant material and social benefits to local people or protect the environmental degradation [sic]" (Smith 1995). The policy implications of such research are particularly disturbing, tantamount as they are to suggesting that policy makers in low-income countries should not promote a sector of the tourism industry that caters overwhelmingly to domestic tourists. Indeed, if the Indian government was to adopt Smith's criterion for acceptable tourist facilities (U.S. standards), then nearly all tourist accommodation in India would have to be shut down, including many of the country's formal-sector tourism facilities. Lacking the resources to stay at the type of tourist facility that Smith endorses, should people in Third World countries simply stay home and leave the cultural and natural attractions of their countries to elite groups and package tourists from the rich countries? What Smith and other researchers fail to recognize is the connection between IIS tourists, both Western and non-Western, and the informal economy in Third World countries.

Another problem with attributing social outcomes solely to specific tourist types is that the types may change. Indeed, as we have seen, the nature of what constitutes a drifter tourist is not always clear. What seemed like an easily discernible type of tourist for Cohen in 1972, what he called "the drifter," became a much more complex category just one year later. Cohen reports (in 1973) the existence of four subtypes of drifter tourists: adventurers, itinerant hippies, mass drifters, and fellow travelers. Turner and Ash observe, "These new, bohemian nomads are characterized by youth, long hair, and an interest in drugs, but this statement must be immediately qualified, since they are not invariably under thirty, long hair does not necessarily entail regular drug use and is hardly a distinguishing characteristic in women" (Turner and Ash 1976, 255).

Pam Riley (1988), based on an extensive study of international long-term budget travelers, compared her findings with Cohen's observations made ten years earlier:

> Budget travelers, as a group, are now different in many respects from those [Cohen] observed earlier. Most do *not* drift aimlessly without concern for destinations. They do *not* beg, and are *no* more hedonistic or anarchistic than members of the larger western culture. They are generally *not* associated with what could be defined as a counterculture. (318, italics in the original)

Finally, we have seen how one of the largest groups of IIS tourists in many Third World countries is not made up of First World drifter travelers at all. Non-Western tourists represent the biggest group of foreign travelers in many low-income countries, and in some countries they are more likely than Western tourists to frequent informal-sector tourism establishments.

In other words, explaining IIS tourist impact on the basis of drifter tourist characteristics is like trying to hit a moving target. Hippie-like drifter-travelers are still found in India, Nepal, Thailand, Mexico, and other Third World tourist destinations but they no longer make up the majority of IIS tourists, not even the majority of Western IIS tourists. We cannot now say that there is any one type of IIS tourist if, indeed, there ever was. We can say that a large number of international tourists travel to destinations in the Third World where informal-sector tourism establishments predominate. Saying anything more than this involves a closer analysis of the particular tourist economy in question. In other words, the impact of IIS tourists, like other groups of tourists, depends as much on the structure of the local economy as it does on the behavioral characteristics of the tourists who travel there.

By ignoring the supply side of the equation, however, tourism researchers often fall prey to an overly deterministic way of evaluating tourist impact that downplays the importance of particular places in shaping the social and economic outcomes associated with IIS tourism. It is an approach that obscures, on the one hand, the relationship between First World IIS tourists (drifters) and the Third World informal-sector enterprises that provide IIS tourists with goods and services and, on the other hand, the fact that IIS tourists and domestic tourists in Third World countries consume the same (or similar) tourism products. That is, it tends to ignore the supply side of the host-guest relationship or at best views the supply side as overdetermined by the demands of international (Western) tourists. With few exceptions, however, the informal guesthouses, cafés, and transport facilities utilized by IIS tourists would continue to operate in the absence of international tourism. Indeed, very few of the informal-sector establishments that provide IIS tourists with goods and services originated specifically in response to perceived IIS tourist demand, particularly in Third World cities. Moreover, the IIS destinations that did arise to serve IIS tourists differ significantly from each other in their social and economic organization (both within and among countries), casting doubt on a simple cause-and-effect relationship between the behavioral characteristics of IIS tourists and the structure and dynamics of individual IIS destinations. Some examples may serve to make my points clearer.

Pahar Ganj

Pahar Ganj is the center of New Delhi's IIS tourism industry. Also known as *Main Bazaar*, it is a fairly large residential and commercial area immediately adjacent to the New Delhi train station and about a 10-minute walk from Connaught Place, New Delhi's main commercial center. A major wholesaling and retailing district, Pahar Ganj has increasingly come to specialize in export products, mainly apparel (Indian-style, lightweight summer clothing in particular); printed bed sheets and similar items; Indian handicrafts; and to a lesser degree, jewelry. Pahar Ganj is also a local market area, with many produce stands, food stalls, grocery stores, hardware stores, tobacconists, sari shops, electronics shops, barbershops, and crockery and cooking utensil stores used by area residents.

The district's reputation as a center for tourism and export has grown considerably since the mid-1980s. The shops dealing with foreigners do a thriving business. One apparel shop owner told me business has never been better. Telecommunications offices have proliferated and now offer e-mail and fax facilities. Shipping agents line the side streets, and signs above many shops are written in English, Russian, and Hebrew. Restaurants catering to the tastes of foreigners are also legion, with many serving such nontraditional Indian dishes as banana pancakes, cornflakes, muesli, beans and eggs, veggie-burgers, and falafel. Informal (that is, illegal or black market) moneychangers do a thriving business, offering between 5 and 10 percent over the official bank rate for U.S. dollars and British pounds.[8] A number of second-hand bookstores have also started up in recent years, specializing in English, German, French, Hebrew, Japanese, and increasingly, Russian books.

Other tourism-related businesses in Pahar Ganj include travel agents and tour operators. Most have tie-ups with private bus companies, charging relatively low rates for bus transport to Rajasthan, Kashmir, Himachal Pradesh, Uttar Pradesh, and places as far afield as Bombay, Pune, and Kathmandu. You can purchase air tickets at many of the travel agencies, usually for much cheaper prices than in the travel agencies found along Connaught Place. Some agencies sell train tickets, as well, and for a fee will arrange for foreign visas and Indian visa extensions.

Some Pahar Ganj hotels with attached restaurants cater almost exclusively to IIS tourists and discourage Indians from renting rooms or dining on the premises. I myself have gone to Pahar Ganj with wealthy Indian friends who were not allowed entry into one hotel restaurant on the grounds that they were not staying at the hotel, even though I was not staying at the hotel and could easily have entered the restaurant. Several of Pahar Ganj's hotels specialize in serving certain foreign nationalities. Israelis, for example, make up the majority of guests at the Veejay Hotel and the Punjabi Guest House,[9] two fairly large (fifty-plus rooms) hotels located opposite one another in an alley adjoining one of the district's busy commercial thoroughfares. The guest book at the Veejay hotel indicates as much, with nearly every entry taken up by an Israeli name. The manager and many of the workers at these two hotels understand and speak some Hebrew. An ultra-orthodox Jewish group, Lubavitch Chabad, even maintains a "Chabad House" in the Veejay Hotel. Other hotels look askance at renting to Israelis, claiming that the young Israeli tourists exhibit loud and obnoxious behavior, intimidate hotel employees, and often underpay for services.

Other hotels cater to both Indian travelers and IIS tourists. The Delhi Hotel, for example, rents about two-thirds of its rooms to IIS tourists and the rest to Indian business travelers and students. The owner told me that his policy is not to discriminate against Indians, as many other hotels do, and he makes a point of renting to both Indians and foreign tourists. The reason hotel owners give for not renting to Indians (and Africans as well, for that matter) is that they cause trouble by stealing things from Western IIS tourists or cheating them in various ways, or that they will not pay their hotel bills. If a particular hotel picks up a reputation among IIS tourists that it is unsafe in any way, the IIS tourists will go elsewhere, and so will a large part of the hotel's profits. In fact, hotel owners are extremely conscious of how authors of travel guidebooks characterize their establishments and try to avoid any undue publicity that may appear in the Lonely Planet or in other travel guides.

Most hotels in Pahar Ganj are small-scale establishments, with some having as few as ten rooms. In addition to their small size, the majority of accommodation facilities in Pahar Ganj, as in New Delhi generally, are unlicensed and illegally operated. According to the New Delhi Police, there are about 650 guesthouses in the city, of which 350 are unlicensed (Anonymous 1996). Delhi hotel owners often ignore formal zoning restrictions governing the construction and operation of accommodation facilities and prefer to remain unlicensed. Owners point to the difficulties of gaining permission from city authorities to build even in an area approved for hotel facilities and to the long time lag between applying for permission to build a structure and actually getting a building permit from the relevant city authorities.[10] Moreover, many could not obtain licenses even if they so desired, because city zoning regulations prohibit the operation of hotels in residential areas.

Some Indian hotel and guesthouse owners lacking the proper operating licenses report having to make unauthorized payments to building inspectors and other city officials. The price of informality in such cases is high and may represent a sizable share of a hotel's revenues. Local authorities may at times inspect the guest books of informal-sector hotels, and then negotiate with the owner for a monthly fee. When owners refuse to pay or when negotiations break down, the authorities may threaten to close the establishment. In an interview with the author, one north Indian guesthouse owner explained:

> I will pay them, but I want to make only one payment per month. But each day another one comes here and demands money from me. Why should I pay so many of them? Let them have my books, they can discuss it and then come for only one payment. Otherwise, they'll take all my money so I should just close the hotel myself.

In another case in north India, the owner and local authorities could not arrive at a mutually satisfactory level of payment; the authorities first harassed a number of hotel guests and eventually closed the hotel. It reopened two weeks later after the two sides reached an agreement.

Accommodation facilities in Pahar Ganj are often unsafe and may represent serious hazards to the welfare of hotel guests and workers. In addition to rat and insect infestation, some informal lodging facilities are fire hazards due to improper electrical wiring, and most lack fire escapes of any kind. They may also be unsafe structurally as well. In 1996, a Pahar Ganj guesthouse collapsed; seventeen people were killed, including eight foreign tourists, and twenty-nine people were injured. In the aftermath of the building collapse, Delhi police launched an "intensive drive" against the illegal hotels (Anonymous 1996). Some New Delhi hotel owners interpreted the building collapse and subsequent police drive as a potential threat to their livelihoods and took steps to remedy obvious health hazards. To the best of my knowledge, however, no guesthouses in Pahar Ganj closed as a result of the crackdown.

Restaurants in Pahar Ganj fall into two categories. The first type caters to both resident Indians and IIS tourists (figure 4.5). There are dozens of such *dhabas* (greasy spoons) in Pahar Ganj, serving traditional Indian dishes: *daal* (lentils), *mattar paneer* (green peas and cheese), *roti* (baked bread), *aloo gobi* (potatoes and cauliflower), *kheer* (sweet rice), and similar dishes (figure 4.6). They are generally very inexpensive and almost always crowded. They are informal because they are small-scale, rarely if ever inspected, and lack the proper health inspection certificates and operating licenses. Because the dhabas are unregulated, they may technically be in violation of the city's health codes. A restaurant owner in south Delhi explained to me that this is not ordinarily a problem, because the authorities in charge of enforcing such regulations accept *baksheesh* for looking the other way. The cost of *baksheesh*, according to this particular owner, is not very high and is factored into his operating costs.

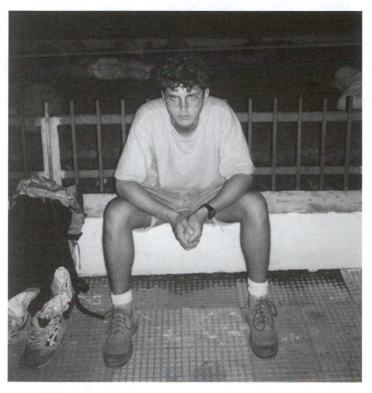

Figure 4.5   IIS tourist, Chandigarh, India

Figure 4.6   Traditional roadside *dhaba*, Uttar Pradesh, India

The other type of restaurant found in Pahar Ganj caters overwhelmingly to IIS tourists, although small numbers of Indians also frequent these establishments. The prices of meals in such establishments are generally much higher than in the traditional Indian *dhabas*, often exceeding U.S.$3 per person. The food is generally of poor quality but somewhat more familiar to Western palates, and the café-restaurants are popular as meeting points for tourists or as places for travelers to eat butter-jam toast, drink coffee, smoke cigarettes, make travel plans, or wait around for their buses, trains, or planes to depart. Most do a thriving business; one owner confided in me that he was able to send his three children to private school in Delhi from the profits he generated in just one of his two restaurants in Pahar Ganj.

One of the reasons for high profits in such establishments is the low wages routinely paid to restaurant and hotel workers in Pahar Ganj. Many employees of Pahar Ganj's tourist-related businesses come from Eastern Uttar Pradesh, Bengal, Bihar, Nepal, and other impoverished regions of the subcontinent. A large number of the hotel and restaurant workers are functionally illiterate; many are young children who work long hours cleaning or serving *chai* (tea) to tourists. Average pay for a restaurant worker is 600–1,000 rupees (U.S.$12–20) per month plus tips, most of which he sends to his family.[11] Those in a position to earn tips do somewhat better but tipping is generally not the rule in IIS tourist establishments and certainly not customary in the more traditional *dhabas*. Although job security is virtually nil, with many workers sacked at a moment's notice, hotel and restaurant workers are usually provided with food and lodging. The work is not ordinarily fast-paced but often tedious and sometimes dangerous. At many small hotels and restaurants, the line between employee and personal servant is usually quite thin.

In contrast to the workers in Pahar Ganj's tourism establishments, the owners are overwhelmingly local. Many of the hotels and restaurants are family owned and operated. Some of the gift shops and travel agents are operated by Kashmiris but generally in partnership with local businessmen. There are currently no hotels, restaurants, or travel agencies in Pahar Ganj owned by foreigners,[12] although nonresident Indians (NRIs) may have some interest in several of the more upscale accommodation facilities.

When asked why they hire workers from other parts of India and from Nepal rather than local workers, the owners say that the Delhi workers insist on higher wages and generally do not work as hard. Almost every owner interviewed expressed the opinion that workers from Eastern Uttar Pradesh, Bihar, and Nepal are superior to local workers because they are willing to work longer hours for lower wages and are generally more grateful for the opportunity to work. One owner expressed a certain fondness for his longer-term employees (one man from Bihar had been with him for over ten years) but during the course of my stay in the hotel did not hesitate to sack another long-term Nepali employee who had been with him nearly as long. In essence, job security does not exist in Delhi's informal tourism sector. Health care, pensions, and other forms of social insurance are also completely lacking for most workers, although some workers interviewed indicated that on at least one occasion, the owner paid for a doctor's visit (30 rupees, about U.S.$0.60).

The import content of the tourism goods and services sold in Pahar Ganj is extremely low. Exceptions include foreign cigarettes, cigarette papers, and goods such as video cameras, laptop computers, and bottles of imported Scotch whiskey. Just about everything hotels and restaurants purchase as inputs are procured in Delhi or in the Delhi region. Gift shops and wholesalers are somewhat different in this regard, with some purchasing their stock (mostly handicrafts) from Rajasthan, Himachal Pradesh, Uttar Pradesh, and Haryana. Apparel is produced either in the Delhi metropolitan area, in Bombay, or in Ahmedabad (Gujarat). Indian brand name electronic equipment (there are no imported brands sold in Pahar Ganj's shops) is manufactured in different parts of the country, usually in one of India's five major metropolitan areas: Delhi, Bombay, Calcutta, Madras, or Bangalore. Thus, there is virtually no leakage of foreign exchange from the domestic economy as a result of IIS tourist spending in Pahar Ganj, although there is significant leakage from the local (Delhi) economy.

IIS tourists in Pahar Ganj rarely come into contact with the local population. The primary form of contact is a commercial one, with IIS tourists purchasing goods and services from Indian merchants, hoteliers, and restaurateurs. Few friendships are formed between local residents and tourists; most tourists keep to themselves and in any event are separated from most of the local population because they do not speak or understand Hindi, Punjabi, or Urdu. Most IIS tourists have only the slightest understanding of Indian languages and customs. For their part, the Indian residents of Pahar Ganj and those who work in nontourist establishments view IIS tourists as low-class individuals with a lot of money. Many Western women do not dress in the customary Indian manner and often wear see-through clothing or petticoats without saris. Most Indians, especially Indian men, interpret such behavior as either indecent or sexually provocative and assume that many of the Western women are "easy," a fact reinforced by cultural stereotypes that Indians harbor of Westerners and Western women in general. Shopkeepers tend to view Western tourists as *chutia* (idiots) who deserve to be cheated (by them), and they often direct foul language at the unsuspecting foreign tourists who lack an understanding of Hindi and thus are unaware of what the shopkeepers are saying.

Pahar Ganj is also a center of prostitution and drugs. Many of the prostitutes who work in Pahar Ganj are from India's northeastern states of Assam, Nagaland, Tripura, Manipur, and Arunachal Pradesh or from Nepal. These girls and women are virtual prisoners, having been trafficked into Delhi by middlemen and sold to the brothels. Some are eventually able to pay off their "debt" to the pimp or brothel owner and leave Delhi, but most remain indebted for long periods of time. A high percentage of the prostitutes in India contract HIV and die prematurely of AIDS and AIDS-related illnesses. Pahar Ganj is no exception; one prostitute informed me that two of her co-workers had tested positive for HIV and that another had died of AIDS-related pneumonia. One reason for a high incidence of HIV among Indian sex workers is a lack of protected sex; in some areas the cost of a condom is nearly the same as the cost of a prostitute, and the customer always decides whether he will use a condom. The young girls working in the industry are often ignorant of the health consequences of unprotected sex or completely unfamiliar with contraception. Another reason for the high incidence of HIV infection among sex workers is their use of shared needles because, as in other countries, many Indian prostitutes engage in prostitution to support their drug habits.

Most brothels and prostitutes in Pahar Ganj cater to local residents, domestic tourists, and the police. Western IIS tourists rarely frequent the city's many brothels or seek out the services of sex workers. This partly reflects a lack of demand on the part of IIS tourists for sexual services; it partly reflects the ignorance of IIS tourists regarding where and how to purchase sex (there is no section in the Lonely Planet guide, for example, with details on finding a prostitute, how much to pay, etc.); and it partly reflects an unwillingness on the part of both brothels and sex workers in India to take foreign men as clients. There are a few European sex workers from the United Kingdom and Russia living in Pahar Ganj as well, women who charge much higher prices and sell their services to wealthy Indians, government officials, and international businessmen who stay in five-star hotels.

In addition to being a center of prostitution, Pahar Ganj is one of Delhi's major distribution points for illicit drugs.[13] Delhi is flooded with heroin and opium; supplies of narcotics flow into the city from India's growing regions, Pakistan, Southeast Asia, and Afghanistan, which in the aftermath of the U.S. invasion has once again become the world's leading supplier of raw opium. Although Delhi has been and remains a major narcotics transshipment point from growing regions to markets in Europe, Africa, and North America, in recent years the city's consumption of heroin has increased dramatically. Delhi's drug-addicted population has soared; addicts are now visible everywhere, including on the sidewalks and alleyways running off of Pahar Ganj's Main Bazaar. Tourists, too, are involved in the city's drug trade, primarily as users but also as traffickers and middlemen. Whereas both the city and the national government recognize the gravity of the situation, a lack of resources has hampered efforts to stem the flow of drugs into and out of Pahar Ganj and the city's other distribution centers.

Zipolite

Playa de Zipolite (Zipolite Beach) is a small *pueblo* (village) in the Mexican state of Oaxaca. Like New Delhi's Pahar Ganj district, Zipolite is a popular destination for both IIS tourists and domestic travelers and has been so since the early 1970s. Unlike New Delhi and Pahar Ganj, Zipolite is neither a city nor part of an urban agglomeration; it is located on a remote part of the Oaxacan coast, eight hours from Oaxaca City and eighteen hours by bus from Mexico City (figure 4.7). Zipolite rarely attracts business travelers. Its chief attractions for both Mexican and international tourists are a mile-long stretch of white sand beach, a rural setting, and a relatively permissive social atmosphere. Nudity is common on the beach, and recreational drugs are widely available. Zipolite features no formal-sector accommodation or restaurant facilities; although the village is supplied with electricity, the water supply is drawn from wells, and until recently the village lacked telephone service. The nearest public telephone was in Puerto Angel, several kilometers away. Pochutla, the nearest population center of any size, is about twenty kilometers away by road.

Zipolite is popular with both domestic and international tourists. International tourists generally outnumber Mexican travelers, although during holidays and especially at Christmas and Easter, relatively large numbers of domestic tourists from Oaxaca City and Mexico City travel to Zipolite and the neighboring village of Puerto Angel. Among the international travelers, most are West European and

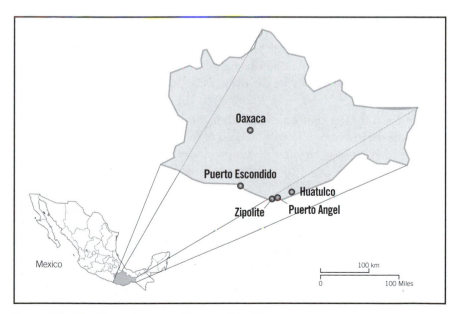

Figure 4.7 Zipolite and surrounding municipalities

Canadian, with fewer numbers of U.S. and South American tourists. According to a survey I conducted in 1997, Italians were the most numerous group of foreign tourists at Zipolite, followed by Germans, Canadians, Americans, English, French, Spanish, Argentines, and Israelis.[14] The average age of a foreign tourist was twenty-seven, with a daily budget of U.S.$20, U.S.$4 of which was spent on accommodation, U.S.$7 on food, and the rest on additional items, mostly alcohol and souvenirs. A large number of the international tourists traveling to Zipolite are students on extended vacations, but many, particularly the West Europeans, are professionals or blue-collar workers on their annual holiday. Many international tourists continue further south to Chiapas and Guatemala before returning to Mexico City and their home countries. During the tourist season, which extends from November through March, an average of between 150 and 200 international tourists stay at Zipolite on any given day. The number of Mexican tourists varies significantly, from virtually none during the week to well over 200 during the Christmas and Easter holiday seasons.

Although Zipolite's strong surf has made it unsuitable for launching fishing boats, neighboring villages are known for their small fishing fleets; fishing comprises the second largest local industry after tourism and the third largest regional industry after tourism and coffee. Both Puerto Angel, a naval center and fishing village just south of Zipolite, and Mazunte, a village a few kilometers to the north, have small fishing fleets. A large stretch of coastline adjacent to Zipolite provides a nesting ground for marine turtles; whereas trade in the endangered turtles and their eggs is now banned in Zipolite and neighboring beaches, local people still collect turtle eggs from unprotected (unpoliced) areas for their own consumption. Although killing turtles for food is not as common today as gathering up their eggs, the practice is not unknown. A reserve for turtles has been established at Mazunte but enforcement of the ban on killing turtles and removing their eggs is lax; those who violate the ban are rarely punished.

Apart from fishing and some handicraft production, there are few local industries based in or around Zipolite. Most of the intermediate goods consumed by tourism businesses in Zipolite are produced outside of the region. Thus, the leakage factor is significant, both locally and regionally. However, just as in the case of the Pahar Ganj tourist district in Delhi, very few commodities consumed by either tourists or tourism businesses in Zipolite are imported into Mexico. The national leakage factor is thus close to zero and compares extremely favorably with international formal-sector resorts such as Ixtapa or Cancún, with their much higher propensity to import goods and services from abroad (see chapter 3). In Zipolite, just about everything consumed by tourists is produced in Mexico, from the automobiles and *colectivos* that bring them to their destination to the *hamacas* that they sleep in to the *mezcal*, tequila, and *cerveza* (beer) that they drink.

Until fairly recently, Zipolite was largely uninhabited. Beginning in the 1960s, people from the region began to settle on the beach, constructing simple shelters for themselves and their families. Many of the original inhabitants came for the purpose of collecting turtle eggs and killing the turtles for their meat. Land tenure is a hotly contested issue in Zipolite, with the federal government seeking to demarcate property boundaries clearly (in Mexico this is known as *regularizacion*) and many of the residents resisting the process on the grounds that they will eventually be forced to sell or, as they say, have their property "expropriated." The problem, the local people say, is that the current form of land tenure, *tierras communales* (communally owned land), where individuals living on the land have usufruct rights but cannot sell it, provides a living to the land's inhabitants but does not offer security to potential investors. Numerous residents of Zipolite point to the process of regularization of communal lands at Santa Cruz, a village that once existed fifty kilometers east of Zipolite, whose inhabitants were expropriated by the federal agencies overseeing the construction of the megaresort of Bahías de Huatulco.

In Zipolite itself, some residents have sought to preserve local autonomy in the face of government pressures to develop their land more intensively. Contrasting what they call their "*turismo rustico*" (rustic or rural tourism) with the intensive tourism development of nearby Puerto Escondido and Huatulco, many of the local residents agree that the privatization of communal lands will lead to the eventual disintegration of the community and their way of life. A locally produced document known as the Zipolite Declaration states that "private property alienates, destroys, and eventually disintegrates the community as people become egotistical and greedy." Many of Zipolite's residents express a clear preference for their present lifestyle and look askance at the prospect of working in a large hotel as gardeners, room attendants, or cooks. They understand very well that local residents rarely receive the better jobs in the resort hotels at Huatulco, Cancún, and other large resorts. As they state in the Zipolite Declaration, "we don't want five-star hotels owned by foreigners; we want progress but only one that accords with our lives under the sky, near the immense sea, secure in our traditions and culture."

Despite local opposition to the privatization of communal lands and the uncertainty of land tenure in many cases, property has been changing hands in Zipolite for quite some time. Outsiders, mostly people from Mexico City, the United States, and Italy, now own several of the larger businesses. (In at least one case, the foreign ownership of beachfront property has resulted from an outsider marrying a local person.) Ownership and control of the tourism businesses in Zipolite remain overwhelmingly local, although the percentage of outsiders with a stake in the local tourism industry has been growing. Local fears that foreigners will buy up the land for five-star hotels do not seem as yet to be well founded. Foreigners are indeed investing in beach properties, constructing hotels, and operating restaurants, but the way in which they are doing so is more in keeping with Zipolite's rustic image than it is with the highly commercialized ambience of Huatulco or Cancún.

The major types of accommodation at Zipolite are thatch-roofed *cabañas* (beach bungalows), *palapas* (lean-tos) under which tourists hang either their own or rented *hamacas* (hammocks), and tents, although camping has become less common in Zipolite over the last few years. In 1997, prior to Hurricane Pauline, there were seventy-two tourism-related businesses located on the beach, with forty-three having some sort of lodging facilities, usually *hamacas* or *cabañas*. The remaining businesses were either restaurants without any attached accommodation facilities or small shops selling cigarettes, fruit, snacks, and other items. In addition to the businesses located on the beach, there are a number of tourism-related establishments located off the beach on access roads and on the main road running through the village.

It is very difficult to estimate the total number of people employed in Zipolite's tourism industry. In addition to resident individuals working in the hotels and restaurants, a great many *ambulantes* (traveling salesmen and saleswomen) move up and down the beach hawking their wares. Wages are generally low, but most tourism-related jobs pay better than agricultural work, about twice the minimum wage. Although many of the workers in tourism-related businesses are family members, a fairly large percentage consists of wage workers who come from surrounding villages. Some have come from as far away as Mexico City, although the majority of tourism workers are Oaxaceños. Working conditions are generally not poor; a majority of the workers surveyed complained less about the working conditions than they did about the low wages. Indeed, many enjoy working at Zipolite because they say it is fun to meet foreigners and the atmosphere is relaxed.

Like IIS tourism destinations in other parts of the world, the atmosphere in Zipolite is socially permissive. This owes something to the history of the destination, because the *jipis* (hippies) were among the first foreigners to travel to Zipolite in the 1960s. Zipolite is reputedly the only nude beach in all of Mexico, it attracts many gay and lesbian travelers, recreational drugs are easy to find, and the alcohol flows freely throughout the day. Generally speaking, most illicit drug use in Zipolite is confined to marijuana, although in recent years the demand for cocaine and heroin by both locals and tourists has increased significantly. Local residents do not generally perceive prostitution as a problem in Zipolite, and few foreigners engage the services of Mexican sex workers.

Zipolite is connected to Pochutla and neighboring villages by a local bus service, by taxis, and by *colectivos* (various forms of shared minibuses or covered pickup trucks). There is frequent bus service from Pochutla to Bahías de Huatulco, Acapulco, Salina Cruz, Mexico City (three buses per day), Oaxaca City (many buses per day), and San Cristobal de las Casas in Chiapas. Armed robbery of buses is becoming more frequent in Oaxaca, particularly on the coastal road connecting Pochutla to Acapulco. One driver told me that, on average, one in every fifteen buses is held up by *banditos* (armed robbers). The *banditos* place large obstacles in the way of an oncoming bus; when the bus stops the bandits board the bus with weapons drawn and rob the passengers.

Crime directed against tourists is also on the upswing in the immediate vicinity of Zipolite. Several IIS tourists and foreign residents reported that they had been the victims of violent crime. One was waiting for a bus late at night in Puerto Angel when masked gunmen abducted him. The gunmen placed a pillowcase over his head and drove him around in their car for approximately an hour. Eventually he was set free but only after he was relieved of his money and other possessions, including even his shoes. Other tourists reported being robbed on the beach late at night as they were returning to their bungalows. Theft from rooms and tents is also common at Zipolite and has increased in recent years. Local residents offer different explanations for the increase, but for some of the more politically astute residents the reason for increased criminal activity is obvious: Mexicans have become much poorer in the wake of successive financial crises and accompanying bouts of structural adjustment. Small farmers (*campesinos*) have been hit particularly hard in the wake of such free trade agreements as NAFTA, particularly in remote parts of the country, such as Oaxaca and Chiapas, and many consider tourists from the North fair game (Barry 1995; Ross 1997).

A number of local residents expressed concern over tourists' behavior and moral laxity. Most, however, felt that the vast majority of tourists were not a problem and did not contribute in any way to a decline in the moral standards of the community. People who were of particular concern to the resident population were the small number of travelers, mostly from the United States, who were either alcoholics or addicted to drugs. The number of such people was sufficiently small, however, so as not to result in any negative perceptions on the part of the local population of tourists in general. In fact, the residents looked on some of the drunken foreigners as a source of entertainment. Understandably, the resident population did not welcome with open arms some of the long-term resident foreigners who supported themselves by selling drugs. This was particularly true of resident drug dealers, who felt that they should have an exclusive right to sell drugs to tourists. "I don't want to compete with the gringos selling marijuana," one drug dealer told me. "They should leave Zipolite if they don't have any money."

Conclusion

Although IIS tourism clearly has its pros and cons, it is rarely disruptive of local communities, as many of its detractors argue. On the contrary, it tends to preserve them because local residents are not displaced, and their villages are not bulldozed to make room for big formal-sector resorts and hotels. Unlike communities in close proximity to Caribbean enclave resorts, for instance, the local people in Zipolite are free to use the beach, and many of them benefit from the tourist trade in a real, tangible sense. In most cases, environmental degradation and cultural decline results from the dynamics of IFS tourism development—not IIS tourism. The local people in Goa (India), for example, certainly understand the difference; they throw rotten tomatoes at tour buses bringing European package tourists to the five-star hotels that despoil their communities, not local buses transporting IIS tourists to informal-sector guesthouses and private residences. In Mexico, the indigenous people who live in IFS resort areas rarely benefit from the influx of tourists; like the village residents of Goa, they understand that formal-sector tourism "development" almost always entails great costs and few benefits for themselves, their families, and their communities. Most would prefer to own their own informal tourism-related businesses than to clean toilets for Western tourists in a five-star hotel owned by some distant transnational corporation or a wealthy family from Mexico City.

What is bad about IIS tourism is what is bad about the informal economic sector in general. Informal-sector tourism workers often earn low wages and frequently work long hours under very poor working conditions. But as the case studies of Pahar Ganj and Zipolite suggest, conditions vary greatly from one IIS tourism destination to the next. In New Delhi, for example, IIS tourism workers, as opposed to owners, do much worse than their counterparts in the city's IFS tourism establishments and would almost certainly prefer jobs in a five-star hotel or similar upscale establishment. In Zipolite, however, the families operating small guesthouses and cafés on the beach generally enjoy what they do, and almost all of them would pass up menial jobs at a five-star hotel in Huatulco in favor of their present situations. As one *palapa* owner expressed it, "there are problems with living in Zipolite, but here we get to spend time with our children and we don't have to work as much as we would have to work in Huatulco."

CHAPTER **5**

The Domestic Formal Sector
New Holidays for the New Middle Classes

Although the South Delhi *barsati* (rooftop apartment) in which I was living was a very comfortable refuge from the 100-degree temperatures of a typical Delhi spring, I jumped at the opportunity to accompany my good friend Parag on one of his many business trips out of the city. Parag is a Bombay-based architect and interior designer whose client list reads like a *Who's Who* of India's rich and famous. On this trip, he was heading to the tourist cities of Agra and Jaipur to check on a project he was undertaking for one of the city's leading jewelers and to source materials for some of his other projects.

There were many transportation options available to us, including air and rail, but Parag decided it would be best to travel by automobile because the distances we would cover would not be great and because it would allow us to visit a few tourist attractions along the way. The Delhi-Jaipur-Agra "triangle" is one of the most heavily touristed regions of the country, and there is no shortage of tourist attractions: The Taj Mahal, one of the country's leading destinations for foreign tourists, is in Agra, and Jaipur's Hawa Mahal, or Palace of the Wind, also attracts many foreign and domestic visitors. Many tour buses carrying both foreign and domestic visitors stop at Fatehpur Sikri, an abandoned city on the Agra-Jaipur road and a United Nations World Heritage site; other palaces that dot the landscape in Rajasthan; and a number of parks showcasing what remains of India's rapidly vanishing wildlife.

The taxi arrived at 7 A.M.; we wanted to leave the city early so as to avoid the heavy morning traffic on the road to Gurgaon, a rapidly developing edge

127

city near Indira Gandhi International Airport. Parag and I had been out to Gurgaon a day earlier, where we went to visit a friend. If I had any doubts about the growth of India's middle class, they were surely put to rest as we drove past the countless new housing blocks, office buildings, and shopping malls coming up everywhere. When I first traveled to India in the mid-1980s, Gurgaon was still overwhelmingly undeveloped and predominantly rural; now new, mammoth housing developments with names such as Wembley Estate and Vatika appear to be literally sprouting out of the dry, dusty earth. The smart, new, air-conditioned shopping malls draw crowds of consumers who browse in the Benetton, Lacoste, and other fashion boutiques, purchase mobile phones in the Sony Ericsson and Nokia kiosks, lunch at Pizza Hut and TGI Friday's, and sip cappuccinos at Barista, a new national chain specializing in international coffees and light snacks.

Gurgaon is, however, much more than a retail center and bedroom community for Delhi commuters. Recall that Parag and I were *leaving* Delhi early in the morning in order to beat the traffic. Gurgaon has become a prime location for international call centers and similar IT businesses that employ thousands of Indians, many of whom commute there from their homes in New Delhi and surrounding areas. American Express, among other global corporations, has located its customer service operations and other back-office operations in Gurgaon. Other multinational corporations with operations in Gurgaon include Siemens, Nestlé, GE Capital, Honda, and IBM. The density of office development and the rapid growth of auxiliary businesses have made Gurgaon a true edge city, one of a number of edge cities in India's major metropolitan areas.

Unfortunately, we didn't leave early enough; traffic swelled on the road out of Delhi, and it took us nearly an hour and a half to leave the metropolitan area. It was still too early to grab a coffee at one of the Barista cafes in Gurgaon so we decided to stop at a *dhaba*, or roadside restaurant, further along the road to Jaipur. We were about ten kilometers out of Gurgaon when I spotted the newest type of *dhaba* on the Indian road: a McDonald's restaurant, complete with U.S. Interstate Highway-style golden arches perched atop a high pylon to alert oncoming traffic. On a long motorcycle trip around North India and Nepal in the mid-1990s, my brother Louis and I had often speculated on the likelihood of ever seeing McDonald's restaurants on the Indian highway, traditionally the preserve of the more traditional Indian *dhaba*. Now, with the tremendous growth of the Indian middle class in the 1980s and 1990s, it had become a reality. Parag told me there was another one on the Delhi-Agra road as well (figure 5.1).

Parag and I continued on our way, arriving in Jaipur early that afternoon. We checked in to a small, family-owned hotel near the city center. The owners and hotel workers recognized Parag immediately because he often stays there when doing business in Jaipur. Jaipur was even hotter than Delhi, so I

Figure 5.1 McDonald's, Delhi-Agra Road, Mathura, India

was happy to learn the hotel had both icy air-conditioning and a swimming pool. The owners had recently renovated the place, and it showed: The hotel was extremely comfortable and had become popular with both Indians and foreign tourists, none of whom as far as I could tell were backpacker tourists, who tend to seek out other, much less expensive accommodation in the city. Jaipur is a very popular destination for backpacker or international informal-sector (IIS) tourists, many of whom stop in the city en route to points further south or who come to the city to purchase items—particularly gems, jewelry, and clothing—for export to their home countries or to sell at other Indian tourist destinations, such as the world-famous Anjuna Beach in the coastal state of Goa.

We spent a couple of days in Jaipur, taking our meals either in the hotel or in one of a number of upscale restaurants scattered around the city and in Jaipur's five-star hotels. I accompanied Parag into one of the city's many bazaars, where he personally sourced materials for his projects around the world. (I would later accompany him to Agra, where he gave me a tour of the workshop where skilled craftsmen worked on his exquisite marble inlay designs, some of which were heading for a Las Vegas casino.)

On the second night in Jaipur, Parag and I visited Chowki Dhani, a popular tourist destination for middle-class Indians on the outskirts of Jaipur. Chowki Dhani is part amusement park, part re-created Rajasthani village, and part resort, what one Indian newspaper reporter claims is "must-see for all those tourists who either don't have the time or inclination to visit the real villages of Rajasthan" (Banerjee 2001). On the night we went there, the park was crowded with Indian families who all seemed to be having a very good time. Children and their parents would take rides on camels and elephants; scream as the Ferris wheel operator spun them up and down on the manually operated ride; view traditional Rajasthani (or what was staged as traditional Rajasthani) puppet shows, magic shows, and dances; and eat a meal sitting down on an earthen floor in a building designed to evoke images of what is supposed to be a typical Rajasthani village dwelling. The tourists were almost all Indians; out of what must have been hundreds of tourists at Chowki Dhani that night, I observed only two foreigners, and they were both the guests of Indian families.

The three-day trip impressed on me even more forcefully than before that international tourism is only the tip of the iceberg in India and other low-income countries, particularly large low-income countries; a much, much larger universe of tourists and the businesses that serve them are domestic in origin. Indeed, on the entire trip through one of India's most heavily touristed regions and a leading draw for foreign visitors, I saw only a handful of foreigners. The vast majority were Indian nationals. The reason for that was also made evident along the way: The Indian middle class is expanding rapidly, as places like Gurgaon make abundantly clear. Along with Benetton, McDonald's, and other trappings of global culture, Indians are increasingly becoming consumers of leisure, not in the traditional forms of pilgrimage to religious shrines, as I will discuss in the following chapter, but rather of Western-style vacations with no loftier goals than fun, entertainment, and "getting away from it all" for a few days.

Of course, I myself was also partaking of another major form of travel in the subcontinent—business travel. Although Parag and I visited a few leisure-oriented tourist attractions along the way, the primary purpose of our trip, or at least Parag's trip, was business. As I will discuss in some detail later, business travel in India has also increased in tandem with other forms of travel, with new facilities coming up in most of the country's metropolitan areas that cater primarily to business travelers. Again, the reason is evident: India is home to millions of small businesses, and not every business traveler or business can afford the high tariffs routinely charged by the country's luxurious five-star hotel chains. For that reason, there has been growth in the three- and four-star range of tourist hotels that cater largely to domestic businessmen and women.

As I noted in chapter 3, most tourism research undertaken in low-income countries deals with the international formal sector of five-star hotels, upscale restaurants, and similar tourist facilities demanded by pleasure and business travelers from the First World. Chapter 4 deals with the much smaller body of research that traces the impact of international low-budget or drifter tourists on the places they visit. The question of domestic tourism in low-income countries is generally overlooked, despite the rather voluminous literature on Third World tourism generated in the Western academy and by market research firms.[1] The oversight is especially surprising in light of numerous accounts, particularly in the business press, that point to the rapid growth of the middle class in low-income countries and the interest that transnational corporations (TNCs) have taken in supplying these middle-class households with goods and services.

Indeed, the middle class has grown rapidly in India and other Third World countries. Estimates of its size vary according to the criteria used to define it, but even a conservative estimate puts the number of middle-class individuals at over 180 million in the case of India, 35 million in Indonesia, 10 million in Thailand, 15 million in Mexico, and 30 million in Brazil (table 5.1). As I will argue in this chapter, the increasing buying power of households has combined with advertising and other media images from the wealthy countries (e.g., film, magazines, satellite television) to create the basis for a consumer society in countries that are on the whole desperately poor.

Evidence of a growing middle class is everywhere in the Third World, particularly in its largest cities. Enclave residential developments are springing up to cater to the new middle classes, once the bastions of only the very rich. McDonald's, Kentucky Fried Chicken, and T.G.I. Friday's restaurants are now ubiquitous sights in Delhi, Mexico City, Bangkok, and other urban centers, as are designer clothes outlets, cellular telephone advertisements, health and

Table 5.1

Estimated Size of the Middle Class in Select Third World Countries, 2003

Country	Population (millions)	Size of the middle class (millions)
Brazil	176.6	35.3
China	1,288.4	257.7
Columbia	44.6	8.9
Egypt	67.6	13.5
Guatemala	12.3	2.5
India	1,064.4	212.9
Indonesia	214.7	42.9
Kenya	31.9	6.4
Mexico	102.3	20.5
Peru	27.1	5.4
Philippines	81.5	16.3
Thailand	62.0	12.4

Source: World Bank 2005.

tennis clubs, new car showrooms, and even bowling alleys. What is true of fast-food outlets, designer clothes, and new subcompact automobiles is also true of leisure activities: The same factors that have given rise to mass tourism in the countries of the First World are now providing the basis for a new kind of tourism in the Third World. Middle-class Indians, Mexicans, Indonesians, Brazilians, and their counterparts in other Third World countries now find themselves with both more disposable income and more leisure time in which to spend it. Consequently, they are increasingly heading for the hills, or the seashore, or to cultural centers, or to cities other than their own as tourists, much like their counterparts in the United States, Western Europe, Australia, New Zealand, Israel, and Japan.

As I will argue in this chapter, the increasing globalization of the international political economy is a chief factor giving rise to domestic formal-sector tourism in most low-income countries. At the same time, however, global economic and political forces are also creating a vast underclass in the Third World. For every member of the new middle classes in India, Indonesia, Brazil, and other low-income countries, there are eight or more poor people, many of whom are desperately poor. For such people, the thought of spending thousands of rupees, rupiah, or pesos on a holiday in a formal resort is completely out of the question. Yet as we will see in chapter 6, poor people in low-income countries also travel but for reasons generally unrelated to those of the middle class. Their motivation for travel is more likely to be religious and less in accord with the travel patterns of those in high-income countries.

Globalization and the New Middle Classes in the Third World

For many people, the Third World is synonymous with poverty and underdevelopment. Indeed, there is much factual evidence to bear this out: lack of infrastructure, war, overpopulation, underinvestment, high rates of disease and illiteracy that, combined with the historical and ongoing exploitation of the Third World by people in the First World countries, have all served to create the conditions for widespread poverty and the growth of a huge underclass of deprived humanity in Africa, Asia, Latin America, the Caribbean, and Oceania. More people live in poverty today than at any time in human history, with more than 60 percent of the world's population earning less than U.S.$3 per day (Chossudovsky 1997).

The deep poverty of Third World societies has not been lost on development economists working in the postwar period (from the First, Second, and Third Worlds) who have grappled with the problem of Third World underdevelopment. Regardless of their political orientation and on what, or whom, they pin the blame for such widespread poverty, most planners and economists who concern themselves with Third World issues have sought to fashion ways for low-income countries to increase their national income or redistribute the benefits of growth in ways that will ultimately reduce the poverty of the majority.

Even though much of the development literature focuses on poverty in the Third World, some scholars and certainly the business press in both low-income and high-income countries have noted the growth of a large middle class in many Third World societies. They differ in orientation from Marxist and neo-Marxist explanations of the "comprador" class, typically defined as a group of domestic industrialists, merchant capitalists, and politicians who ally themselves with foreign imperialists in a joint effort to exploit their country's material and human resources. In contrast, the more recent accounts of the middle class focus on the growing number of households in low-income countries with rising disposable incomes, households that come closest to approximating the lifestyles and consumption habits of the Western middle classes, including their demands for more leisure goods and services.

The Magnitude of the Middle Class in the Third World

An analysis of income distribution data for low-income countries reveals that most of these societies are characterized by highly unequal social structures. In most low-income countries, the top two income quintiles (the richest 40 percent of the population) account for over 70 percent of total national income. In some countries, the richest 40 percent of the population accounts for over 80 percent of the national income. Other countries exhibit even more extreme forms of income inequality: In Kenya, for example, the top income quintile alone (the richest 20 percent) accounts for over 60 percent of national income, and in Brazil the top 20 percent accounts for an astounding 70 percent share of GNP.

The case of Brazil sheds light on the fact that countries with relatively high GNPs may still contain vast numbers of impoverished people, one of the reasons why average measures such as GNP per capita are often extremely misleading indicators of general well-being. Indeed, it is an open question as to whether World Bank statistics on income distribution in the Third World reveal the existence of a *middle* class in the Western sense at all, as opposed to an expanded upper class. In the context of the high-income societies, the middle class almost by definition accounts for the bulk of the population. The social structure of most First World countries is diamond-shaped, with most households falling somewhere in the middle with respect to income (if not wealth). Third World societies, in contrast, have income structures that more closely resemble an upside-down champagne glass: a small group of households take most of the income, relatively few people fall into the "middle," and the bulk of the population is poor. Thus, my use of the term *middle class* to describe certain groups of people in Third World societies is based more on the groups' cultural and consumer-oriented characteristics than it is on any affinity with the structural or demographic aspects of the First World model.

Differing definitions of the middle class notwithstanding, there is enough evidence to suggest that large numbers of people in the Third World receive fairly high incomes. In a number of low-income countries in Asia, Africa, and Latin America, the richest 40 percent earn on average over U.S.$5,000 per year. In Brazil, the richest 20 percent earn close to U.S.$10,000 per year.

GNP per capita expressed in dollar terms, however, often understates the true purchasing power of individuals and households in the Third World, another reason why traditional measures of GNP per capita are often misleading indicators of national prosperity. It is for this reason that World Bank economists provide an alternative measure that they call *purchasing power parity* (PPP) estimates of GNP and GNP per capita. The Bank defines the PPP conversion factor as "the number of units of a country's currency required to buy the same amounts of goods and services in the domestic market as one dollar would buy in the United States" (World Bank 1996, 225). Using this alternative measure, we see that countries such as China and India rival the First World nations with respect to the value of their overall production. In addition, the purchasing power of middle-class households in low-income countries expressed in dollar terms expands considerably when PPP levels are taken into consideration.

Socioeconomic strata (SES) analysis is an alternative, albeit related way of measuring the buying power of middle-class households in low-income countries (Walker 1995). The SES approach, developed and utilized largely by market research firms, divides a country's household population into distinct groups (e.g., upper, upper-middle, middle, lower-middle, and lower classes) based on the householders' ability to consume goods and services and according to what types of goods and services they wish to consume. It differs from PPP analyses largely in terms of identifying the types of products that households at different levels of the income hierarchy are likely to demand. Thus, while the very rich may constitute a market for Italian sports cars and luxury yachts, the upper-middle class may demand designer clothing, vacations at Disney World, and a Ford Escort, the middle class may want to shop at Wal-Mart and eat at a McDonald's restaurant, and the lower-middle class may represent an important market for color television sets. One report found that in 1995, there were 133,800 upper-class or "A-level" households in Brazil and 57,700 similar households in Mexico, with an average buying power of U.S.$143,000 and U.S.$261,000, respectively, representing a small but important overseas market for luxury goods and services (Strategy Research Corporation 1995).

Explanations for the Rise of a Middle Class in Third World Countries

The middle class in Third World countries has traditionally been very small. On the eve of Indian independence (1947), for example, the Indian middle class of professionals, government bureaucrats, traders, small-scale industrialists, black marketers, and a small portion of the peasantry did not exceed 10 percent of the country's total population (Varma 1998). Although longitudinal studies of the middle class in Third World countries are few and far between, there is enough evidence to suggest that in India and many other low-income countries, the middle classes have been growing rapidly in recent years. To what factors, then, should we attribute the growth of the middle class in countries as otherwise diverse as Brazil, Kenya, and India?

There are numerous explanations for the growth of the middle class. One of the earliest attempts to account for the rise of the middle class in low-income countries is the Marxist-Leninist theory of the comprador class or the *comprador bourgeoisie*, a group whose interests are intimately tied to those of the imperial bourgeoisie or the colonial or neocolonial power. Whether the comprador class represents a true *middle* class is open to interpretation: Historically, the comprador bourgeoisie has been involved in trading, money lending, real estate speculation, and government service and has played an intermediary role between the ruling colonial or neocolonial class and the population at large. It is thus a "middle" class in this structural sense only because it has never accounted for a large percentage of a country's (or colony's) population. As we will see later, however, theories of the comprador bourgeoisie have reappeared in recent years to account for the growth of relative affluence among large sections of Third World society.

A second explanation for a growing middle class in Third World countries may be derived from the economic policies pursued by the newly independent former colonies of Asia, Africa, and Latin America. In the 1950s and 1960s, many Third World countries embarked on a regime of import substitution industrialization (ISI), a policy designed to promote indigenous production of commodities that had previously been imported from the metropolitan centers. Historically, import-substituting industries have ranged from consumer durables to heavy industrial products such as steel and automobiles. Although ISI as a development strategy is now debunked by most academic economists and by most in the mainstream business press, it is important to note that nearly every society in the world today that most economists would consider "developed," including all of the First World countries and the Asian "miracles" or "newly industrializing countries" (NICs), got that way through the adoption of and strict adherence to ISI policies (Amirahmadi and Gladstone 1996).

A theory of the middle class is implicit in theories of ISI; the link between ISI and an increase in middle-class households lies in the employment opportunities that this particular development strategy creates for key segments of the domestic population. The rapid rates of industrialization that accompanied ISI in Brazil, Mexico, India, and other large Third World countries in the 1950s and 1960s led to an increased demand for managers and both skilled and semiskilled workers. Because many of the import-substituting industries are highly unionized, pay scales tend to be much higher than those found in the traditional or unorganized industrial sectors. In addition, ISI creates large numbers of jobs in government service because another hallmark of an ISI regime of accumulation is extensive government oversight of industrial production. The increased incomes of the workers and managers in the import-substituting industries who make up the new middle classes in turn provide an important market for the commodities produced in the new factories. The connection between the increased purchasing power of the "masses" and the new industries emerging under the ISI regime form a central component of what regulation theorist Alain Lipietz (1982) calls "peripheral Fordism," a theory of Third World industrialization based on the historical experience of the United States, Europe, and Japan.

*Peripheral Fordism, the Debt Crisis, and the Transition to a
"Global" Political Economy*

The productivity increases on which central Fordism was based began to taper off by the mid-1960s. The demise of Fordism, however, did not have the same effects in the periphery as it did in the core. Growth in the high-income market economies was slowing down while countries as diverse as South Korea, Iran, Brazil, and Mexico were registering high growth rates. And contrary to the New International Division of Labor (NIDL) thesis, not all of these countries were merely re-export platforms providing TNCs with pools of cheap labor. Some were actually pursuing a strategy of peripheral Fordism, a model of accumulation that couples an internal growth in effective demand with a policy of export promotion centered around either labor-intensive commodities or raw materials, a combination of import-substitution and export promotion (Lipietz 1987).

Peripheral Fordism is genuine Fordism in that it links intensive accumulation to an expanding internal market. It remains peripheral, however, in that (1) many elements of what Marx called *Department One* (producer goods, technology) remain external to the economy; (2) the model is predicated in the final analysis on the growth of world demand; (3) large sections of the population do not share in the fruits of development; and (4) the model is heavily dependent on loans from banks and other investors in the North. The link between what Lipietz calls the "mirage" of independent or autocentered industrialization in the South and a more recent "opening" of Third World countries to capital and cultural flows from the North, also known as *global-ization*, is the so-called debt crisis of the 1980s.

According to the regulation school, during the mid- to late-1970s, capitalists in the North began reacting to declining profits in three distinct ways. Their first reaction, what Lipietz characterizes as genuinely Fordist, took the form of increased trade and investment within the core countries themselves in an effort to generate fresh productivity gains through an expanding market. Their second response, the search for cheaper labor power, resulted in the reloca-tion of entire sectors of Northern industry to the Third World, one instance of what David Harvey (1989) calls the "spatial fix." In Marxist terms, capital's movement to those areas with a surplus of labor-power was an attempt to in-crease the mass of surplus value—in short, to drive up the rate of exploitation, a phenomenon dealt with at length by the NIDL theorists (Froebel, Heinrichs, and Kreye 1979).

For many people in the Third World, however, the most significant result of less profitable investment outlets in the First World was the rapid growth of fi-nance capital and the large increases in the amount of credit extended by banks in the North to members of political and economic elites in the countries of the South. The phenomenal growth of the Eurodollar market and the billions of so-called petrodollars parked in U.S., European, and Japanese banks trans-lated into cheap money for Third World elites. International inflation fueled by the Vietnam War and the devaluation of the dollar made borrowing costless, at least in the short-term. The onslaught of Thatcherism and Reaganomics had not yet undermined the mass purchasing power of the working classes in the rich countries of the North. Heavily indebted Third World countries could escape the consequences of balance of payments crises as long as increased ex-ports and fresh loans could cover their debt servicing requirements. However, because the growth strategies of the South hinged on the maintenance of Keynesian demand policies in the North, the Reagan-Thatcher monetarist shock could forebode only disaster for nascent Third World Fordism.

The coup de grâce of central Fordism came in the form of the so-called supply-side offensive of the late 1970s and early 1980s. Although the crisis of Fordism initially took the form of a productivity slowdown and a squeeze on profits, it was only after the second oil shock in 1979 that the crisis led to a concerted attack on the mass purchasing power of the Northern working classes. As traditional export markets dried up in the North, Third World re-gimes found it increasingly difficult to service their debts, which by the early 1980s totaled well over half a trillion dollars. Compounding their debt ser-vicing problems was the question of interest rates: Most loans made to the Third World by Northern banks were adjustable-rate loans, usually tied to the London Interbank Offered Rate (LIBOR). As the U.S. Federal Reserve drove up interest rates in an effort to curb inflation and create a recession, Third

World long-term debt nearly doubled. Compounding the problem were the massive budget deficits run up under the Reagan administration to finance a global arms race: Third World debtors now found themselves in the dubious position of having to compete with the U.S. government in capital markets. It is easy to see who would win that game.

Needless to say, the Third World lost. Third World elites had invested in a model of development that proved unsustainable over the long term. What one *New York Times* reporter calls the "harsher realities of capitalism" (Bohlen 1993) were once more brought to the fore as cadres of the International Monetary Fund (IMF) and the World Bank descended on debtor nations to impose austerity in the name of what author Jeremy Seabrook refers to as *international monetary fundamentalism*. Structural adjustment and similar policies achieved their intended goals of drastically reducing wages and public spending, devaluing the currency, and restoring a large trade surplus. Billions of dollars are currently flowing from debtor nations to Northern banks while the "harsher realities" of disease, illiteracy, homelessness, crime, hunger, and war are on the increase throughout the Third World.

From Peripheral Fordism to Globalization

One casualty of structural adjustment and similar policies proved to be peripheral Fordism itself. In most of the Third World countries that had adopted it, Fordism is now a thing of the past. It has been superseded by a new set of economic, political, cultural, and social practices that together make up what is today referred to as *globalization* or, in the case of the Third World, *neoliberalism*. Under the aegis of such supranational bodies as the IMF, the World Bank, and the World Trade Organization (WTO), which are themselves ascendant "global" institutions, Third World nations have been forced to dismantle state controls over industrial production, "open up" their countries to foreign capital and commodity flows, devalue their currencies, and eliminate subsidies for education, health care, and even essential food items. The impact of such policies for billions of people have been severe and include rising levels of poverty, social dislocation, malnutrition, unemployment, disease, criminal activity, and environmental destruction.

Although neoliberal policies have had disastrous consequences for large numbers of people in every Third World country that has adopted them, not all groups have lost out in the process. Indeed, people whose interests are tied to transnational capital and global production processes (multinational corporations, export industries, international financial institutions, etc.) have in many instances seen their standards of living improve. In India, for example, managers of multinational branch plants and retail outlets in the large urban areas earn significantly more than their counterparts in domestic industries. It is important to note, however, that the benefits of the new social and economic policies are not restricted to urban centers in low-income countries: Although there are more poor rural Indians today than there were Indians in 1947, not everyone in the countryside lives in poverty. Large landowners, farmers using green revolution technology and benefiting from state subsidies, grain traders, and some business owners in market towns form a rural elite that has grown considerably since the Rao-IMF reforms went into effect nearly a decade ago.

Globalization has in effect created a new kind of comprador class, a much larger one than had existed under colonial regimes. In India, Mexico, and other Third World countries, the classes tied to global capital flows are prospering while the majority of the population sinks deeper into poverty. As sociologist William Robinson observes:

> Transnationalized fractions in the Third World are "junior" partners: they oversee at the local level, and under the tutelage of their "senior" counterparts in the North, the sweeping economic, political, social and cultural changes involved in globalisation, including free-market reform, the fomenting of "democratic" systems in place of dictatorships, and the dissemination of the culture/ideology of consumerism and individualism. (1996, 18)

It is this last point, the growth of a consumer culture among Third World elites, that helps to explain the rise of new forms of leisure in the low-income countries. In the next section, I look more closely at the case of India.

A New Culture of Consumption: The Growth of India's Consumer Society

> Aye, kya bolti tu? Aati kya PVR? McDonald jayenge, McBurger khayenge, McLove manayenge, aur kya. And why not, yaar. V-day and V-mail comes but once a year, no? One day for us to play . . . the MTV way. So . . . be you my Valentine?
>
> —Nikhat Kazmi, *The Sunday Times of India*,
> February 14, 1999 (Valentine's Day)

To even the casual observer, India's "opening up" to the West has brought momentous change to its popular, and particularly its middle-class, culture. One of the most evident changes is the shift in both official government rhetoric and the attitude of ordinary citizens from a view of India as a land of poverty and scarcity where "mindless" consumption has no place to a rampant consumerism characterized by its glorification of the market and its indifference to the sufferings of the poor. The cultural shift to a middle class "in perpetual search of self-gratification," as a recent op-ed piece in a leading Indian newspaper puts it, mirrors the fact that India has become one of the most unequal societies in the world. "What's more tragic than the mere existence of such inequality," the author continues, "is the widespread acceptance of it, the large-scale indifference to it" (Philipose 1999). Consumerism has come to fill the ideological vacuum left by a declining Gandhian-Nehruvian ideology of self-restraint and socialism, as have divisive social movements such as communalism and Hindu chauvinism (Varma 1998).

The signs of middle-class consumerism are everywhere in India but are particularly evident in the country's larger metropolitan areas. What political scientist Benjamin Barber (1992) calls "McWorld," the forces that "mesmerize the world with fast music, fast computers, and fast food—with MTV, Macintosh, and McDonald's, pressing nations into one commercially homogeneous global network," has burst onto the Indian scene with a vengeance, closely paralleling India's embrace of IMF-dictated structural reforms. Western-based fast-food outlets such as McDonald's, Wimpy's, Pizza Hut, and Kentucky Fried Chicken are ubiquitous sights in Delhi, Bombay, Bangalore, Madras, and Calcutta— and now even in India's smaller cities. Bennetton, Lacoste, and Ralph Lauren boutiques fill the retail spaces in the country's central business districts and shopping plazas, catering to the crowds that spill out of new multiplex cinema halls featuring Hollywood, as well as the more traditional Bollywood, films. Whereas a decade ago the Indian middle class had the choice of only a few automobile models, all produced by domestically owned firms, there are today close to twenty production models manufactured in India and include nearly all of the major international automobile companies. Financing for those automobiles and other consumer products has also gone global, with firms such as Citibank, Barclays, and Bank of America offering a plethora of loans to the country's new consuming classes. Even children have become big business, with children's clothing boutiques catering to middle-class households and beauty salons offering "head massage for Sikh kids once a month, free computerised hair styling, free health counciling [*sic*], free party make-up annually and manicure and pedicure once a month" (Singh 1999).

One of the most important factors fueling the growth of consumerism in India and other Third World countries is the rapid globalization of the media and the greater exposure of urban elites to Western culture, both through travel and through consumption of Western media production. India's elite culture has changed dramatically over the last fifteen years in ways that are directly attributable to the country's growing integration into global media flows. Valentines Day, unheard of in India just a decade ago, is now a major gift-giving holiday among the urban elite, with plenty of radio and TV air time devoted to it, as well as daily features in the country's English-language newspapers. Discos in Delhi, Bombay, and Calcutta buzz to the same types of music distributed by the same global distributors (e.g., Bertelsmann, Time Warner, Sony) as discos in London, Amsterdam, and

New York. In a much larger sense, the very idea of the "good life" for middle-class India—a nuclear family, new car, Ralph Lauren shirt, outings to McDonalds, and vacations spent "sipping on Bacardi rum," as a popular commercial proclaims—has been drawn almost entirely from Western media portrayals.

India provides a good example of how a rapidly globalizing media industry can revolutionize broadcasting and, in turn, transform popular culture in low-income countries.[2] Whereas only fifteen years ago India had no commercial television stations and the only nationwide network was the state-owned Doordarshan, today satellite feeds and cable operators provide the Indian middle-class consumer with dozens of stations from which to choose. Foreign-owned broadcasters such as the British Broadcasting Company (BBC), Time Warner's Cable News Network (CNN), Music Television (MTV), The Discovery Channel, and Rupert Murdoch's Star TV Network compete directly not only with the government-owned Doordarshan but also with domestic commercial broadcasters, such as Zee TV. New commercial media outlets are not restricted to television: Radio, books, magazines, the Internet, and telecommunications providers have increasingly come to depend on advertising revenues and the rupees, pesos, and dollars of those with "effective" demand to justify their operations in the Third World.[3]

Although access to the global media is still highly restricted in India, with only a miniscule percentage of Indians currently enjoying the fruits of India's broadcasting revolution, most of these are urban-based, middle-class households. Since 1995, the demand for commercial broadcasting has grown quickly, with satellite broadcasting now within the reach of the urban poor and a growing percentage of India's vast rural population. The thrust of programming, however, is still directed primarily at the urban-based upper-middle class, the "globalizing" consumers of India's restructured post-1991 economy. This makes sense from a marketing perspective, because the profits accruing to commercial media are dependent not only on their viewer base but also on the sale of that base to commercial advertisers (see figure 5.2).

The social pathologies attendant to a consumer society are now as evident in India as they are in the West, perhaps even more so when contrasted with the vast gulf separating the new globalizing classes from the vast majority of Indians (see figure 5.3). Diet and "slimming" centers have sprung up in the major cities and have grown in tandem with such eating disorders as anorexia and bulimia. *The Times of India* reports that close to 50 percent of middle-class teenage girls are on a "starvation diet," a trend it attributes to television, media, and the fashion industry (Khan 1999). The report adds, "a mother of two college-going daughters hit the nail on the head: 'In today's market-driven society, young people see themselves as products meant to be packaged well, hence the premium on looks.'"

Figure 5.2 Parvati Valley, India

Figure 5.3 Shopping Mall, Gurgaon, India

India Today, a leading weekly newsmagazine, recently ran a cover story on the dangers of widely available "designer drugs," such as LSD, ecstasy, and cocaine. Unlike *bhang*, *charas*, and opium, traditional psychotropics and narcotics used since antiquity on the Indian subcontinent by large numbers of people, the newer synthetic drugs are restricted to the urban elite of the country's largest cities. The *India Today* reporters trace the influence of the new drugs to a "designer culture" created not by the "foreign junkies" and "hippies" in the cheap hotels of Pahar Ganj and Colaba, who the Indian media have traditionally associated with domestic drug addiction, but by the ubiquity of the international advertising industry:

> For this Armani-suited, gelled, city-slick segment, cocaine isn't a problem. It's just the latest fashion accessory. And there is an openness about the entire thing as they blow white lines inside their steel and chrome BMWs and Porsches or pop multi-coloured pills in huge rave parties, jiving to some hypnotic techno beat. People who do drugs in this rich brat pack aren't perceived as losers. In fact, they're the winners. . . . These rich kids become role models for others who break into this elite circle and start equating drugs with coolness. (Ramani and Thapa 1999, 52–53)

The economic reforms ushered in by the P. V. Narasimha Rao government in 1991 have proven extremely resilient, continuing apace despite two changes at the center, first with the establishment of a Bharatiya Janata Party (BJP) government in 1998, then with a Congress-led coalition in 2004. Given the nationalistic rhetoric of many BJP politicians, who often spoke and continue to speak of the evils of multinational capital and advocate a return to the Swadeshi (self-reliance) policies of the past, the rise of the Jana Sangh-affiliated BJP in the late 1990s did not bode well for continued liberalization of the Indian economy. As Hansen wrote at the time:

> The RSS's campaigns against foreign investments in the consumer goods sector and foreign fast-food chains which are "contaminating Indian culture and food habits," and the restrictions on foreign investment to high-technology sectors ("Potato chips, no; Computer chips, yes!" as the slogan went in 1996), all seem to point toward the notion of "patriotic capitalism." (Hansen 1999, 220)

If anything, the economic plank of the BJP-led coalition that came to power in 1998 was more reminiscent of Nehruvian socialism and what its detractors call the "license Raj" than of the more recent neoliberal reform vision espoused by P.V. Narasimha Rao; his minister of state for commerce (and now finance minister), Palaniappan Chidambaram; and his finance minister (now Prime Minister), Manmohan Singh.

Despite the rhetoric, however, BJP governments have been as welcoming—in practice if not ideologically—of neoliberal reforms and India's greater integration in the world economy as their Congress Party predecessors and successors.

One reason is structural: India has a very large foreign debt and remains subject to the pressures of international lending agencies, such as the IMF and its private-sector creditors. The Rao government undertook its reforms chiefly because of India's debt and shortage of foreign exchange reserves, which by the early 1990s had dwindled to virtually nothing. Another reason is political, because the BJP draws much of its support from the growing ranks of India's urban middle class, the members of which tend to be pro-globalization. As Gurcharan Das, former head of Proctor & Gamble India, points out, "We start off the twenty-first century with a dynamic and rapidly growing middle class which is pushing the politicians to liberalize and globalize . . . and it is enthusiastically embracing consumerist values and lifestyles" (Das 2002, 287).

One of the new consumerist values and a central part of the new middle-class lifestyle is leisure travel, which has certainly not showed any signs of slowing down under BJP governments. People's concepts of travel and leisure have changed, along with other aspects of Indian elite and middle-class culture. Until fairly recently, orthodox Hindus refused to undertake sea voyages because crossing the ocean would entail losing one's (upper) caste status. Travel was not pleasurable and was rarely undertaken for recreational reasons. Traditional Indian concepts of travel are primarily religious in nature: People travel to see and experience the sacred, in the form of a temple, a mountain, a river, a cave, and so on (see chapter 6). Today, however, travel and recreation have been packaged and marketed as commodities, the consumption of which is an end in itself and devoid of any religious connotations. Advertisements in newspapers and color glossy magazines tout travel "experiences" to both domestic and overseas destinations. As one Indian journalist observes, "from erstwhile shopping jaunts to Singapore and Hong Kong, holidays are now an opportunity to collect unique and unforgettable experiences" (Bahal 1998, 62). Indian outbound tourists, recruited almost entirely from India's new globalizing elite groups, reached 3.7 million in 1997, double the number of foreign tourists India hosted that year. The number of domestic "leisure" tourists in India has also mushroomed in recent years, although no one knows for sure how many more middle-class Indians are traveling: Neither the Indian government nor the majority of India's state governments keeps track of domestic tourist arrivals.

It is clearly the case, however, that the number of people who travel for purely recreational purposes—to "get away from it all," to "get away for the weekend," to "get away with the kids"—has increased rapidly over the past ten to fifteen years. The evidence of a growing desire among middle-class Indians to consume travel holidays is perhaps nowhere so evident as at the destinations themselves. Resorts and vacation destinations catering to middle-class Indians who travel for purely secular reasons have proliferated in recent years, with both new resorts getting built and old ones getting redeveloped to cater to ever-growing numbers of tourists. Himachal Pradesh, a mountainous state in northern India and a prominent domestic tourism destination, features a relatively large number of formal-sector resort areas. In the following section, I will first discuss tourism in Himachal Pradesh generally, then will look more closely at the Kulu Valley, a destination in Himachal Pradesh that has seen its annual domestic arrivals increase by over 500 percent since the late 1960s.

Holidays for the New Middle Classes: Hill Stations in Himachal Pradesh

Himachal Pradesh is a large, sparsely populated state in northern India. A largely mountainous region (*Himachal* means "land of snowy mountains"), the state is known for its many summer resorts or hill stations. During the colonial period, India's British rulers escaped the heat of the northern plains by traveling to Shimla, Mussoorie, Almora, Dalhousie, Dharamshala, Kangra, and other mountain villages in what are today the states of Uttaranchal and Himachal Pradesh. The country's hill stations were also known as centers of rest and relaxation, complete with spas and sanitariums. They were, in fact, early tourist destinations, even if the only tourists able to go there were wealthy British colonialists and Indian kings and princes.

The British penchant for attempting to recreate England in the midst of the peoples they colonized is perhaps nowhere so evident as in Shimla, a medium-sized village that by the early twentieth century had become the summer capital of the British Raj (figure 5.4). Like other British colonial settlements in

Figure 5.4 Shimla, India

India, Shimla featured both a "native town" located near the *bazaar* (market) that winds its way down the side of a hill, and an area for the Europeans and the Indian ruling class (the maharajas)—the "civil lines"—what in Shimla is still referred to today as "The Ridge." The British supervised construction of a mall built in gingerbread style, complete with Victorian tea shops, a village church, a recreation park and amphitheater (Annadale), a clubhouse, library, billiard hall, theaters (the Gaiety and the Ritz), and even a replica of an English public school. Even though Shimla was and remains the quintessential British hill station in India, the city's architecture and planning resembled—and still resembles even today—many other Indian hill resorts constructed during the British Raj: Dalhousie, Landsdowne, and Mussoorie in the North, and Ooty and Kodaikanal in the South of the country.

Manali, the major tourist destination of the Kulu Valley, differs from most other hill stations in that it developed as a tourist resort after India gained its independence in 1947. Although a number of British families operated small inns and guesthouses in the area during the mid- to late nineteenth century, Manali was never a popular destination for European travelers during the colonial period, largely due to the region's difficult access. Unlike Shimla, Mussoorie, Ooty, Kodaikanal, and other hill stations built prior to 1947, Manali developed primarily to service the recreational needs of the Indian upper and middle classes in the post-independence period. Some historians point to Prime Minister Jawahar Lal Nehru's two visits to Manali in 1958 and again in 1959 as the catalyst for the resort's subsequent tourism boom (Shabab 1996).

Other factors that served to increase Manali's popularity with both Indian and foreign tourists were the opening of an airstrip at Bhuntar in the late 1950s (about forty kilometers south of Manali near Kulu) and, a decade later, the completion of National Highway 21 linking Manali and Kulu with the rest of the country and particularly with the population centers of the Punjab, Haryana, Delhi, and Uttar Pradesh, Manali's general market area. Advertising is also a factor behind Manali's and other hill stations' rising popularity with middle-class Indians, with "advertisements for hill stations pitched to local tourists in terms similar to those that publicized them first among colonial elites" (Crossette 1998). Full-page color advertisements in the *Times of India*, *Hindustan Times*, *Indian Express*, and other leading English-language newspapers tout the prospect of cool mountains and exquisite scenery to northern India's 40 million English speakers.

The Structure of the Tourism Industry in Himachal Pradesh

In many respects, Himachal Pradesh mirrors the rest of India with respect to the structure of its tourism industry: Foreign tourists represent less than 2 percent of total tourist arrivals statewide, religious tourists make up a considerable part of the total tourist traffic, and informal-sector tourism establishments far outnumber those in the formal sector (table 5.2).

Despite the similarities, however, Himachal's tourism industry differs from other Indian states in some important respects. For one thing, in some areas of Himachal Pradesh, the number of international tourist arrivals approximates or, in the case of the remote trekking region of Lahaul and Spiti, even exceeds domestic tourist arrivals. The state's tourism industry is also relatively larger and more formalized than that of most other Indian states. Although Himachal Pradesh ranks sixteenth among India's 31 states and union territories in terms of the percentage of buildings used for hotels and similar accommodation facilities, it ranks third with respect to the percentage of buildings in urban areas used for lodging purposes. Not surprisingly, there are more hotels per capita in Himachal Pradesh than in any other Indian state except Nagaland, Kerala, Goa, and Arunachal Pradesh.

The formal hotel sector is arguably larger in Himachal Pradesh than it is elsewhere in India. Stating this with any degree of certainty is fraught with difficulties, however, because one of the major problems with measuring formality and informality in Himachal Pradesh's tourism industry, as in other parts of India, is a dearth of accurate statistics on formal- and informal-sector

Table 5.2
Himachal Pradesh Tourist Arrivals by Religious Orientation, 1997

	Domestic arrivals	International arrivals	International (%)
January	235,646	1,452	0.6
February	205,783	2,128	1.0
March	211,197	3,003	1.4
April	510,387	3,486	0.7
May	415,105	4,293	1.0
June	517,175	4,890	0.9
July	285,584	9,852	3.3
August	232,554	14,208	5.8
September	283,011	7,846	2.7
October	496,083	6,687	1.3
November	193,094	3,091	1.6
December	244,801	1,591	0.6
Total arrivals, 1997	3,830,420	62,527	1.6
Nonreligious arrivals (%)	41.8	82.1	

Source: The Department of Tourism & Civil Aviation, Government of Himachal Pradesh, unpublished data

accommodation and other tourist facilities. Nonetheless, there are still a number of ways one might go about estimating the size of the formal hotel sector in Himachal Pradesh generally and Kulu-Manali in particular.

One way is to equate the formal accommodation sector with the public hotel sector and privately owned accommodation facilities approved and classified by either the government of India or the Himachal Pradesh tourism department. As regards the former, the state-owned Himachal Pradesh Tourism Development Corporation (HPTDC) currently owns and operates fifty-three hotels and sixty restaurants throughout the state, making it the largest hotel chain in Himachal Pradesh and one of the largest in India. As regards the latter, 1,689 hotels and other lodging facilities in Himachal Pradesh had been approved in 1998 by the state or central government. Although comparable census data is lacking for 1998, in 2001, government-approved accommodation facilities represented 30 percent of all lodging facilities statewide. It appears at first glance, therefore, that the number of formal-sector hotels in Himachal Pradesh, although perhaps larger than in other parts of India, nevertheless represents a relatively small share of the state's supply of hotels.

A second criterion for determining which hotels are in the formal sector is price: The assumption here is that those hotels that cost more are presumably more likely to display formal-sector characteristics. Himachal Pradesh is one of the few states in India that publishes a statewide listing of hotels, guesthouses, forest rest houses, and other types of accommodation facilities according to price. The Himachal Pradesh Ministry of Tourism and Civil Aviation gathers the information on a biannual basis and publishes the names of hotels, along with the number of rooms and the room rates. Of the 1,689 hotels and other lodging facilities in Himachal Pradesh recognized by the Himachal Pradesh Ministry of Tourism, 15 percent charge more than U.S.$25 per night for lodging, and 40 percent charge more than U.S.$12.50. Without comparable statistics from other Indian states, it is difficult to compare formality in Himachal Pradesh's tourism industry with that elsewhere in India. However, based on what information we do have, it appears very likely that Himachal Pradesh's tourism industry, particularly its hotel sector, is more developed than the hotel sectors of other Indian states.

The Case of Kulu-Manali

The word *Kulu* is derived from *Kulanthapitha*, which means, depending on the translator, "end of the civilized world" or "end of the habitable world." (*Kulu* refers to a district of Himachal Pradesh, to the capital of that district, and also to the mountain valley that bears its name.) Indeed, until the early decades of the twentieth century, the Kulu Valley was largely cut off from the rest of India, accessible only by steep mountain paths during the summer months and completely inaccessible during the winter. The Kulu and adjacent valleys were originally populated by *adivasis* (indigenous peoples). Migrants from other parts of India followed, as did a small group of European settlers, mainly English and Scottish. It was the latter group of Europeans who first introduced apple growing to the Kulu Valley during the late part of the nineteenth century, an industry that today ranks as one of Kulu's largest, along with agriculture, tourism, and handicrafts (figure 5.5).

The Kulu Valley is eighty kilometers long but only two kilometers across at its widest point near Katrain. The Beas River bisects the valley, dividing it into two halves, or "banks." As the river flows southwesterly from its source at *Beas Kund* (Lake Beas) in the high Himalaya (near the Rohtang Pass, about forty

Figure 5.5   Kulu-Manali.

kilometers from Manali), it is fed by numerous smaller rivers and rivulets (*nullahs*, in the local parlance) that drain adjacent valleys such as the Parvati and Solang. The Kulu-Manali tourism corridor extends from the town of Bhuntar, just south of Kulu and site of the regional airport, through Manali and Vashisht to the Rohtang Pass at an elevation of 4,000 meters (13,000 feet). The village of Manali, named after the mythical Indian lawgiver Manu, is located about forty kilometers northeast of Kulu at an elevation of 2,000 meters (6,500 feet). Other tourist centers in the Kulu Valley include Naggar, Katrain, Vashisht, and smaller villages along the route to the Rohtang Pass.

Despite the region's relative inaccessibility, travel and tourism has a long history in the Kulu Valley, predating by centuries the introduction of air and road transport. Manali, Jagatsukh, Naggar, and other villages and towns in the Valley were located along ancient trading routes connecting China with India and Persia, and evolved as important supply depots and market centers. British settlers began opening inns as early as the mid- to late-nineteenth century but almost always as a subsidiary business to their major apple growing and other horticultural pursuits.

The evolution of Kulu-Manali as a mass tourism destination, however, is closely connected to the road-building activities carried out by the British colonial administration beginning in the early part of the twentieth century. Roads brought "modernity" to the Kulu Valley and surrounding areas and radically altered traditional social arrangements and cultural practices. Road building in the Kulu Valley, as in other parts of the Himalayas (indeed, as in other parts of India and the Third World in general), meant the introduction of market relations, a "cash crop" economy, increasing social differentiation, and rapid cultural change.

Roads and the people who increasingly came to travel on them have also brought about extensive environmental change, most notably large-scale deforestation, in much the same way as they have in other parts of the Third World. There is a strong correlation between road building in Himachal Pradesh and the state's rapid rate of deforestation. Whereas in 1940 over 60 percent of Himachal Pradesh was covered by forests, by the 1990s the amount of land under forest cover had declined to less than 40 percent (Shabab 1996). During the same period, road construction increased rapidly in Himachal Pradesh and other mountain areas of India, extending further into the delicate Himalayan ecosystems. The link between road building and deforestation is more evident than ever today: In the Parvati Valley (adjacent to the Kulu Valley), both sides of the new road extending from the present road head at Manikaran up to the small village of Pulga, about fifteen kilometers away, have been cleared of forest as part of a large hydroelectric project. The Parvati River is literally choked with trees that have been cut and floated down to Manikaran for transport to Punjab, Haryana, Delhi, and Uttar Pradesh.

By 1928, the British authorities completed a road from Mandi (a lower-elevation district capital) to Kulu; by 1932, they widened it for vehicular traffic. Although construction of the road from Kulu to Manali began during the 1930s, it was not until the 1970s that it was completed by the Indian Border Roads Organisation and renamed National Highway 21. The World Bank financed much of the road construction in the area for the ostensible purpose of linking the apple-growing areas of the Kulu Valley with distribution centers in the Punjab and Haryana. Tourism was a key factor associated with the benefits that development and modernization would bring to the Kulu Valley, beginning in the early 1970s. As we will see, however, not everyone in the Kulu Valley prospered to the same extent from the tourist trade—or even at all.

The Kulu Valley is today one of the leading tourist destinations in the state of Himachal Pradesh. In 1997, the Kulu-Manali tourism corridor attracted over 700,000 tourists, more than any other district except Shimla (the capital district of Himachal Pradesh). Just under half (47 percent) of the tourists who visited Kulu-Manali in 1997 did so for religious reasons, with the balance traveling to the area for leisure pursuits or to visit family and friends. There is wide variation among the various tourist centers in Kulu-Manali with respect to the motivations of individual travelers. For instance, Kulu attracts far fewer pleasure tourists than does Manali: The annual Dussehra Festival held there each year to celebrate Rama's victory over the Ceylonese demon-king Ravana attracts upward of 100,000 religious worshippers. Compared with other areas in Himachal Pradesh, where up to 95 percent of the tourists are religious pilgrims, Manali is overwhelmingly a secular-oriented resort destination.

Change has come rapidly to the Kulu-Manali region. The road from the district capital of Kulu to the resort center of Manali is littered with billboard signs advertising the many hotels that have been built in Manali since the early 1980s. Yet only thirty years ago, Manali was still a small village with only a few guesthouses, several small *dhabas* (local restaurants), and a Tibetan bazaar. Less than 19,000 tourists visited Kulu-Manali in 1965, compared with over 740,000 in 1997. Today, Manali features over 350 licensed hotels, dozens of restaurants (both formal and informal), and dozens of informal guesthouses (figure 5.6). The Mall, the major retail and commercial strip running through Manali's main business district, is suffused with signs of the new affluence of the Indian middle classes: Late-model Maruti-Suzuki, Honda, Toyota, Hyundai, and General Motors automobiles crowd the streets, honeymooning couples stroll up and down in their finery, camera shops and expensive restaurants serving just about every regional cuisine cater to Indian tourists on short holiday jaunts, and shops selling woolen embroidery, saris, jewelry, and other luxury items line the Mall, as well as the many side streets running off it.

In 1991 there were 2,433 people living in Manali, divided into 633 households. The town is not unlike other small Third World villages that have become

Figure 5.6 Manali, India

well-known tourist destinations where the number of tourists greatly outnumber the local residents. During the high seasons (April to June and September to November), the inflow of tourists to Manali may exceed 6,000 daily, resulting in a tourist-to-host ratio of nearly 3:1 on any given day. Manali ranks first in the state with respect to the number of its workers engaged in "trade and commerce," a census category that includes hotel and restaurant workers. The town also ranks among the highest in Himachal Pradesh with respect to the percentage of its workers in "household industry," due to the large number of (mostly female) workers engaged in the household production of tourist-related gifts and souvenirs.

The Development and Growth of Tourism in Manali

Although the Kulu-Manali tourism corridor is in many ways an integrated resort area, I have focused primarily on the resort town of Manali. I have done so for a number of reasons. First, most tourists visiting the Kulu-Manali area stay in Manali for at least part of their holiday, and many tourists stay only in Manali. Consequently, Manali's tourism sector is much larger than Kulu's or any other part of the Kulu-Manali corridor. Second, Manali has experienced a prolonged hotel-building boom since the early 1980s and attracts primarily domestic, middle-class tourists. Third, most of the hotels and other tourist-related businesses in Manali are formal-sector establishments:

Whereas informal-sector businesses certainly operate in Manali, it is clear that the formal sector predominates. Finally, most visitors to Manali are leisure tourists whose motivations for travel (to Manali, at least) are similar to those of their Western counterparts.

Tourists in Manali

Tej Vir Singh is among the few tourism researchers to have undertaken a detailed investigation of Kulu-Manali's tourism industry and one of the few to have conducted a detailed sample survey of domestic tourists who visit Manali. According to Singh:

> Indian tourism, unfortunately, has still to consider research on "tourists" important to the sound growth of the industry. The little data base that has been prepared pertains to foreign tourists. . . . No sincere effort has been made to prepare minimum [*sic*] data base on domestic tourists. There is a crisis of information on Himalayan resorts, where visitors are overwhelmingly in-tourists [domestic tourists]. (Singh 1989, 138)

The lack of reliable data on domestic tourist characteristics is as true of Manali's tourism industry as it is of the country as a whole. As Singh (1989, 139) points out, "not much dependable information exists on [tourists'] geographic origin, socio-economic status, lifestyle behaviour and expenditure patterns." Nevertheless, Singh's 1987 survey of tourists in Manali provides a good baseline with which to compare the characteristics of tourists traveling to Manali in the late 1990s.

Singh (1989, 156) found (in 1987) that "the profile of the [Kulu] Valley tourist is of an average middle class Indian, young salaried class [*sic*] with good education who visits the Valley and Manali for relaxation and recreation." Singh also found that most tourists visiting Manali stayed for one to five days and came from one of India's four largest cities (Bombay, Calcutta, Madras, and New Delhi), with the most arriving from Calcutta (31 percent) and New Delhi (23 percent).

Comparing 1999 survey data with Singh's figures from a decade earlier indicates that Manali attracts an even more affluent, "upmarket" crowd than it did before (table 5.3). In 1999, domestic tourists in Manali are more likely than in 1987 to be university educated; older; and from professional, business, or managerial occupational backgrounds. They are more likely to have higher incomes than their counterparts in 1987. Moreover, more tourists arrive by automobile and stay for shorter periods of time, due partly to the fact that Manali now attracts more tourists from its immediate hinterland than heretofore. In short, Manali has gone upscale and attracts more of an upper-middle-class clientele than it was attracting in the late 1980s.

Table 5.3

Manali Tourist Characteristics, 1987 and 1999

Geographic origin of tourists			
Area of origin	**1987 (%)**	**1999 (%)**	**% Change 1987–1999**
Bihar	3	2	−1
Chandigarh	2	7	5
Delhi	23	19	−4
Gujarat	2	5	3
Himachal Pradesh	3	4	1
Haryana	1	8	7
Maharashtra	14	9	−5
Punjab	4	17	13
Rajasthan	3	5	2
Tamil Nadu	2	2	0
Uttar Pradesh	9	9	0
West Bengal	31	13	−18

Length of stay (days)	**1987 (%)**	**1999 (%)**	**% Change 1987–1999**
One to three	14	28	14
Four to five	31	38	7
More than five	19	26	7
Unknown	36	8	−28

Educational level	**1987 (%)**	**1999 (%)**	**% Change 1987–1999**
Primary	2	0	−2
Secondary	7	4	−3
Technical	18	12	−6
University	73	84	11

Income level[a]	**1987 (%)**	**1999 (%)**	**% Change 1987–1999**
Below $65	8	3	−5
$65–195	28	10	−18
$196–325	37	45	8
$326–520	8	30	22
Above $520	11	10	−1
No response	8	2	−6

Table 5.3 (continued)
Manali Tourist Characteristics, 1987 and 1999

Mode of transport	1987[b] (%)	1999 (%)	% Change 1987–1999
HPTDC Bus	51	18	−33
Private bus	27	38	11
Taxi	20	8	−12
Private automobiles	7	36	29

Occupation	1987 (%)	1999 (%)	% Change 1987–1999
Agriculture	1	0	−1
Business	18	22	4
Homemaker	2	8	6
Industrialist	2	5	3
Service	55	60	5
Student	11	2	−9
Other	12	3	−9

[a] For purposes of comparability, rupees have been converted to U.S. dollars at an exchange rate of 15 rupees per dollar for the 1987 data and 40 rupees per dollar for the 1999 data.
[b] Numbers do not equal 100 percent.
Source: Author's survey 1999; Singh 1989.

Building Boom in Manali

Manali has experienced a sustained hotel-building boom since the early 1980s. Whereas in the 1970s the village had few hotels and even fewer formal-sector tourist-related establishments, Manali now features over 350 hotels with more than 4,000 hotel rooms. During the 1990s alone, the number of hotels in Manali tripled. In addition to hotel construction, the resort town has seen tremendous growth in the number of nonhotel tourist-related businesses: The number of restaurants, retail shops, photography studios, travel agencies, and similar businesses has mushroomed since the late 1970s. Moreover, the growth in Manali's hotel stock occurred overwhelmingly in the high-end "luxury" sector: The 1990–1998 period registered a 1,012 percent increase in higher-priced hotel establishments, whereas growth in the low-end "budget" sector was only 18 percent during the same period.[4]

There are at least three major reasons for the rapid growth of Manali's hotel sector during the 1980s and 1990s. The first is one I have already touched on—the steady growth of tourist arrivals in the Kulu-Manali tourism corridor. Whereas the Kulu-Manali region attracted only 10,000 tourists in the mid-1960s and fewer than 20,000 in the early 1970s, by the mid-1990s, Kulu-Manali was hosting more than 400,000 recreational tourists annually. If we include religious pilgrims in the total number of tourist arrivals, the number exceeds 700,000 arrivals annually. The growth in tourist arrivals has not only been absolutely large in Kulu-Manali; it has also been relatively large. Kulu-Manali ranks second among districts in Himachal Pradesh with respect to the total number of tourist arrivals (only the capital district of Shimla attracts more tourists), and it ranks first with respect to the growth in tourist arrivals. From 1988–1996, the number of domestic tourist arrivals in Kulu-Manali grew by 176.2 percent, more rapidly than any other district in the state of comparable size. (Shimla's tourist arrivals, for example, grew by only 32.1 percent during the same 1988–1996 period.)

A second reason for the growth of Manali's hotel sector is the growth of the Indian middle class and the changing class background of tourists who travel to Manali. The majority of tourists who visit Manali are middle to upper-middle class. Like their counterparts in the West, they travel primarily for leisure and recreational reasons. In the late 1980s, Singh (1989) found that 80 percent of tourists in Manali traveled there for recreational reasons. By the late 1990s, an even larger percentage of tourists surveyed (100 percent) characterized their motivation for visiting Manali as primarily nonreligious. Moreover, the tourists who visit Manali are generally higher-paid professionals and salaried individuals who can afford to pay more for and expect more from their chosen accommodation. They insist on clean, comfortable rooms with television, heat, room service, no insects, and car parking, at a minimum.

A third reason for the rapid growth of Manali's hotel sector is the generous subsidies extended to hotel developers by the state and national governments (Singh 1989). Through state-owned banks, the Himachal Pradesh Finance Corporation provides up to 90 percent of the financing for new hotel construction, 65 percent in the form of loans and 25 percent in the form of grants and direct subsidies. In addition, state government subsidies may cover up to 25 percent of the construction costs of cafeterias and restaurants, federal and state income tax exemptions are available to tourism entrepreneurs, and there are few remaining restrictions on foreign ownership of tourism-related businesses. Whereas in the past, foreigners could hold a maximum 49 percent equity interest in hotels, after 1989 they were able to hold a 100 percent ownership interest (Crossette 1989). Nearly all of the subsidies for large hotels in Manali have benefited "outsiders" from Shimla, Delhi, Bombay, and even other countries. One notable example is the Holiday Inn resort at Prini (near Manali), which, according to local sources, was once owned by the family of India's former Prime Minister, Atul Bihari Vajpayee.

Who Benefits from Tourism in Manali?

As the last paragraph intimates, the growth of Manali's formal tourism sector has tended to benefit outsiders and not the local inhabitants. Local people generally lack the capital resources and connections in the state capital (Shimla) and the national capital (New Delhi) that are often prerequisites in India for obtaining subsidies and other forms of largesse from the state. Local residents certainly participate in the Kulu-Manali tourism economy but only to a limited degree. Local ownership of hotel and other tourism facilities is less than 40 percent, if one counts as "ownership" even minimal equity participation; local management of tourism enterprises is even lower, at approximately 10 percent. Local residents even lose out in labor markets, because migrants from other parts of India and Nepal are willing to work for a much lower wage.

Current (1999) wages for formal-sector hotel workers in Manali are not much higher than in the informal sector and average about 1,000 rupees (U.S.$20) per month for waiters, room attendants, cooks, and similar occupations. Job security is virtually nonexistent, and almost all of the work is seasonal in nature. Managers of the larger hotels tend to earn higher wages, but management employees are drawn almost entirely from outside the region. Many come from New Delhi, Bombay, and other large urban centers.

But not all locals are bereft of opportunities. Many continue to own and operate farms and grow apples and other produce that they sell to the tourism enterprises. Some operate taxis and work as trekking guides, utilizing their knowledge of the Kulu Valley and surrounding areas. Many engage in informal economic activity to supplement their earnings from agriculture, including the operation of informal-sector hotels, restaurants, and other tourism-related enterprises. Still others (many others) engage in the production of *charas*, a substance similar to hashish. The risks from producing *charas* are low, and the profits are often very high. In fact, during the 1980s and 1990s, Himachal Pradesh and especially Kulu District became one of the leading producers of *charas* in India. The market for *charas* is primarily made up of foreigners from Italy, France, the United Kingdom, and Israel, buyers who are willing to pay up to 100,000 rupees (about U.S.$2,000) per kilogram for the finest quality *charas*, known locally as *malai* (cream).

Local residents are much more likely to benefit from their interaction with foreign tourists than they are with domestic tourists, particularly the international informal-sector (IFS) tourists that I discussed at length in chapter 4. Although less than 5 percent of the tourists visiting Manali are foreigners, they disproportionately avail themselves of the tourism services provided by the local population, including renting rooms in locally owned farmhouses, buying crafts and other handmade items, and dealing in *charas*.[5] Singh took note of the phenomenon, what he calls "craft tourism," over a decade ago:

Many visitors, chiefly foreign tourists partake of such rural joys, valley mores, traditions, and rustic charm. Many of them stay there with farmers in their poor dwellings for experiencing such bizarre and exotic living style. A kind of "craft tourism" has been coming up in these Valley villages, and this must be taken note of by the planners and resource managers. It is here that tourism establishes some links with farming community [sic] for their economic benefit. (Singh 1989, 119)

Unfortunately, the same thing cannot be said of Manali's rapidly expanding formal tourism sector, which tends to exclude local residents from the benefits—but not the costs—of the tourist trade.

Residents' Perceptions of Tourism

In the late 1980s, Singh conducted a survey to determine how local residents view tourism development in Manali and the Kulu Valley generally.[6] Summing up his findings, Singh (1989, 163) states that the "majority of opinion [sic] was that tourism has enhanced scenic beauty, brought in ecological awareness, [and] promoted cleanliness." Singh found that local residents believe that tourism leads to income and job creation and to economic diversification of the local economy. Interestingly, the survey revealed that whereas the local residents feel tourism aids in the preservation of local culture, they also believe that it serves to undermine local traditions through Westernizing influences. On the negative side, Singh's survey revealed that local residents blame tourism for inflationary pressures on the local economy, most notably land inflation, and feel that the local residents tend to get the worst jobs in an industry that is highly seasonal in nature.

Resident perceptions of tourism are today not much different than they were in the 1980s, although people tend to stress the negative factors associated with tourism development more now than they did when Singh surveyed the local population in 1987. A common refrain voiced by long-time Manali residents is that the benefits of tourism development flow out of the region—to Delhi, Shimla, and other faraway places—whereas the costs of tourism development—congestion, inflation, environmental degradation, and loss of traditional culture—remain local. Many Manali residents blame the state and national governments for not addressing the lack of local equity participation and local employment opportunities in the Kulu-Manali tourist economy; some even say that the government is actively working against the local people in league with outsiders, an attitude that is beginning to result in direct political actions against the state. In one instance, a state-operated hotel and hot spring complex in the village of Vashisht (a few kilometers from Manali) was sabotaged by locals who claimed that all of the income from the tourist complex was being taken out of the area by corrupt government officials. The facility remained closed throughout the busy spring 1999 season.

Planning for Tourism in Manali

Unlike other hill stations in India that have suffered from haphazard and un-planned growth, Manali has benefited from a fairly comprehensive planning effort first launched in the 1970s, long before the resort began attracting large numbers of tourists. The State Department of Town and Country Planning drew up Manali's first development plan in 1977. The major thrust of the plan was to preserve the town's ecology because the planners realized that uncon-trolled development in the Upper Kulu Valley would threaten the viability not only of the tourism industry but of the region's agricultural and horticultural industries as well.[7] The Manali Plan of 1977 states, therefore, that "the forest belts . . . shall remain intact, orchards shall be maintained and the rural char-acter of the place shall be preserved without infringement upon the natural setting and cultural features of the resort" (quoted in Singh 1989, 121).

In a more general sense, the planners sought to preserve the pastoral nature of Manali by prohibiting construction of major roads, confining development to certain zones of the town while placing strict limits on it in other areas and limiting such things as architectural styles and building height. The Plan divides the town and surrounding villages into five zones, with each zone tar-geted for a different level of tourism, residential, agricultural, and horticultural development. Each zone has a different tourist-to-resident population, rang-ing from zero (no tourists) to 4 (high tourist population). Although it is clearly evident that private developers have been allowed to circumvent numerous provisions of the 1977 Manali Plan, most notably the provisions limiting con-gestion of tourist facilities and the provisions on architectural style, the overall guidelines of the Plan have been more or less followed. As Singh (1989, 124) points out, "any discerning eye can discover that the Manali development pro-cesses and structures have closely followed the 1977 Plan and it is for this rea-son that the landscape appeal and the resort image has been fairly maintained, despite the speedy growth of tourism."

Conclusion

The Kulu-Manali corridor is a rapidly growing tourism region that attracts mostly middle-class domestic tourists from India's largest urban centers. Most of the growth occurring within the Kulu-Manali tourist economy is taking place within the formal sector. The benefits from tourism development in Kulu-Manali, especially the benefits of formal-sector tourism development, flow mainly to outsiders, although, like tourism development everywhere, the costs are borne disproportionately by the local population. Unlike tourism development in other parts of the Himalaya, the growth of tourism in Kulu-Manali has proceeded more or less in an orderly fashion, due no doubt to an effective physical planning process that has eliminated some of the worst environmental and ecological impact of unplanned tourism development.

In key respects, Manali residents' experience of the tourism industry is not unique. In many places throughout the world where an overwhelmingly formal-sector tourism industry has taken hold, the local culture has often had to bear the brunt of "development." Moreover, the benefits from tourism development have often flowed to outside investors who have no historic stake in the local community. Although such an outcome is more common in low-income countries, there are certainly many examples in the First World (Greece and Hawaii come to mind) where local residents feel cheated and put out by the rapid growth of the tourism industry.

Interestingly, in formal-sector tourism resorts, the background of the tourists (domestic or foreign) does not appear significantly to influence the outcomes for the local population. Whether the local residents are Mayan Indians or Himachali mountain folk and whether the tourists are New Yorkers or New Delhiites, local residents are generally bypassed in favor of outsiders in the government's allocation of credit and subsidies for tourism-related businesses, as well as in the allocation of employment opportunities in all but the most menial and low-paying occupations. The reason is straightforward: Formal-sector tourism resorts in the Third World are usually found in remote areas, and local residents rarely command the resources and political clout necessary to compete with other potential investors.

Where local residents have benefited from tourism development, however, they have almost always commanded their own resources and, not surprisingly, have been successful in excluding outside investors from participating in or at least dominating the local tourist trade. In the Third World, cases of successful local participation in the tourism industry almost always entail a high degree of informal economic activity because local residents rarely command the political and economic resources to engage in formal-sector real estate development. Although it is clearly not the case that everyone engaged in the informal tourism sector benefits to the same degree (see chapter 4), in some instances, members of the local community in informal-sector tourism destinations do much better than their counterparts in formal-sector tourism resorts. In the next chapter, I consider one such community in Pushkar, a popular pilgrimage center in the Indian state of Rajasthan.

CHAPTER **6**

The Domestic Informal Sector

Migrants, Pilgrims, and Other Poor Travelers

The train we had boarded in New Delhi the previous evening, the Ashram Express, arrived at Haridwar station early in the morning. Even though it was barely 6:00 A.M., the platform and station were already abuzz with travelers and pilgrims; some were followed by porters hired on the spot to transport trunks and suitcases from the train to waiting taxis; and others carried only small satchels or blankets; still others had no belongings at all except the *lungis* (loincloths) wrapped around their waists. Outside the station entrance, the shop-lined street was crowded with taxis, rickshaws, and buses, all jostling for position amidst clouds of bluish-purple exhaust fumes. The sides of the road were full of people, many of whom, like me, had come to Haridwar from somewhere else. My travel companions and I stopped for hot milk and *fen* (croissants) in a dilapidated booth by the side of the road near the bus stand. The ramshackle building was propped up on one side with a pole. I lit up the single cigarette I had purchased from a passing cigarette and bidi (Indian cigarette) seller for 1.50 rupees (about U.S.3¢) and asked the proprietor how to get to Rishikesh.

Haridwar, a major pilgrimage center in the northern Indian state of Uttar Pradesh, is the place where the Ganges River emerges out onto the plains from the Himalayan Mountains. *Haridwar* literally means "gateway (*war*) of the Lord (*Hari*)"; along with Varanasi, Mathura, Puri, Ayodhya, Dwarka, and Kanchi, it is one of the seven sacred cities of India. Haridwar is also one of the four cities in India to host the *Kumbha Mela* (Aquarius Festival). In 1998,

161

the last time the *Kumbha* was held at Haridwar, an estimated 10 million pilgrims came from all over India and the world to bathe in the Ganges. On this particular day, however, there was no great festival to celebrate, and the city, although bustling as usual, was not extraordinarily busy.

The *chai-wallah* (tea maker) told us where we could find a bus to Rishikesh. He also told us where we could find an unregistered taxi ("very cheap," he said) that would transport us for the same price. My companions and I decided on the bus because the bus stand was nearby, and soon we were rumbling along on the way to Rishikesh, our final destination. (It was actually only my final destination. My travel companions, three Krishna devotees from Vrindavan, were planning on making a pilgrimage to Badrinath, the source of the Ganges River and about twelve hours by bus from Rishikesh.)

Rishikesh is a large town in the Himalayan foothills about twenty-four kilometers from Haridwar. It is a religious center known for its many *ashrams* (monastic retreats) and yoga centers. Although the vast majority of visitors to both Haridwar and Rishikesh are Indians and Hindu, many foreigners also visit the two pilgrimage centers. Rishikesh, in particular, attracts a fairly large number of European and North American travelers, who go there for yoga instruction and other spiritual pursuits, as well as for sightseeing. Rishikesh, like Haridwar, is built along the banks of the Ganges River, or *Ma Ganga*, as the local people and many pilgrims refer to the sacred river. Two pedestrian suspension bridges, Lakshman Jhoola and Ram Jhoola, span the Ganges at Rishikesh (the river is wide there as it emerges from the mountains); dozens of *mandirs* (temples), *ashrams*, and *dharamshalas* (pilgrims' rest houses) line the river's banks and dot the hills in the background; numerous bathing *ghats* (steps) lead down to water's edge; and hundreds of small shops selling trinkets, food, religious paraphernalia, and other items crowd both sides of the river. Of course, there are always multitudes of pilgrims, tourists, and other travelers (figure 6.1).

Indeed, since the time my friends and I had left Vrindavan a couple of days before, we had been in the midst of great crowds of travelers fitting just about every possible description. The variety of travelers in India is enormous, as almost anyone passing through an Indian railway station can attest: entire families on holiday, elderly couples on their way to visit relatives, farmers transporting produce to market, ordinary pilgrims traveling to one of the innumerable holy places found throughout South Asia, wandering *sadhus* (holy men and, sometimes, women), and foreign tourists, to name just a few. A factor common to most Indian travelers, however, is a lack of material resources, especially when compared with the Indian upper classes and to people in high-income countries. Another characteristic most Indian travelers have in common, and one clearly related to the first, is their patronage of and reliance

Figure 6.1 Rishikesh, India

on informal-sector tourism and travel-related establishments. In fact, apart from the train journey itself (Indian Railways is state-owned, capital-intensive, and employs hundreds of thousands of people), my friends and I, along with most of the travelers we had encountered on our trip from Vrindavan to Rishikesh, moved almost exclusively through informal tourism space; the formal sector was literally nowhere in sight.

The reason is not difficult to fathom: Most people in India and other low-income countries, whether they are on the road or at home, spend most of their time in "informal space." In fact, informal economic space, no matter how it is defined, is the largest economic "space" in most Third World countries (see chapter 2). In chapter 4, we saw how one informal tourism destination, New Delhi's Pahar Ganj, thrives just one kilometer away from Delhi's main formal-sector commercial center, Connaught Circus (and, incidentally, only three kilometers away from the Prime Minister's residence). The context of chapter 4, however, was international informal-sector (IIS) tourism. In this chapter, I will consider domestic informal-sector (DIS) tourism, a much larger and more extensive phenomenon than IIS tourism. In India alone, domestic tourist arrivals easily account for more than three times the *entire world's* annual international arrivals, as reported by the World Tourism Organization (WTO).

The Extent of Domestic Informal-Sector Tourism

The WTO (2005e) defines *tourism* as "the activities of persons traveling to and staying in places outside their usual environment for not more than one consecutive year for leisure, business, and other purposes." The WTO further categorizes travel away from one's home into leisure, recreation, and holidays; visiting friends and relatives; business and professional; health treatment; religion and pilgrimage; and other. It defines *other* as "transit and other unknown activities." With the WTO's definition of tourism in place, we are better able to evaluate travel and tourism practices in poor Third World societies.

At the outset, it is clear that we are dealing with a worldwide phenomenon of immense proportions. In China alone, for example, there were 744 *million* domestic tourist arrivals in 2000, many more than the total number of international tourist arrivals *in the entire world* in that year (table 6.1). The number of travelers in India is even larger: In 1997, Indian Railways reported over 1.5 *billion* long-distance railway passengers who journeyed an average of 178 kilometers per trip (table 6.2). Other low-income countries, although not accounting for as many journeys due to smaller overall populations, may have relatively more travelers; Mexican tourism authorities, for instance, reported over 100 million domestic tourist arrivals annually in the mid-1990s (Secretaría de Turismo 1996). Although data are lacking for most low-income countries, it is safe to assume that many people in the Third World travel away from home ("their usual environment") for extended periods of time and would thus qualify as tourists, according to the WTO's definition.

Table 6.1
China's International and Domestic Tourism, 1980–2000

Year	Total arrivals (millions)	Foreigners[a] (millions)	Tourist receipts (U.S.$millions)	Domestic arrivals (millions)	Tourist receipts (RMB millions)
1980	5.7	0.5	617	—	—
1985	17.8	1.4	1,250	—	—
1990	27.5	1.7	2,218	—	—
1995	46.4	5.9	8,733	629	137,570
1996	51.1	6.7	10,200	639	163,712
1997	57.6	7.4	12,074	644	211,361
1998	63.5	7.1	12,602	694	239,083
1999	72.8	8.4	14,099	719	283,286
2000	83.5	10.2	16,231	744	317,554

RMB = renmimbi, the official currency of the People's Republic of China.
[a] Non-Chinese international arrivals.
[b] No data
Source: China National Tourism Administration (2005)

Table 6.2
Indian Railways Passengers, 1950–1997

Year	Suburban (all classes)	Nonsuburban (upper class)	Nonsuburban (second-class mail and express trains)	Nonsuburban (second-class ordinary trains)	Nonsuburban (second-class total)	Nonsuburban (total)	All trains (total)
1950–1951	412	25	52	795	847	872	1,284
1960–1961	680	15	96	803	899	914	1,594
1970–1971	1,219	16	155	1,041	1,196	1,212	2,431
1980–1981	2,000	11	260	1,342	1,602	1,613	3,613
1990–1991	2,259	19	357	1,223	1,580	1,599	3,858
1991–1992	2,412	20	371	1,246	1,617	1,637	4,049
1992–1993	2,282	20	332	1,115	1,447	1,467	3,749
1993–1994	2,302	21	314	1,071	1,385	1,406	3,708
1994–1995	2,430	23	335	1,127	1,462	1,485	3,915
1995–1996	2,484	27	380	1,127	1,534	1,507	4,018
1996–1997	2,578	27	403	1,145	1,548	1,575	4,153

All figures in millions
Source: Indian Railways 1999

In many respects, the reasons poor people have for traveling from point A to point B are as varied (or as similar) as any other group of people, including the "golden hordes" of middle-class tourists from rich countries whose travel habits tourism researchers and market analysts have so well documented (Turner and Ash 1976). Many travel for pleasure, for business, "to see the world," and to visit their friends and families. Their mode of transport usually differs from First World middle-class travelers—trains, buses, and walking versus planes, cruise ships, and automobiles. Their average length of stay may also be different because they are less likely than First World tourists to adhere to rigid work schedules ("9-to-5" jobs) when they are not traveling, more likely to work in agriculture or informal-sector activities, and more likely to be unemployed or underemployed. Poor people in Third World countries are, of course, much less likely to patronize expensive formal-sector hotels and resorts and much more likely to frequent informal-sector guesthouses, restaurants, transport, and other tourist facilities. They are also more likely to participate in pilgrimages to religious centers.

Although there is not to my knowledge any body of theoretical work that deals explicitly with poor Third World tourists (in the Western sense of the word), there are two bodies of literature that pertain explicitly to human mobility and travel patterns in Third World societies and that address at least some of the motivations poor people in the Third World may have for embarking on temporary journeys. The first deals with migration and the second with the anthropology and sociology of pilgrimage. I will consider each in turn and begin with the relationship between migration and tourism in the Third World.

Migration and Circulation

The root of the word *migration* is the Latin *migrare*, which means to transport, to move, or to change residence (du Toit 1990, 305). Although we do not normally associate migration with the movement of people for leisure and recreational purposes, anyone who lives or works in a seasonal resort area, such as South Florida or Spain's Costa Brava, is well aware of Northerners' propensity to migrate south in search of warmer climes during the winter season. From November through March, major north-south transport routes, such as I-95 in the United States and the Autoroute du Soleil in France, are crowded with tourists who temporarily escape the cold winters of the Northeastern and Midwestern United States and Northern Europe by moving south to the beaches of Florida, the Riviera, the Costa Brava, and the Costa del Sol. Similarly, winter resort areas, such as Aspen, Telluride, and Chamonix, swell with skiers, snowboarders, and snowmobilers—almost all of whom migrate from somewhere else—during the height of the winter tourist season.

In contrast, high rates of unemployment and underemployment, particularly in rural areas, are one of the reasons for the large-scale rural-to-urban migration that has characterized much of the Third World since the 1940s. Whether people traveling in search of employment qualify as tourists is open to interpretation. They are clearly not leisure tourists in the Western sense. But is a poor person who travels in search of employment a type of business traveler? Many of the migrants I have interviewed in large Third World cities stated that they came to the city for noneconomic as well economic reasons, including to see the sights and to have fun, and many stated that they did not intend to stay in the city for an extended period of time. They considered their homes to be elsewhere. Regardless of their motives for traveling from point A to point B, however, all migrants avail themselves of travel- and tourism-related goods and services, many of which are produced in the informal sector.

Although a number of authors have recognized the growing importance of geographic regions devoted exclusively to tourism and leisure pursuits, they focus more on the characteristics of the places themselves than on the movement of people into and out of them. Sociologist Jószef Böröcz (1996), however, explicitly places tourism within the larger context of migration studies. By conceptualizing tourists as "strangers," or as a type of migrant, he claims to provide tourism with a theoretical frame of reference, the rather extensive literature on migration:

> The tourist can be demarcated from the other main social types subsumed under the stranger—the rich varieties of the migrant and the expatriate expert—by *not* performing income earning activities away from home. *The tourist is the leisure migrant.* . . . One advantage of the leisure migration approach is that it provides the study of tourism with a point of reference—the literature on labor migration and refugee flows. (Böröcz 1996, 7, italics in original)

Böröcz's analysis of tourism is theoretically significant because it links tourism with migration and the geography of population movements. His theory of leisure migration suffers, however, from many of the same shortcomings that plague traditional accounts of travel and tourism. For example, like many other tourism researchers, Böröcz conflates the international tourism industry with all forms of tourism and assumes, implicitly if not explicitly, that all tourists are from rich industrial societies and that poor people do not travel for leisure purposes. He claims that a necessary condition of tourism is that "free time be regulated and packaged in weekly and annual blocks" and that a "singular characteristic of leisure migration among all human flows is that it is mediated by a transnationally organized institutional structure, the tourism industry" (Böröcz 1996, 28, 12). Thus, even though Böröcz intimates that leisure travel is possible in non-Western societies, his analysis remains anthropologically un-informed. As the present investigation reveals, travel and tourism is not only, or even primarily, a condition of advanced industrial capitalism; it is much more prevalent in the Third World (at least in terms of absolute numbers), even though it may not always take the same form that it does in wealthy First World countries.

As we saw in chapter 5, many people in low-income countries are opting for the same kinds of travel experiences and for many of the same reasons as their counterparts in the First World. They are, to use Böröcz's terminology, leisure migrants. Yet from both a cultural and a historical perspective, travel and tour-ism in low-income countries does not begin with the growth of a Westernized middle class. Nash (1981, 463) points to several nonindustrial (hunter-gath-erer) cultures in Africa (!Kung San), Australia (Pidjandjara), North America (Washo), and South America (Ye'cuana) in which, during their seasonal mi-grations, "people engage in a great deal of what is obviously leisure activity." Similarly, the centuries-old traditions of *pay thiaw* (to go wandering for fun and enjoyment) in northeast Thailand, *merantau* among the Minangkapau people of Indonesia, and *bejalai* (going around) in East Malaysia exhort young men to travel outside their villages in search of experience and knowledge (Parnwell 1993). In India, the Rabari and other nomadic groups spend a good part of the year traveling with their camel herds; as anyone who has spent time with the Rabari will know, a great deal of their time "on the road" is spent pur-suing leisure activities—in other words, having fun.

Regardless of their ethnic and cultural origin, however, it is clear that ever-growing numbers of people in the Third World are packing up and moving. In fact, more people are on the move today than at any other time in human his-tory. The reasons vary with the country, the region, and the individual migrant. Sometimes migration is state-sponsored, as in the case of Indonesia's World Bank-funded *Transmigrasi Swarkasa* (transmigration program). Sometimes migration is forced: Dozens of hot and cold wars since the mid-1940s have resulted in large-scale refugee flows and created millions of refugees in Latin America, Africa, the Middle East, and Asia. Migration is often economically induced as people move from rural to urban areas, from one urban area to another, and in many cases from one country to another in search of employ-ment and better lives for themselves and their families. A rapid influx of peo-ple in search of work has swelled the populations of Mexico City, Shanghai, São Paulo, Bombay, Bangkok, Cairo, Los Angeles, and other emerging Third World megacities. Accordingly, in Latin America, Asia, Africa, and other Third World regions, urban populations are growing much more rapidly than rural ones. Most migrants are not in search of leisure but they demand goods and services from tourism-related enterprises and qualify as tourists, according to the WTO definition.

China's Floating Population

Although many migrants leave their villages for work-related reasons, the same people may also have noneconomic reasons for moving, and still others may not move for economic reasons at all. China, with one of the largest migrant populations in the world, is also one of the few Third World countries to conduct periodic surveys of its *liudong renkou* ("floating population"), the name given to the "several tens, or perhaps hundreds of millions [of people] on the move during China's industrial revolution" (Bakken 1998, 10). China's floating population, which the government estimates at 80 million people, is defined as the total of all persons without permanent household registration (*hukou*) in their current places of residence. It includes not only rural-to-urban migrant laborers but "include[s] temporary residents, contract rural workers, short term [*sic*] visitors [i.e., tourists], people on business trips, etc." (Cheng 1998). Surveys of migrants in Shanghai, Beijing, and other large Chinese cities reveal that the number of migrants in China is very large; that most are not permanent migrants but travel away from their homes for less than a year; and that a surprisingly large number of migrants migrate for other than work-related reasons, including tourism.

Temporary migration to China's urban areas has increased rapidly over the last two decades. Beijing and Shanghai attract the most migrants; by the mid-1990s, Shanghai was host to over 3 million temporary migrants, and Beijing's floating population numbered well over 1.5 million. The floating population has grown faster than the permanent one so that in almost every large Chinese city, the share of temporary migrants has increased. By the late 1980s, the floating population represented about 25 percent of the total population in Beijing, Shanghai, and other Chinese urban areas. Shanghai, in particular, has seen its floating population grow very rapidly, from 500,000 temporary migrants in 1982 to over 2.8 million in 1993, registering average annual growth rates that in some years have been more than 40 times higher than the growth of the permanent population.

In addition to their large numbers, temporary migrants tend to remain temporary. A 1993 survey of 44,484 temporary migrants in Shanghai found that over 70 percent of migrants remain in the city for less than one year. Another survey of Shanghai's floating population found that 60 percent of migrants traveled to the city for a "visit" and stayed an average of 5.5 months (Goldstein, Goldstein, and Guo 1991).

Finally, many temporary migrants in China migrate for noneconomic reasons. Commenting on peoples' motivations for moving to Beijing and Shanghai, demographers Alice Goldstein and Shenyang Guo (1992, 48) observe that:

> Reasons can be inferred directly for those migrants on construction teams and in free markets—they have clearly come to the city for economic reasons. Among the migrants staying in Beijing's hotels and hostels, over half the men and almost one-third of the women also cited business as their motivation. Others came for training (which may have been work-related) and *tourism* (italics added).

Temporary migrants living in households (as opposed to hotels, outdoors, etc.) are even more likely to travel to the metropolis for noneconomic reasons; 46.4 percent of Beijing's and 56.8 percent of Shanghai's temporary migrants living in households migrate for reasons other than work (Goldstein and Guo 1992). The 1993 Shanghai survey likewise reveals that nearly half the temporary migrants in Shanghai had come for either social (visiting family and friends), cultural, or business reasons and would thus qualify as tourists, according to the WTO.

Temporary migration is not, of course, unique to China. There are large floating populations of men, women, and children in many (if not most) Third World countries who do many, if not most, of the things that tourists with more money do in the First World: They travel on buses and trains, they eat in restaurants, they stay in hotels and guesthouses, they visit with friends and family, they conduct business, and they sightsee. Whether we would consider them tourists in the Western sense of the word is open to question; clearly, they are not akin to a typical middle-class American family visiting Disney World or bronzed German tourists lying on the beach in Mexico. Most are probably not searching for authenticity, what Dean MacCannell (1976) claims many "modern" tourists are doing (unsuccessfully, it turns out) in an effort to reclaim some lost sense of the sacred and their place in the cosmos.

There is, however, a Third World counterpart to MacCannell's modern-day tourist-pilgrim who searches unsuccessfully for meaning in the lives of others: a real modern-day pilgrim for whom the problem of inauthenticity is not nearly as acute as it is in the West. In the next section, I look more closely at pilgrimage and its relationship to tourism in the Third World.

Pilgrimage

A tourist is half a pilgrim, if a pilgrim is half a tourist.
— Turner and Turner 1978

Stated simply, a pilgrimage is a journey to a shrine or a sacred place. Correspondingly, a pilgrimage center is a place where the divine is made (or has been made) manifest or where a saint has worked miracles. Nearly every major world religion, and many minor ones, identifies some points on the earth's surface as in some way partaking of divine reality. Pilgrimage sites are found on every continent (with the obvious exception of Antarctica) and in many countries of both the First and Third Worlds. Mecca, Jerusalem, and Bethlehem are some of the more well-known international pilgrimage destinations (at least to Westerners) and attract millions of pilgrims each year.[1] Other sites are more regionally focused but may attract even more worshippers: Lourdes Cathedral in France, for example, attracts 5 million visitors annually and features "the largest number of hotels and guesthouses (30,000) [in France] outside Paris" (Eade 1992, 22). The shrine of Medjugorge in the Yugoslavian province of Herzegovina attracts 3,000–5,000 pilgrims daily and three times as many on religious holidays. Poland's 500 pilgrimage centers attract 6–7 million Catholics each year, with the major center of Czestochowa drawing 4–5 million annual visitors. Temple Square in Salt Lake City, Utah, an important site for Mormons, attracted "4.7 million visitors . . . in 1990, more than any national park in the western United States, including Grand Canyon or Yellowstone, and twice as many as the number of pilgrims to Mecca each year" (Hudman and Jackson 1992, 116). Other countries with well-developed pilgrimage centers include Iran, India, Mexico, Thailand, and many countries in Central and South America.[2]

Of the major world religions, travel is perhaps most often associated with Islam, because one of Islam's five pillars of faith is pilgrimage to Mecca, a city in the Hejaz (Saudi Arabia) visited by millions of men and women every year. Although like Judaism, Christianity, Hinduism, and other faiths, it is difficult to generalize about Islam because of the varieties of Muslim religious practice and belief, Islam enjoins its adherents to perform not only the *hajj* (pilgrimage to Mecca) but also *hijra* (movement away from unbelief), *ziyaras* (visits to holy sites), and *rihla* (travel for educative purposes, to acquire knowledge; Eickelman and Piscatori 1990). As with Hindu pilgrimage, however, a literal understanding of the *hajj* and other forms of Islamic exhortations to travel are not always accurate; as Eickelman and Piscatori (1990, xii) point out, for many devout Muslims, religious travel is less movement along the surface of the earth and more "a journey of the mind."

Regardless of how one conceives of Islamic pilgrimage, however, physical journeys along the earth's surface have always formed an important part of Islamic practice and continue to do so today, not only in the Hejaz but also in South Asia, Iran, Iraq, and North Africa. Fueled by decreases in travel costs and rising per capita incomes for many Muslims, the number of people making the annual *hajj* (pilgrimage to Mecca) alone increased 20-fold from 1950 to 2000 (Bianchi 2004).[3] Because the number of people wishing to make the *hajj* (pilgrimage to Mecca) now outstrips the carrying capacity of the facilities set up by the Saudis to accommodate pilgrims, an international Islamic group, the Organization of the Islamic Conference, has set up a quota system based on each country's population size. Fewer restrictions apply to devout Muslims who wish to undertake an *umra* (lesser pilgrimage) out of season, as many are increasingly doing. Indeed, as political scientist Robert Bianchi points out, *umra* has become a "niche business" in the Muslim world, a form of "quasi-secular tourism," and in many respects *hajjis* (pilgrims to Mecca) are indistinguishable from "well-heeled tourists" (Bianchi 2004, 37, 71).

Tourism and pilgrimage share many characteristics. Both involve temporary journeys from one's home to some other, often distant place. Both involve "attractions," even though the attractions may be as different from each other as the Lourdes Cathedral in France and a beach in Thailand. Both tourism—at least in its leisure forms—and pilgrimage are things people do in their spare time and are not work-related activities. Both are socially and culturally sanctioned, with the annual trek to the mountains or the beach, or a holiday in some foreign country—"you just *have* to go to France this year"—as much an obligatory rite for middle-class, secular Westerners as a pilgrimage to the holy land can be for those more religiously inclined. Both tourism and pilgrimage are markers of status: The *hajji* (pilgrim to Mecca) who returns to his village is accorded a respect that may rival in many ways that accorded to the office worker in New York who just returned from two weeks of cruising around the Caribbean with her boyfriend. Finally, and most pertinent to the present investigation, both tourists and pilgrims avail themselves of tourism-related goods and services: hotels, hostels, travel agents, restaurants, cafés, buses, trains, planes, and other parts of the tourism infrastructure.[4] In fact, pilgrims and tourists share so many characteristics that we may, like the WTO, subsume pilgrimage under the larger rubric of tourism but with the proviso that it is a form of tourism with special characteristics.

Until fairly recently, anthropologists have generally avoided the subject of pilgrimage for a number of reasons: Pilgrimage partakes of the exceptional rather than the ordinary, it is not a fixed sociocultural unit, it is syncretic and involves a patchwork of different beliefs and practices, and it is not as easily interpreted by social scientists as other social and cultural practices (Morinis 1992). In recent years, however, the number of historical and ethnographic accounts of pilgrimage has expanded considerably (Fuller 1992; Gold 1988; Morinis 1992).

Basing their work on van Gennep's idea of *rites de passage* in traditional societies, Edith and Victor Turner were among the first anthropologists to theorize the practice of pilgrimage, viewing it as a liminal (*limen* means "threshold" in Latin) activity in which participants transcend the boundaries of life's everyday structures and partake of the "antistructure" of *communitas*, "a relational quality of full unmediated communication, even communion, between definite and determinate identities, which arises spontaneously in all kinds of groups, situations, and circumstances" (Turner and Turner 1978, 250). The Turners note how modern-day tourism and pilgrimage often overlap, pointing to the travel and tourism infrastructure common to both activities: "The most characteristic modern pilgrimage is blended with tourism, and involves a major journey, usually by modern means of transportation, to a national or international shrine" (Turner and Turner 1978, 240).

Although the Turners only touch on the similarities of pilgrimage and tourism and never explicitly deal with the anthropology of tourism as distinct from pilgrimage, other scholars have explicitly adopted the Turners' approach and much of their terminology in analyzing tourism and tourist behavior. Graburn (1989, 26), for instance, notes the alternating cycle of the "sacred/nonordinary/touristic and the profane/workaday/stay-at-home" that characterizes the passing of time for people in both industrial and agricultural societies. It is obvious from a reading of Western and increasingly non-Western culture that many people eagerly await the annual vacation, viewing it as a needed respite from the workaday world and a way of re-creating themselves anew through nonstructured or differently structured interactions with others. (It is no coincidence that the root of the word *holiday* is the old English *halig doeg* or "holy day.") Ethnographic accounts of both leisure tourism and pilgrimage demonstrate that each type of travel contains elements of the other, thus validating the Turners' insight into pilgrims' ludic behavior. Whereas pilgrims often have fun on their journeys (Gold 1988), leisure tourists, particularly those Dean MacCannell (1973; 1976) identifies in his work, may take what they are doing very seriously. Whether the communitas of pilgrims is the same as that of Club Méditerranée merrymakers, both types of activity are clearly liminal in the Turnerian sense of the word.

Erik Cohen (1988) even refers to a "Turnerian tradition" in tourism social science. Most studies that compare tourism and pilgrimage, however, focus on the similarities between today's First World tourists and either European pilgrims of the past or Third World pilgrims today. But to what extent are today's Third World pilgrims leisure tourists, and vice versa? The categories are decidedly blurred; in India, for example, many pilgrims claim to be tourists, and many middle-class tourists combine a pleasure holiday with at least some stops at a temple or other sacred center, with "a tendency among many white collar visitors to holy places [in India] to call themselves just 'tourists' rather than pilgrims" (Bhardwaj 1985, 247). Anthropologist Ann Grodzins Gold (1988, 282), in her ethnographic account of Rajasthani pilgrims, found that the highlight of the trip for most of the pilgrims was bathing in the Bay of Bengal, an act with no religious significance. Ironically, she states, "if Victor Turner's general vision of pilgrimage as 'liminoid' and 'antistructural' is anywhere directly pertinent to Rajasthanis' journeys, it is here on the beach at Puri."

As in the case of temporary migrants, however, whether we view pilgrims as a type of tourist or tourists as a type of pilgrim is to consider the phenomenon of pilgrimage only from the point of view of the individual traveler, or emically; it begs the question of the larger institutional and structural context in which pilgrimage occurs. Consequently, we gain little understanding of the social, cultural, and economic impact of pilgrimage—or indeed, of other types of travel—solely from an analysis of travelers' behavior and psychology.

For instance, the role and impact of pilgrimage varies greatly from one country to the next and even from one region to the next within the same country. In many cases, pilgrimage centers double as more mundane tourist destinations; as we have seen, determining who is a pilgrim and who is a tourist is not always an easy matter. In other cases, pilgrim way stations predominantly cater to other types of travelers. Pahar Ganj, which I discussed at length in chapter 4, is certainly no pilgrimage center, although many of the people passing through it are pilgrims. It is, however, an informal tourism destination where domestic tourists far outnumber international travelers and where the number of informal tourism-related businesses greatly exceeds those in the formal sector. What pilgrims passing through Pahar Ganj share with other travelers who stay in its relatively cheap hostels and guesthouses is a reliance on informal-sector goods and services and the informal economy more generally.

In the next section, I consider the characteristics of the industry that caters to the travel needs of temporary migrants, pilgrims, and other poor travelers in low-income countries. After a brief discussion of pilgrimage in India, I will look more closely at the small town of Pushkar, a religious and tourism center in Rajasthan that is also host to a major annual commercial fair and regional tourist event, the Pushkar *Mela*, or Pushkar Camel Fair.

Pilgrimage in India

Tirtha-yatra is the Hindi phrase that comes closest in meaning to the Western concept of pilgrimage.[5] It literally means "journey (*yatra*) to a river crossing (*tirtha*)." It may also mean, depending on the context, a devoted wife, one's parents, a sacred shrine, or a spiritual teacher, among other things, and *yatra* need not entail a physical journey on the earth's surface but may refer to a journey undertaken within one's soul. Alan Morinis (1992) defines *pilgrimage* (in India and elsewhere) as "a journey undertaken by a person in quest of a place or a state that he or she believes to embody a valued ideal," where "journey" is understood in both a physical and nonphysical sense. Thus, a journey to the "Vrindavana of the mind," for instance, the celestial Vrindavan accessible to the true devotee of Krishna, is as much a pilgrimage as physically going to the town of Vrindavan located on the earth, along the Yamuna River, in Uttar Pradesh, India. Similarly, one of the major pilgrimage centers in India, Benaras (also known as *Kashi* or *Varanasi*), is said to be present in other *tirthas*, and they in turn are present in Benaras.[6]

Thus, *tirtha-yatra* (pilgrimage) has both a literal and a figurative meaning for most Hindus: it can either mean a literal, physical journey on the earth's surface from one's present position to some other sacred place or it can mean a crossing from mundane existence to the sacred realm or to some higher level of consciousness that need not entail bodily movement through space. Many *tirthas* (shrines) are indeed found near water (oceans, lakes, rivers, streams, etc.) and may in fact actually be a ford or river crossing because Indian purification rites often involve bathing in water (figure 6.2). For most Hindus, however, the symbolic meaning of *tirtha* is more important than the literal meaning, although it should be noted that Western notions of what is literal and what is symbolic are not in all cases directly applicable to the Indian religious experience (Bhardwaj 1973, 32).

As I discussed previously, pilgrimage and tourism share many characteristics. One of them is the fact that both tourists and pilgrims travel to a place in order to see its sights (or sites), to sightsee; in pilgrimage centers such as Pushkar and Vrindavan, temples are the repositories of deities, the sights that pilgrims come to see. In fact, the Hindi word for revelation of the deity, *darshan*, means "to view the deity" or "to see the deity." An Indian pilgrim, however, does not exactly see in the same way as a tourist, even the tourists MacCannell (1976)

Figure 6.2 Pilgrims Bathing in the Ganges River, Uttar Pradesh, India

believes are searching for authenticity in the sites they visit. For an Indian pilgrim, the sight is alive; it looks back. As Fuller (1992, 59–60) explains, "*darshana* is not merely a passive sight of the deity in its image form; the deity is also gazing on the devotee with eyes that never blink."

The practice of pilgrimage in India, in the sense of a religious pilgrim physically moving through space, is of ancient origin and probably predates the Vedas because many pilgrim shrines in India were worshipped as holy sites prior to the Aryan conquest of India and their subsequent absorption into Hinduism. Shiva, Vishnu, and the mother goddess—each with his or her roots in pre-Aryan India—are the deities that have been and continue to be most commonly associated with *tirthas* in India. Pilgrimage has historically played a major role in opening up new trade routes on the subcontinent, particularly between the sedentarized Aryan population of the north and the Dravidian population of the south, and was probably instrumental in forging a pan-Indian consciousness and eventually a national identity from the diverse cultures and regional distinctiveness found throughout India (Bhardwaj 1973; Mandelbaum 1970.) Thus, it may be no coincidence that the cult of *Bharat Mata* (Mother India), complete with its own temple in Benaras where the presiding deity is a map of India, emerged in the late nineteenth century, coinciding with the beginnings of Indian nationalism and the anti-British Quit India movement.

Pilgrimage in India Today

Over time, and particularly during the twentieth century, pilgrimage has increased in popularity in both relative and absolute terms; more Indians are undertaking pilgrimages than ever before, and a larger share of the population is visiting the country's *tirthas*. As Surinder Bhardwaj (1973, 5–6) observes in the late 1960s, "one can maintain, without fear of contradiction, that more people now visit more sacred places than ever before in the history of India . . . because modern means of mass transportation have made it possible for larger numbers of individuals to undertake pilgrimages." Whereas in the past pilgrimages were difficult and fraught with the dangers of wild animals, brigands, and disease, today most pilgrims undertake their journeys by rail and bus. In the late 1960s, Bhardwaj estimated the number of Indian pilgrims at "several millions" annually, with important religious events such as the *Kumbha Mela* attracting "over 1 million devotees"; thirty years later, tens of millions of pilgrims set out on sacred journeys each year, and the last *Kumbha Mela*, in 2001, attracted over 60 million travelers.

There are literally thousands and possibly tens of thousands of *tirthas* in India, Nepal, and Tibet. They range in size from large cities such as Varanasi (Benaras) and Allahabad (Prayaga) to small towns such as Manikaran and

Pushkar to Himalayan outposts with semi- or nonpermanent populations such as Badrinath in Uttar Pradesh and Mount Kailash in Tibet. Whereas some *tirthas* attract a steady flow of pilgrims, others are inundated with travelers during certain times of the year or even at multiyear periods. Some *tirthas* are national in scope and draw pilgrims from all over the subcontinent and from abroad. Others, however, are more regionally focused, and still others are known only locally.

One factor that emerges from just about every study of pilgrimage in modern India is the way in which religious travel on the subcontinent has become a mass phenomenon, with no clear distinction between pilgrimage and secular forms of travel. Now an integral part of India's domestic tourism industry, travel agencies specialize in pilgrimage tours in much the same way as they specialize in other forms of leisure travel (figure 6.3). Moreover, pilgrims share

Figure 6.3 New Delhi, India

the same tourism infrastructure with other tourists. They travel by bus and train.[7] They stay at hotels and guesthouses. They eat in restaurants, they purchase souvenirs, and they increasingly combine travel to holy places with more mundane forms of sightseeing.

The Case of Pushkar, Rajasthan

The best sacred place of all sacred places

—Padma Purana

Pushkar, a small town in the north Indian state of Rajasthan, is one of the most important pilgrimage centers in India. Although the town's permanent population is made up of only 500 families (approximately 12,000 people), nearly a million leisure and religious travelers visit Pushkar every year. On particularly auspicious days, thousands of pilgrims flock to Pushkar in order to bathe in the waters of its holy lake, *Jyestha* (Elder) Pushkar, an act reputed to wash away the sins of a thousand lifetimes. Pushkar provides a good example of a "pure" pilgrimage/tourist center because virtually its entire economy, society, and culture is based on accommodating travelers. With dozens of hotels, guesthouses, *dharamshalas*, restaurants, *chai* (tea) stalls, and gift shops, the town caters to visitors year round; during important festivals, the tourist population may swell to over 200,000. Although the number of foreign tourists has increased dramatically since the early 1980s, domestic travelers greatly outnumber foreign tourists; the vast majority of business establishments are unregulated, of small scale, and informal; and DIS tourism clearly predominates (figure 6.4).

Pushkar is located about thirteen kilometers from the much larger city of Ajmer. The road connecting Ajmer with Pushkar, constructed during the British administration in the mid-nineteenth century, crosses the *Nag Pahar* (Serpent Mountains), which form part of the Aravalli range. The town is nestled among low-lying hills, two of which are crowned with temples. Pushkar is built up around the lake, its whitewashed buildings forming a semicircle around the water, with a pedestrian bridge spanning the lake's southern shore. *Ghats* (steps), where pilgrims perform *puja* (worship), ring the lake on the three built-up sides, leading down to the water's edge and into the water (figure 6.5). Most of Pushkar consists of a maze of narrow streets and alleyways running off of the main road encircling the lake. There are a fairgrounds and two bus stands on the outskirts of town. Although Pushkar was once surrounded by verdant forests, the landscape is today dry and barren. The deforestation of the surrounding area and loss of topsoil has led to increased siltation of the lake; water levels drop precipitously during the spring and early summer as much of the lake—once home to crocodiles—literally dries up.

Figure 6.4 Pushkar, India.

Historical and Mythological Origins

Like other pilgrimage centers in India, Pushkar's origins are shrouded in myth; local accounts of the town's beginnings differ not only from one an-

Figure 6.5 Pushkar, India.

other, but also from a more rigorous historical analysis.[8] Pushkar is certainly very old and probably dates back to the fifth century B.C. The town was already known as an important pilgrimage center during the time of the great Indian epics, the Mahabharata and Ramayana. In the *Aranyakaparvan* (a part of the Mahabharata devoted to pilgrimage), Pushkar is accorded the highest significance; it is the *tirtha* from which all pilgrimages should begin and end. Although over the subsequent centuries Pushkar declined in importance relative to other *tirthas* such as Prayaga (Allahabad) and Varanasi, it is still revered in the Puranas (A.D. 300–1000) as the *tirtha* from which every sacred journey should ideally originate.

Pushkar has had a violent political history; the town and surrounding areas were conquered and reconquered over the centuries by Turks, Afghans, Rajputs, Mughals, and Marathas. Many of its temples were destroyed by Muslim invaders, only to be rebuilt by succeeding Hindu royal families. The collapse of the Mughal Empire in the late eighteenth century created a power vacuum in *Rajputana* (Rajasthan), an area that included Pushkar and the neighboring city of Ajmer. Marathas from the south and Pindari (Pathan) tribesman from the northwest would routinely plunder towns and disrupt trade routes throughout the region. A British observer at the time noted how "nothing was safe from the pursuit of Pindaree lust or avarice; it was their common practice to burn and destroy what could not be carried away and, in the wantonness of barbarity, to ravish and murder women and children, under the eyes of their husbands and parents" (Prinsep 1972, 39–40). Divided and often at war with one another, the Rajput kingdoms were unable to contain the Pathan invasions.

In light of their political and military weakness and consequent inability to fend off violent incursions into their territories, the Rajputs entered into a series of treaties with the British in 1817–1818. The British East India Company, which had been rapidly increasing the territories under its control, allowed the Rajput states to remain nominally independent but took control of their external relations and demanded a fixed annual tribute, among other things (Banerjee 1980). In return, the British agreed to protect *Rajputana* (Rajasthan) from neighboring warlords and other violent aggressors. Unlike most other Rajasthani princely states, however, Ajmer and surrounding areas (including Pushkar) did not become a British protectorate but were forcibly ceded to the British East India Company in 1818 when the Maratha ruler, Scindia of Gwalior, did not honor his pledge to assist the British armies in their campaign against the Pindarees. The Ajmer area remained under direct British administration until Indian independence in 1947, when it became part of the state of Rajasthan.

Although the British administration of India was as rapacious as its predecessors, British rule ushered in a period of relative political stability in Rajasthan and elsewhere on the subcontinent. In the case of Ajmer and other princely states in *Rajputana*, the incessant warfare and *dacoity* (banditry) that plagued the region for decades was considerably reduced. In exchange, the British exacted a tremendous toll in tribute from agricultural producers. In line with their activities in other parts of India, the British also invested in rail and road improvements. In the 1840s, the British supervised construction of a railhead at Ajmer and a road linking Ajmer and Pushkar, infrastructural improvements that significantly increased pilgrimage traffic to the holy *tirtha*.

Mythical accounts of Pushkar's origins differ markedly in their scope from the political and historical record. Pushkar is among the few places in India with a temple dedicated to Brahma and the only place where *puja* (worship) of Brahma is conducted on a daily basis (Joseph 1994). According to local legend, Pushkar was created when Lord Brahma, despairing of no *vedi* (place of worship) dedicated to him, let a lotus flower drop from his hand; the flower touched the earth in three places, and there were formed the *tirthas* of *Jyestha* Pushkar, *Madhya* Pushkar, and *Kanistha* or *Buddha* Pushkar.[9] Brahma then proceeded to perform his *yagya* (sacrifice) in the Pushkar forest without his wife Savitri. Brahma, who could not proceed without a female consort, purified the shepherdess Gayatri in Savitri's place. When Savitri finally arrived, she was outraged; she cursed Brahma and declared that he would be worshipped only in Pushkar and nowhere else on earth (Joseph 1994).

After Brahma had created Pushkar, the local legend continues, the town became well known among men and women as the *tirtha* of *tirthas*; a dip in the holy Pushkar Lake would erase all worldly sins and lead immediately to *moksha* (release from the cycle of reincarnation). The pilgrim would attain a heavenly state after death and would break the cycle of rebirth. The other gods complained to Brahma, however, that because he had made attaining *moksha* (release) so easy for mortals, people were neglecting their sacrificial responsibilities and engaging in all sorts of sinful activities. Brahma decreed that only on the five days of the year leading up the full moon (*poornima*) of the Hindu month of Kartik (October–November) would pilgrims be able to avail themselves of the full power of the Pushkar *tirtha*. Consequently, Kartik Poornima is the busiest part of the pilgrimage season in Pushkar, with close to 200,000 pilgrims arriving to bathe in the lake over the course of a one-week period.

Caste and Occupational Structure

With approximately 12,000 people living in 2,000 households, Pushkar is one of the smallest towns in Rajasthan. The town's population has grown moderately over the past six decades: It doubled from 1941 to 1991 and increased 23 percent from 1981 to 1991. As in other parts of Rajasthan (and India), men significantly outnumber women; Pushkar's male-to-female ratio is 15:1. Pushkar's male literacy rate (73 percent) is much higher than the state average, owing to the large number of upper-caste Brahmins who live there and for whom literacy is a prerequisite of religious employment. (Female literacy, although higher than the state average, is still less than 50 percent.) Whereas Brahmins are the dominant caste group and make up over half the town's population, the scheduled castes and tribes (otherwise known as *harijans*, or untouchables) account for 21.4 percent of the population (up from 17 percent in 1981). The balance of the population consists primarily of Rajputs and Muslims.

Although Brahmins are the demographically, economically, and socially dominant group in Pushkar, they are divided into two rival factions. One group, known locally as the *Badi Basti* (big neighborhood) or Parashar Brahmins, claim descent from Parashar Muni, the founder of the Parashar community; the *Badi Basti* Brahmins believe Parashar Muni was present when Brahma created Pushkar. The other group is known as the *Choti Basti* (small neighborhood) Brahmins; they claim to be the true Brahmins of Pushkar because, as they say, the *Badi Basti* Brahmins are not really Brahmins at all. Disputes between the two Brahmin communities, especially with respect to property rights, date back hundreds of years. On many occasions, the communities have sued each other in civil courts (in both the pre- and postindependence periods) to determine which has the rightful claim to *jagirdari* (estate) rights concerning lands in and around Pushkar. Although violence between the two groups rarely breaks out today, it was fairly common in the past. Intermarriage and social relations are, however, extremely limited (Joseph 1994).

The occupational structure of Pushkar's resident population is heavily skewed toward trade and services. There is very little farming or manufacturing industry in Pushkar; the bulk of employment is in trade, commerce, and the category of "other services," a broad occupational grouping that includes *pandagiri* (the pilgrimage priesthood) and other activities connected with officiating at religious ceremonies. On a statewide basis, Pushkar ranks eighteenth out of Rajasthan's 272 towns in terms of the share of its workforce employed in "other services" (which includes *pandagiri*), an indicator of the town's specialization in religion and religious activities. (The district of Ajmer, of which Pushkar is a part, ranks second only to the capital district of Jaipur with respect to the number of places of worship.)

Pilgrim and Tourist Arrivals

In 1998, Pushkar hosted about 1 million domestic and foreign tourists.[10] As in other Indian tourist centers, domestic travelers greatly outnumbered international visitors; in 1998, foreign tourists represented only 5 percent of Pushkar's total arrivals (table 6.3), a significant increase over 1995 when foreigners made up only 2 percent of the town's arrivals. (Not surprisingly, Ajmer district is the leading tourist destination in Rajasthan, surpassing even the capital district of Jaipur in the total number of arrivals.) Both domestic and international visitor flows are marked by seasonal variation; domestic arrivals peak during the months of May, August, and November, whereas international visitors generally avoid Pushkar during the hot summer months (table 6.3). Pushkar's busiest month is the Hindu month of Kartik (October and November), the time of both *Kartik Poornima* (the full moon celebration when bathing in Pushkar Lake is believed to be especially propitious) and the *Kartik Mela* (Pushkar Camel Fair). During the *Kartik Poornima* festival in 1998, over 200,000 tourists visited the town.

Table 6.3
Pushkar's Foreign and Domestic Visitor Arrivals, 1998[a]

Month	Foreign	Domestic[b]	Share of foreign arrivals (%)
January	4,521		
February	5,502		
March	4,498		
April	3,106		
May	2,254		
June	1,897		
July	1,678		
August	2,086		
September	2,854		
October	5,799		
November	8,357		
December	4,788		
Total	47,340	912,500	5.2

[a] Tourists registered in hotels and guesthouses
[b] Estimated
Source: C.I.D. Office, Pushkar

Most of Pushkar's domestic visitors are from Rajasthan and neighboring states who have journeyed to Pushkar on a pilgrimage. The majority of visitors are poor agriculturalists who have traveled to Pushkar by some form of public transportation (bus or rail). Nearly every domestic visitor to Pushkar travels in family- or caste-based tour groups, many as part of longer pilgrimage tours that include other *tirthas* in India.[11] Their presence is conspicuous, with large groups of pilgrims (first men, then women and children) walking barefoot through the town and down the *ghats* by the lakeside. Most pilgrims remain in Pushkar for short periods of time and do not spend more than a few days in the town and the surrounding area.

Gopal and Vina

Although the bulk of Pushkar's visitors are pilgrims, not every domestic visitor to Pushkar comes strictly for religious reasons. Many visitors combine *tirtha-yatra* (pilgrimage) with more mundane forms of sightseeing and tourism-related activities. Gopal and Vina visited Pushkar on their honeymoon, accompanied by two of Gopal's brothers.[12] Gopal is a *mukut-wallah* (adornment-maker for temple deities) from Mathura in the state of Uttar Pradesh (about eight hours from Pushkar). Vina now lives with Gopal's family in Mathura, although she is originally from the nearby town of Bharatpur in Rajasthan. The four family members traveled by train from Mathura to Ajmer, then by local bus from the Ajmer train station to Pushkar. They rented two rooms at one of Pushkar's numerous guesthouses and either ate at *halwais* (sweet shops) or the guesthouse. Vina kept her head and face covered with a kerchief, as is the custom in her native area, and spoke through her husband. The couple stayed in Pushkar for three days before returning to Mathura.

Gopal was quick to point out the religious importance of Pushkar. "Lord Brahma is worshipped in Pushkar but so is Lord Shiva, and Krishna too." Gopal pointed to the *ghat* (steps) where he and Vina had performed *puja* (worship) earlier in the day, as well as the temple they had just visited. He did not hold the *pandas* (pilgrimage priests) in high regard: "They are *chor* (thieves)," he said, "and unwilling to work." Nevertheless, he claimed to have paid one of them ten rupees (U.S.20¢) for saying a prayer, not a small amount of money for the newly married couple (Gopal's monthly income is less than U.S.$50, and Vina works mostly at home). "*Behenchod* (sister-fucker)," Gopal added, "he should give me money because I am *Brij Basi* (native of Braja Mandal, an important pilgrimage center in Uttar Pradesh that includes Gopal's native city of Mathura); he should be happy that I have come to Pushkar and not ask me for money." Gopal felt that the *pandas* looked down on him because he was not Brahmin and had to work for a living. Even so, he felt that Brahmins are necessary in places such as Pushkar because they are, after all, priests and therefore indispensable to pilgrims who simply have to put up with them.

Gopal and Vina did not come to Pushkar for religious reasons only. They also came to have fun and to drum up business for Gopal's workshop in Mathura. The two honeymooners were thus not only *tirtha-yatris* (pilgrims); they were also *ghoom-yatris* (sightseers) and business travelers as well. The trip to Pushkar was especially interesting for Vina because she had rarely traveled outside of her home village near Bharatpur and her new home in Mathura. (She said, through her husband, that she had once been to Delhi as a child.) Gopal had been to Pushkar on numerous occasions in the past, mostly on business but also for religious reasons. The couple was planning on taking another trip to Badrinath (the source of the Ganges in the Himalayan Mountains) but that would have to wait until they could save enough money.

Middle-Class Visitors

Not all Indian tourists who visit Pushkar are poor; many are from the middle and upper-middle classes and harbor the same world view as those who visit Manali and other nonreligious tourist destinations (see chapter 5). Although few middle-class tourists visit Pushkar solely for secular reasons, they clearly engage in leisure activities during their stay. For instance, along with foreign tourists, they gather by the lakeside at sunset at a place the locals call *Angrezon ka Ghat* (Foreigner's Ghat), order *chai* from the Sunset Café, and snap pictures of the foreign tourists who juggle fire and bang tabla drums. As in other Indian tourist settings, backpacker tourists have ironically become an attraction for Indian travelers, a tourist "site" in and of themselves.

Many of the middle- and upper-middle-class tourists who visit Pushkar arrive early in the morning by automobile from nearby towns and cities and stay only for the day. Others lodge at one of the town's few formal-sector hotels. Author Pankaj Mishra (1995), commenting on Pushkar's tourism industry from a decidedly middle-class perspective, has this to say about his accommodation at the government-owned and -operated Tourist Bungalow:

> The name was a misnomer; it wasn't a bungalow at all, but a modern seventies-style building tacked onto an old palace . . . As in a lot of state-run hotels, the initial planning was done right. Then, on the day it opened, things began to go steadily downhill, and never looked up. Apathy and neglect were visible everywhere. The place was overstaffed; waiters and bell-boys hung around the lobby looking underworked; but things still moved in a sluggish, indifferent manner. (Mishra 1995, 71)

Although he is an Indian, Mishra's experience in Pushkar was remarkably similar to that of many foreign tourists. Upon arriving in town, he and his traveling companions were not besieged by *pandas*, as are many of the poor pilgrims, but by the same hotel, shop, and travel agency touts that Western tourists encounter during their stay in Pushkar. As he remarks, "We kept driving through the outskirts [of Pushkar] and ended up on the far side of the lake where touts besieged us, and all sorts of 'guides' began volunteering unsolicited information in the expectation of being paid in the end" (Mishra 1995, 70). It is clear from Mishra's account that Pushkar's touts view wealthy, and even middle-class Indians, in much the same way as they do foreign tourists.

Pushkar's Dual Tourism Industry

By just about any measure of informality, Pushkar's tourism industry is overwhelmingly informal. Nearly all of the town's hotels, guesthouses, restaurants, and other tourism-related establishments are unlicensed, small-scale, family-owned, and unregulated. The only exceptions are the Pushkar Hotel, Peacock Holiday Resort, and the Sarovar Tourist Bungalow operated by the Rajasthan Tourism Development Corporation (RTDC). Accordingly, over 95 percent of lodging establishments in Pushkar are either *dharamshalas* or family-owned guesthouses. The incidence of informality among other types of tourism establishments, particularly restaurants, is even higher and approaches 100 percent.

There are clear differences between the accommodation and other tourism-related establishment frequented by foreigners and those catering mainly to pilgrims. Whereas international tourists tend to stay at hotels and guesthouses, Indian pilgrims are more likely to stay in *dharamshalas*. (Some hotels and a small number of *dharamshalas* provide accommodation to both groups of tourists.) Similarly, the types of dining establishments frequented by the two groups also differ: Foreigners patronize the "all-you-can-eat" buffets and restaurants serving Western-style food, and the Indians eat at *dhabas* (greasy spoons) and *halwais*. Even the retail businesses that line Pushkar's main street attract different groups of customers. The religious souvenir, trinket, and bangle (jewelry) shops cater to domestic visitors; and international tourists make up the largest market for finished clothing, books, pirated music cassettes, and telecommunications services, such as email and long-distance telephone service. The greater propensity of foreign tourists to spend money in Pushkar is reflected in the fact that they make up about 5 percent of Pushkar's visitor arrivals but represent 15 percent of visitor spending (figure 6.6).

The character of Pushkar's main street has notably changed since the early 1990s. Many traditional businesses have relocated to other locations in Pushkar

Figure 6.6 Pushkar, India

Figure 6.7 Camel for Hire, Pushkar, India

or closed altogether, largely because the shop owners were able to sell or rent their shops to others for relatively large sums of money. Real estate prices have increased rapidly in Pushkar, particularly since the early 1990s. From the mid-1980s to the late 1990s, the cost of renting retail space along the main road in two of town's centrally located markets, Narsingh Bazaar and Sadar Bazaar, increased more than 300 percent, from 300 rupees to over 1,000 rupees per square yard. The rapid growth of gift shops and merchants dealing in tourism-oriented goods (mostly clothing and textiles) and the decline of more traditional shops, such as *halwai* (sweet), *paan* (betel nut), and general merchandise stores, are due in part to the higher profits the tourism-oriented shops generate (figure 6.7).

Pandas and Pandagiri

The major business of Pushkar, however, is the business of religion. As we have seen, the largest occupational grouping in Pushkar is *pandagiri* (the pilgrimage priesthood). *Pandas* or *tirthpurohits* (pilgrimage priests), who are always Brahmins and who hail from both communities in Pushkar (Choti Basti and Badi Basti), make up more than 50 percent of the workers in Pushkar's major industries. (*Pujaris*, or temple priests, are not as numerous as the *pandas* and often look down on them.) *Pandas* perform a number of functions for pilgrims: They guide them to temples and other holy sites, assist in the pilgrims' performance of *puja* (worship), and may even provide information relating to their patrons' family history. Although many *pandas* (actually families of *pandas*) have maintained *jajmani* (heriditary) relations with clients for decades (even centuries), competition for new business is fierce; groups of *pandas* wait by the bus stand and descend on pilgrims alighting from buses, offering their services through a combination of threats and persuasion. *Pandas* generally have a bad reputation with pilgrims, who often perceive them as corrupt, lazy, and greedy.[13]

In defense of their behavior, *pandas* in Pushkar are quick to point out how the times have changed and how the pilgrims who come to Pushkar have changed along with them. Whereas the *pandas* claim that in years past, pilgrims were wealthy and refined individuals who donated large sums of money for the upkeep of temples and other holy places, they are now mostly poor, ignorant people who arrive in Pushkar on tour buses and who give very little to the *pandas* and the temples. Many *pandas* resign themselves to the present state of affairs on the grounds that the world is in *kalyuga* (the age of Kali), a cosmic period of eroded morality and general spiritual decline. It is particularly telling, some of the *pandas* assert, when people in the holiest of holy places, such as Pushkar, Vrindavan, and Varanasi, both residents and pilgrims alike, succumb to ignorance, avarice, and fear (but particularly avarice).

The age of Kalyuga notwithstanding, the *pandas'* assertion that the times have changed is not without basis in the historical record of the last fifty years. The types of pilgrims visiting Pushkar and the nature of pilgrimage in India have changed significantly since 1947. As we have seen, pilgrimage in India has become both more democratic and more of a mass phenomenon. A cheap public transportation system and the elimination (or reduction) of many hazards associated with travel on the subcontinent (brigands, disease, etc.) have led to an increased flow of pilgrims to the country's many *tirthas*.[14] Moreover, the government's elimination of the Maharajas' privy purses put an end to what had subsidized the *pandas* for centuries—the charity of India's royal families. Postindependence legislation aimed at curbing absentee landlordism in India, most notably the Zamindari Abolition Act, entailed the loss of thousands of acres that wealthy individuals had bequeathed or given to the *pandas* (as well as the temples) as gifts and from which the *pandas* received payment in kind from the cultivators (Joseph 1994). Due to the changing nature of pilgrimage traffic and the loss of hereditary land rights, a large share of Pushkar's Brahmin community (from both *Bastis*) has had to look elsewhere for employment.

Change in Pushkar's Tourism Industry

One place they have found employment is in Pushkar's hotel and guesthouse industry.[15] Beginning in the early 1980s, many Brahmin families began converting their homes, or a part of their homes, into small hotels, guesthouses, and restaurants. Whereas some families own and operate their own guesthouses, others rent the space to other Brahmins or to outsiders who invest their own funds and manage the business. The number of guesthouses grew most rapidly during the 1980s, from one in 1980 to over thirty in 1989. By the late 1990s there were thirty-six family-owned hotels and guesthouses in Pushkar, representing approximately half of Pushkar's lodging establishments (figure 6.8).

Foreign tourists represent the largest market for the new accommodation facilities, a fact that has sown further division within Pushkar's Brahmin community. Many Brahmins object on religious grounds to the growing presence of foreigners because they claim that foreign tourists use and sell drugs, engage in lascivious behavior, eat meat, urinate in the lake, and otherwise pollute the town's holy places. The Brahmins who own or operate the lodging facilities, although they acknowledge that some foreigners may have caused problems in the past, claim that the situation is under control and that the other Brahmins are lazy, unwilling to work, and complain about foreign tourists only because they are not the ones making money from the international tourist trade. Even so, hotel and guesthouse proprietors who cater to foreigners remain sensitive to the issue of foreigners' activities in the town: A list of dos and don'ts for foreign tourists, ranging from no use of drugs to no kissing in public, are prominently posted in most accommodation facilities (figure 6.9).

Most tourism-related businesses in Pushkar (indeed, most businesses of any kind in Pushkar) are family-owned and -operated, with the profits from the

Figure 6.8 Locally Owned Guesthouse, Pushkar, India

Figure 6.9 Tourist Dos and Don'ts, Pushkar, India

business divided among male family members. Profits are meager, and many hotel owners complain that they have difficulty supporting their families. Business owners also hire workers from surrounding villages (oftentimes children) to work as waiters, cooks, helpers, cleaners, and so on. Like informal wage work generally in India, remuneration is very low, and the hours are long. A child working in a restaurant twelve to fourteen hours per day, six days per week, will receive two or three meals per day, and his parents will receive about 300–400 rupees (U.S.$6–8) a month from the restaurant or hotel owner.

Residents' Perception of Tourists in Pushkar

The local residents of Pushkar classify tourists into three major groups: Indian pilgrims, "poor" Westerners or backpackers, and "rich" Westerners on package tours. Most local residents do not view pilgrims as tourists at all; they are *yatris*, pilgrims who have come to Pushkar for the merit that attaches to such a journey. For most residents, *Pushkarraj* (Pushkar and adjoining areas) without pilgrims would not be Pushkar; such a state of affairs would be unthinkable.

Foreign tourists, however, are another story. In 1982, the Pushkar Bachao Samiti (Save Pushkar Committee) began what would be a series of demonstrations against the foreign "takeover" of Pushkar, among other things. As anthropologist Christina Joseph (1994, 227–228) observed in the 1980s:

Their [Pushkar Samiti Bachao's] main agenda is to remove hotels on the ghats as they infringe upon the lake and deprive pilgrims of a place to bathe. They have staged rallies and processions, held town meetings in the middle of the main street and organized protests on a regular basis to build up grass roots support. At one town meeting in 1988 they presented an agenda for the preservation of the lake ... The speakers contended that the purity of the lake had been besmirched by sewage and all kinds of garbage including cigarettes, beetle leaf spittle, and condoms. They also demanded the rigorous enforcement of the ban on liquor, meat, and drugs and called upon the pandas to be ready to sacrifice themselves for Pushkar's sanctity if necessary.

A decade later and despite the rise to national prominence of the Hindu-oriented Bharitiya Janata Party (Indian People's Party), the Pushkar Bachao Samiti members had not had much success in realizing any of their goals; the lake is still polluted, the hotels on the lake are still operating, and foreigners continue to pollute Pushkar with their vices. Joseph (1994) argues that the Pushkar Bachao Samiti was ineffective because Pushkar's residents perceived the organization as corrupt and overly political. A number of respondents indicated more recently (in 1999) that the Pushkar Bachao Samiti was initially formed by outsiders, not for its professed goals of protecting the lake and other holy places in Pushkar, but to drum up support for political organizations that were themselves "foreign" to Pushkar. Moreover, the industry it has sought to undermine (tourism) is economically important to many in Pushkar's Brahmin community.

Although the Pushkar Bachao Samiti members were unable to achieve all of their goals, Pushkar's residents continue to express concern over the effects on the local youth of exposure to more permissive Western ways. Topping the list is what the locals perceive as excessive drug use among the tourist population, although most people claim that the problem is not nearly as acute as it once was. Whereas there is certainly a market for hard drugs such as heroin and alcohol in Pushkar, the most widely used psychotropic substance is *bhang*, a mixture of ground marijuana leaves, water, and spices that is normally eaten in the morning or early afternoon. A café in the center of the village serves *bhang lassi* (marijuana mixed with yoghurt) and *bhang chai* (marijuana mixed with tea), mostly to Western tourists, for very high prices. Many more Indians than Western tourists use *bhang*, however, because it is cheap, socially acceptable, and legally available throughout India at government-licensed shops.

Who Benefits from Tourism in Pushkar?

Almost any resident of Pushkar, and most visitors, will proclaim that everyone who either lives in or visits Pushkar benefits enormously. Performing *puja* (worship) on the shores of Pushkar *Jyestha* in the proper way will wash away the sins of a thousand lifetimes. Pushkar, as the Puranas declare, is "the best sacred place of all sacred places," and in the words of a local hotel owner, "Who could not benefit from the power and goodness of such a special place, of such a holy place?" There are few atheists living in Pushkar; most residents of the town strongly believe in the town's mythical origins and its continuing religious significance. Similarly, nearly every pilgrim who arrives in Pushkar believes strongly in the sanctity and splendor of the town and what it promises to those who travel there.

Nevertheless, on the more mundane material plane, it is clearly the case that some of Pushkar's residents benefit more than others from the steady influx of pilgrims and tourists. Topping the list are the mostly upper-caste (Brahmin) families with property in and around the town. Despite the competition between the two *bastis* (neighborhoods), the *Badi Basti* and the *Choti Basti*, for control of communal lands and other potentially lucrative aspects of the pilgrimage trade, both groups have benefited because of their priestly status (*pandagiri*) and through their ownership of property. The conversion of Brahmin family homes into guesthouses and hotels, a trend that became popular in the 1980s, is a particularly salient example of how property ownership in Pushkar is tied directly to the question of who benefits from the travel and tourism trade.

Conclusion

Holy *tirthas* in India have been catering to travelers for hundreds, if not thousands, of years and receive far more visitors annually than Disney World, Las Vegas, and Cancún combined. But unlike districts and villages in formal-sector resort areas of the Third World, local communities in informal tourism destinations generally remain intact and are not "expropriated" by outside interests, their residents reduced to scrubbing toilets for Western tourists on lands they once owned themselves. Profits from informal-sector tourism enterprises may not be high—and certainly not higher than the profits accruing to five-star resorts and other formal-sector tourist establishments—but at informal tourist destinations, most of the profits generated by the tourist trade remain in local hands. Communities remain intact.

The growth of Pushkar as both a pilgrimage center and more recently as a foreign tourist destination has distinct implications for theories of Third World tourism development as well as for effective tourism planning in low-income countries. Pushkar has no formal tourism sector; only 4 percent of its hotels and none of its restaurants or retail shops are formal-sector enterprises. There are no formal-sector travel agents, tour guides, American Express offices, or rental car agencies. The equity participation of transnational corporations (TNCs) in Pushkar's tourism industry is zero. (There are even few banks and other "national" formal-sector enterprises.) The town's tourism industry, with a few notable exceptions, is almost entirely in the hands of the local Brahmin community; most of the profits generated in Pushkar's tourism-related businesses stay in Pushkar and surrounding villages. Despite the growth of international tourism in recent years, the continuing trend of local ownership and management continues unabated. Pushkar's residents, unlike those of Manali or India's other formal-sector resorts, have not been pushed aside by tourism "development" but have been able to mediate the rapid growth of both domestic and foreign tourism, largely on their own terms.

Pushkar and other Indian pilgrimage centers overwhelmingly attract domestic tourists but, as we have seen, the numbers of foreigners visiting the community has increased in recent years. As in other Indian tourist centers, local residents have had mixed feelings about the influx of international tourists. Many residents express concern over the lax morality of Westerners; they also resent the lack of respect that the foreigners pay to the holy sites in and around the town. Few complain about the money, however, and many residents protest about Western decadence even as they collect room rents and grossly overcharge Westerners for basic services, such as *puja* (worship) by the lakeside. Even though a small minority of residents wishes to ban foreign tourism altogether, townspeople have worked out some solutions to the problem of untoward foreign influence in recent years by banning "rave parties" and by conspicuously posting lists of "dos and don'ts" around the town and in hotels catering to Westerners, among other things. Despite their concerns about Western vices, most Pushkar residents continue to view tourism, both domestic and foreign, as a good thing for a very simple reason: They benefit from it in a real, tangible sense.

In the concluding chapter, I will further elaborate on the differences between formal- and informal-sector tourism, focusing on the environmental and community sustainability of the four tourism sectors.

CHAPTER 7

An Alternative to the Alternative?

Informality and Sustainable Tourism in the Third World

In place of the old wants . . . we find new wants, requiring for their satisfaction the products of distant lands and distant climes.

—Karl Marx and Frederick Engels

Most discussions of tourism in contemporary societies focus on mass tourism, the movement of large numbers of people to destinations in both the First and Third Worlds. For sociologist John Urry (1988, 35), "it is movement or travel which is the defining characteristic of modernity; and in turn it is travel which is the absolute precondition for the emergence of mass tourism—surely one of the quintessential features of modern life." It is important to note, however, that what Urry and most tourism scholars understand as mass tourism is formal-sector tourism and, in the case of the Third World, international formal-sector (IFS) tourism. Even though domestic tourism is much more pervasive in the Third World than international tourism, for most Western scholars and even those who write extensively about tourism, people in low-income countries somehow do not seem to qualify as tourists. We have seen, however, that in India, one of the world's largest "very poor societies," domestic tourism dwarfs international tourism, both in terms of the number of travelers and in terms of the number of informal-sector tourism-related enterprises. India's thousands of tourist destinations attract hundreds of millions of domestic visitors every year, visitors who overwhelmingly consume informal-sector commodities. What India's tourist sites do not attract a lot of, relatively speaking, are wealthy package tourists from North America, Western Europe, and Japan. The same

195

is true of China, Indonesia, Brazil, and other large Third World countries that neither have large IFS tourism industries nor attract relatively large numbers of Western travelers.

Despite the fact that it accounts for relatively few travelers in low-income countries, IFS tourism figures prominently in Western disquisitions on tourism in the Third World, probably because of its higher visibility and economic importance in foreign exchange terms. Early discussions of IFS tourism largely cast it in a positive light as a "clean" industry with few economic or sociocultural drawbacks. By the early 1980s, however, the international tourism industry came under increasing scrutiny, particularly in low-income countries. As we saw in chapter 3, IFS tourism may contribute to a country's foreign exchange reserves and provide limited employment opportunities to local residents, but the benefits flow disproportionately to national elites and to the airline, cruise-ship, and resort transnational corporations (TNCs) that dominate the industry. The costs of IFS tourism, however, remain overwhelmingly local and include the destruction of local communities and displacement of residents, the institution of virtual apartheid at five-star resort complexes, pedophilia and other forms of sexual exploitation of women and children by Western men, extensive ocean dumping by the cruise ship industry, and the devastation of marine and land-based ecosystems, to name just a few. For all of these reasons, the 1982 Manila Declaration on World Tourism, issued by what would later become the Ecumenical Coalition on Third World Tourism (Holden 1984, 7), concludes, "[International] tourism wreak[ed] more havoc than brought benefit to recipient Third World countries."

Alternative tourism, also known as *appropriate tourism, sustainable tourism, green tourism*, and *ecotourism*, is the travel industry's response to charges that traditional forms of mass IFS tourism are ecologically damaging and culturally destructive. Proponents of alternative tourism recognize that the negative effects of IFS tourism generally outweigh the industry's positive impact in low-income countries and, in some cases, high-income countries as well; they seek to fashion new forms of tourism that are less taxing on the local environment and society. With an emphasis on small-scale establishments, use of local materials whenever and wherever possible, and respect for traditional cultures, ecotourism promoters claim that tourism can be beneficial to both foreign tourists *and* local communities. The dual criteria of environmental awareness and cultural sensitivity are reflected in the International Ecotourism Society's definition of ecotourism: "responsible travel to natural areas that conserves the environment and improves the well-being of local people" (International Ecotourism Society 2005). As we have seen in chapter 3, however, the rapid growth of ecotourism, particularly IFS ecotourism,[1] in the Third World often creates the same kinds of problems that it is ostensibly designed to avoid.

Apart from the adverse social, economic, cultural, and environmental impact of mass tourism in both the First and Third Worlds, numerous authors have taken issue with the superficial, inauthentic, and decontextualized nature of the mass tourist experience. In Boorstin's view, tourist facilities are designed with the superficial tourist—not the serious traveler—in mind. The image prevails over reality, historical tableaux over actual history, and the fake over the original. The trivial nature of modern-day tourist attractions is taken to its extreme in the hyperreal and simulational worlds of Disneyland and other theme parks, a fact not lost on subsequent cultural critics.[2] In Third World tourist centers, performances ranging from limbo dancing in the Caribbean to snake charming in India are staged exclusively for the benefit of Western tourists, many of whom are duped into believing that what they are seeing is an "authentic" expression of "native" culture. Daniel Alarcón (1997) notes an added twist of irony in the case of Mexico's mega-resort of Cancún, where the resort's planners have tried to fashion a sense of "Mexicanness" from *their* interpretation of Disney's presentation of "authentic" Mexican culture!

As we saw in chapter 1, the standardized and hyperreal quality of most formal-sector tourist attractions has its basis in the international political economy of the post–World War II era. The rapid growth of mass formal-sector tourism, fueled by declining transportation costs and rising standards of living for many people in the high-income countries, has resulted in a commodified and standardized tourist experience shaped largely by TNCs. For Guy Debord (1992, 120), "the economic management of travel to different places suffices in itself to ensure those places' interchangeability," with tourism affording the average person "the chance to go and see what has been made trite."

Debord and other postmodern critics, taking note of an increasingly consumer-driven and socially polarized Western society, link tourists' experience with social capital formation and claim that what tourists are really buying are signifiers pointing to the prospect of some contrived experience (Bourdieu 1984). Travel has become a sign of social status so that, "returning to Canada with a suntan in February is like driving a Porsche" (Reimer 1990, 505). Precisely because tourism is a culturally constituted consumer good, it comes as no surprise that it serves as an indicator of one's class status, particularly in an increasingly fragmented and unequal post-Fordist world.

Alternative tourism is a buzzword that serves to distinguish—at least in the eyes of its First World practitioners—the more "enlightened" or "worldly" travelers from the run-of-the-mill mass of ordinary tourists. A small but growing body of literature is concerned with understanding the motivations of these tourists, a group that Ian Munt refers to as "ego-tourists." Munt and other authors seek to ground the growth of alternative tourism in a class analysis of contemporary society, demonstrating how the travel industry has become more "flexibly" organized and how new class fractions have appropriated certain forms of travel ranging from culture tours of "exotic" regions to adventure travel in remote areas as distinctively their own. A much larger body of work on alternative tourism focuses less on the motivations and class origins of individual travelers and more on the pros and cons of alternative tourism (and particularly what has become its most popular expression, ecotourism) for destination countries and regions. In this chapter, I will first discuss alternative tourists; then, after critically reviewing the impact of alternative tourism on Third World destinations, I will assess the merits and drawbacks of Third World formal- and informal-sector tourism in light of the 1990s sustainability and ecotourism discourse.

Alternative Tourists

The best place to begin a discussion of alternative tourists is with a definition of *alternative tourism*, not an easy task because existing definitions vary considerably. Alternative tourism is commonsensically defined in terms of mass tourism, because it is ostensibly everything that mass tourism is not. Mass tourism involves large movements of people; alternative tourism involves relatively few travelers. Mass tourism takes a heavy toll on destination areas; alternative tourism is relatively benign. Mass tourism overwhelmingly benefits TNCs and national elites; alternative tourism extends more benefits to local communities and people of color. According to most scholarly definitions, alternative travel shares only one characteristic with mass tourism: First World residents are its only practitioners. People in low-income countries cannot be alternative tourists because they cannot be tourists. Although the definition of alternative tourism appears fairly straightforward, we will shortly see that it becomes somewhat more complicated because alternative tourism often takes on characteristics of its opposite, mass tourism.

If we provisionally define alternative tourists as a relatively small group of First World travelers who attempt to seek out "unspoiled" or "untouristed" parts of the world, we find that they have been around for quite some time and probably as long as mass tourism itself. In an early formulation of the resort cycle, Walter Christaller (1963) notes that artists are often the first people to visit what will later become mass tourism destinations. Ascona, for example, a small town in the Swiss canton of Ticino, was at one time an artist colony that has since become an upscale destination catering mainly to wealthy German tourists. (The nearby town of Minusio, bordering Locarno, was also the home of Russian anarchist Michael Bakunin.) Similarly, backpacker, low-budget, or "drifter" tourists, the international informal-sector (IIS) tourists whom I have described at length in chapter 4, also qualify as alternative tourists because there are relatively few of them, and they often travel independently to "exotic" Third World destinations. Exoticism is important, because one of the hallmarks of alternative tourist psychology is the sense of "being there first," not necessarily the first person to visit a site but one of the first Westerners and certainly one of the first tourists.

Most critical discussions of alternative *tourists*, as opposed to alternative *tourism*, generally focus on tourists' behavioral and class characteristics and not their impact on the places they visit. Munt (1994, 51) refers to alternative tourists as people who practice "the 'other' post-modern tourism," drawing a distinction between the hyperreal and simulational tourist spaces of festival marketplaces, Disney Worlds, and heritage sites; and the growing number of upper-middle-class "ego-tourists," who he claims are "united both by their ability to make relatively expensive journeys overseas and by seeking a classificatory distinction from run of the mill tourists." For Munt and other critics of "posttourism," alternative tourism is rooted in the "classificatory struggles" of the new class fractions taking shape in a post-Fordist First World. Tour agencies have been keen to pick up on what Urry (1988) calls the "decentring of identity" and the need of the new middle classes to distance themselves from the lower middle class. Thousands of alternative tourism firms now cater to the needs of what Urry (1990) refers to as the "service class."

This is where discussions of alternative tourism dovetail with the larger body of work on flexible specialization, because one of the major premises of the flexible specialization literature is that the decline of Fordism and the rise of flexible production systems correspond to class realignments and a more fragmented social structure.[3] Due to the decline of Fordist mass production and heightened social differentiation, firms must now tailor their products to narrower groups of consumers. In other words, tourism- and travel-related businesses now confront smaller "niche" markets and engage in more highly specialized, small-batch production.[4]

Alternative Tourism: Marketing Gimmick or Genuine Article?

As we saw in chapter 3, what passes for ecotourism and alternative travel in many parts of the Third World is usually a nature- or culture-based variant of traditional IFS tourism, with all the attendant ills of that form of travel. More often than not, the expected benefits of ecotourism and other forms of alternative travel do not materialize.[5] The very people and communities that alternative tourism is ostensibly supposed to help are alienated from the industry and receive few material benefits. IFS ecotourism development often entails high levels of foreign investment and consequent profit repatriation, loss of local control, and inflationary pressures on local economies. As the ecotourism industry becomes more "internationalized" in Belize, Costa Rica, Dominica, Kenya, Guyana, and other Third World countries that cater to First World nature tourists, the percentage of funds spent by ecotourists at their destinations, relative to funds advanced in their home countries, falls precipitously (Cater 1994). Even the sine qua non of ecotourism, protection of the local culture and environment, is often eroded as ecotourism takes on more qualities of its "mass" IFS progenitor. With few exceptions, the evidence suggests that IFS ecotourism is less of an "alternative" to conventional mass tourism than it is a marketing gimmick aimed at well-meaning consumers from the world's wealthiest countries.

In many ways, the growing popularity of ecotourism and other alternative forms of travel highlights yet another variant of Western imperialism. After European and later U.S. colonial and neocolonial practices destroyed most indigenous societies and in numerous ways caused the present worldwide environmental crisis, representatives of the wealthy countries now call for the poor countries to cordon off their remaining natural areas for the benefit of all humankind or, more correctly, for that part of humankind with the money to go on ecotours, to own pharmaceutical companies, and otherwise to benefit from a less rapid depletion of the Third World's nature reserves. The forests and savannas, lakes and rivers, coral reefs and fisheries of the Third World have now become the poor countries' comparative advantage, they are told, a valuable export they can sell to the wealthy classes of the North.[6] The hypocrisy of ecotourism and other nature-based "solutions" touted by the World Bank and other Western development agencies is not lost on the people of the South, who often cannot afford the entry fees to parks and nature preserves in their own communities.

The growth of ecotourism also underscores differences between First and Third World concepts of the environment and between corresponding notions of environmental protection. Whereas Northerners view the environment as something to gaze upon and re-create in (the museumization of nature or "reserves," as in capital reserves) many people in low-income countries, and in particular the indigenous groups that inhabit the Fourth World ecospaces that First World alternative tourists are interested in gazing upon, are less likely to draw a distinction between themselves and the surrounding natural space. As Michael Hall (1995, 19) observes:

> The concept of ecotourism reflects Western ideas about environmental conservation which tend to separate humankind from nature. In traditional societies, there is no division between the natural and cultural components of the landscape—the physical environment is an everyday lived-in experience. However, many advocates of tourism either ignore or fail to understand the relationship of indigenous people to their environment.

The result is often disastrous for the cultures that inhabit the forests and other areas slated for IFS ecotourism development or IFS tourism development generally. A notable example is the industry's marginalization of traditional societies that had formerly inhabited the wildlife game reserves in Kenya, Tanzania, and South Africa; people fenced out of lands that they have traditionally considered their own. As a Maasai schoolteacher in the Serengeti poignantly observes, "We don't get any benefits from the tourists, from the national parks, from the wild animals" (quoted in Honey 1999, 222). In her study of ecotourism in Africa, Martha Honey (1999, 222) corroborates the schoolteacher's claims, drawing a parallel between the colonial period and the present:

> Since the colonial period, the Maasai have been barred from using prime grazing lands and water sources within the Serengeti, and in recent years they have witnessed the growth of tourism bypassing their impoverished communities. They see the tourist dollars flowing in and out of what they contend is their land, and yet they receive almost no benefit.

The parallel between the Maasai in Africa, the Maya in Mexico, the mountainfolk of the Kulu and Parvati Valleys in India, and other indigenous groups on all continents is readily apparent and underscores the contention that not every aspect of sustainable IFS tourism may be realizable in all low-income countries (Wall 1996). For instance, protection of the environment (in the Western sense) and local ownership or control of tourism enterprises may be incompatible objectives.

Is Informal-Sector Tourism Ecofriendly?

What tourism researchers have generally overlooked in the debate on the advantages and disadvantages of alternative tourism development, however, is the degree to which informal-sector tourism in low-income countries is "environmentally friendly" and represents a real alternative to the dominant models of formal-sector tourism development in the Third World: enclave resorts, five-star hotels, package tours, and more recently, ecotourism. The degree to which the informal tourism sector meets the criterion of ecotourism as defined in the literature is important, both because of its size (in most countries, it is much larger than the formal tourism sector) and because of what it tells us about the nature of tourism social science—that Western scholars tend to focus on the travel needs and impact of middle- and upper-middle-class individuals from the wealthy countries and neglect domestic tourism in low-income countries, as well as the sizable number of foreign tourists who overwhelmingly consume informal-sector tourism goods and services at Third World destinations.

Although definitions of ecotourism vary, most include at least some reference to sustainability. Butler (1999, 35) provides the following commonsensical definition of sustainable development within the context of tourism:

> Tourism which is developed and maintained in an area (community, environment) in such a manner and at such a scale that it remains viable over an indefinite period and does not degrade or alter the environment (human, physical) in which it exists to such a degree that it prohibits the successful development and well-being of other activities and processes.

Similarly, as we have seen, the International Ecotourism Society defines ecotourism as "responsible travel to natural areas that conserves the environment and improves the well-being of local people" (International Ecotourism Society 2005). For obvious reasons, the emphasis on sustainability and conservation is implicit or explicit in all definitions of alternative tourism and ecotourism.

Ecotourism expert Erlet Cater (1994) argues that a genuine ecotourism should emphasize locally owned and managed tourist facilities and a keen sensitivity to the local environment. In this view, shared by many alternative tourism advocates, ecotourism will benefit low-income countries in several ways. It requires less in the way of expensive infrastructural development; it provides an opportunity for a country, region, or locality to benefit from international tourism, even if the funds for large-scale tourism are not available; it requires fewer imports or "leakages," more local inputs and thus a higher multiplier effect; and it allows for profits to remain in the locality and the region. It is also less likely than IFS tourism to foster apartheid-like practices in the provisioning of tourist spaces. Golf courses and "private" beaches do not supplant the communities that once regarded such spaces as their own (figure 7.1).

Large-scale IFS tourism is not ecofriendly because outsiders own most facilities, community- and cooperatively owned lands are privatized, formal-sector investors seek to maximize profits only in the short term (or at most, the medium term), and high-density tourism development wreaks havoc on the local culture and the environment. As we have seen in chapter 3, Mexico's IFS tourism industry clearly fits this pattern, particularly with respect to the expropriation of local communities and the level of outside investment. So too do resort areas in Asia, the Caribbean, and other regions. Commenting on tourism development in the Caribbean, for instance, Polly Pattullo (1996, 204) points out, "The conclusions reached by many specialists is that high-density [IFS] mass tourism and the open economies and closed ecosystems of small islands are not compatible with sustainable development."

Informal-sector tourism development at first glance seems to meet all of the requirements for sustainability. Most informal tourist facilities found in both IIS and domestic informal-sector (DIS) destinations are locally owned

Figure 7.1 Pulga, India

small-scale establishments that have only a minimal impact on the local culture and the environment. Unlike IFS and domestic formal-sector (DFS) tourism, in very few cases are the local inhabitants marginalized from the tourism industry and the benefits that flow from it. In the three informal-sector case studies presented in this book, Pahar Ganj, Pushkar, and Zipolite, it has generally been the local population and not outsiders who have benefited most from the growth of the tourism industry. Furthermore, most informal-sector tourist destinations in low-income countries have remained viable over an extended period of time, in some cases for hundreds if not thousands of years. Additionally, it is clearly *not* the case that informal tourism destinations are more sustainable than formal-sector destinations because they receive fewer visitors. Vrindavan, a pilgrimage center in Uttar Pradesh, India, receives over 2.5 million tourists a year, 25 percent more than the total number of international tourists the entire country receives during the same period. Pushkar hosts nearly a million tourists annually and has been attracting visitors for thousands of years.

Compared with IIS, DIS, and even DFS tourists, traditional IFS tourists and IFS ecotourists have a much greater impact on the places they visit for a very simple reason: Recreating First World environments in poor, Third World societies is very expensive, capital-intensive, and socially exclusive. Informal-sector tourist facilities are generally much less taxing on the local resource base than are formal-sector tourist facilities, particularly IFS facilities. A lack of air conditioning, refrigeration, hot and cold running water, and other "essentials" demanded by most First World tourists clearly lessens the environmental toll of informal-sector tourism. In addition, the displacement and expropriation of local communities often associated with formal-sector tourism development (both IFS and, to a lesser degree, DFS tourism development) is highly destructive of local culture and social organization. Informal-sector tourism development is rarely destructive of local culture, because most of the tourism-related enterprises are locally owned and form a part of the larger community and because most informal tourists are domestic tourists who share similar cultural and social backgrounds with the host residents.

The above observations are not meant to suggest that informal-sector tourism is without any social, cultural, and environmental costs. Informal-sector tourism destinations in low-income countries are mostly unplanned and, as in many formal-sector destinations, their residents may be poor and underemployed, a situation that informal-sector tourism development has done little to change because many jobs in the industry are poorly paid. New Delhi's Main Bazaar, Pahar Ganj, provides a notable example. Moreover, the environmental costs of informal-sector tourism—water pollution, deforestation, and inadequate garbage disposal, among other things—are certainly significant, even if informal tourists on a per capita basis consume fewer commodities and generate less waste than their formal-sector counterparts.

Conclusions

Contrary to much scholarly opinion, the global travel and tourism business is not a monolithic industry dominated by TNCs that cater primarily to people from First World countries and, to a lesser extent, Third World elites. To be sure, a large part of it is and does just that, but another and perhaps much larger part of the world's tourism industry caters to poor people in low-income countries and, to a much lesser extent, to First World travelers who forego the comforts often associated with Third World luxury hotels and enclave resorts. In other words, like most other global industries, the tourism industry is bifurcated into formal and informal sectors. Unlike other industries, however, and stemming from the fact that tourism is a commodity consumed at the point of production, the tourism industry is further divided into domestically and internationally oriented sectors corresponding to distinctive tourism spaces or destinations. Although each low-income country is characterized by a different mix of IFS, IIS, DFS, and DIS tourism, most contain elements of all four sectors, with the exact proportion determined by a host of factors ranging from proximity to First World markets to the general level of the country's industrial development.

The four distinct Third World tourism sectors and corresponding spaces are associated with different developmental outcomes. In other words, each sector is associated with distinct costs and benefits. IFS and IIS tourism, for example, generate foreign exchange but may result in social activities destructive of traditional cultural practices. IFS tourism in particular, with at least the potential to employ many people and earn large amounts of foreign exchange, is import-intensive and often associated with foreign control of the industry, the sexual exploitation of women and children, the destruction of local communities, and apartheid-like divisions in enclave resort areas. DFS tourism, although less likely than IFS tourism to earn large amounts of foreign exchange, is also less import-intensive and may create employment opportunities for resident nationals if not members of the local community. DIS and IIS tourism destinations are almost always unplanned and less capital intensive than either IFS or DFS destinations, but unlike IFS and DFS tourism, the industry is more likely to benefit local communities and to support traditional cultural practices; in most cases, it is more environmentally sound than formal-sector tourism and much IFS ecotourism.

The four-part division of the tourism industry in low-income countries carries distinct implications for tourism planning and for evaluating the costs and benefits of any national tourism development strategy. To begin with, as with other industries, there are clear trade-offs involved in Third World tourism development. One is that in order to maximize foreign exchange earnings from IFS tourism, as Mexico and many Caribbean and South Pacific Island nations have attempted to do, governments must be willing to dispense with democratic decision-making procedures at the local level because most indigenous societies oppose formal-sector tourism development. A second related trade-off is the degree of foreign investment and control Third World governments wish to promote in their tourism industries. Although the current international climate fosters increased investment by TNCs in low-income societies, the reasons are as often political in nature as they are economic. There are many grounds for curtailing the flow of direct foreign investment (DFI) in the Third World and for limiting the influence of TNCs in the economic decision making of low-income countries. In the tourism industry, they extend from excessive profit repatriation and government subsidies of TNC hotel and resort operations to the fickleness of tour operators who play one Third World resort destination against another. A third trade-off is cultural and, increasingly, political: the degree to which policy makers in low-income countries wish to subject their people to the depredations of foreign tourists. The sexual exploitation of women and children is perhaps the vilest expression of Western imperialism in the tourism industry, but the enforced separation of predominantly white, First World tourists in five-star hotels and resort complexes from the "natives" in surrounding spaces is not much better and is eerily reminiscent of the not-too-distant colonial past.

What is true of other industries that operate in low-income countries is equally true of tourism; the interests of big national and transnational hospitality corporations are often directly opposed to the interests of people who live in the coastal regions, forest ecosystems, and urban areas most valued by First World tourists and the transnational hotel and resort chains that serve them. Third World policy makers, even those who implement tourism strategies, often recognize that formal-sector tourism development, particularly IFS tourism development, benefits local communities the least.[7] Even critics of IFS tourism, however, claim that it generates foreign exchange more than agriculture and even extractive industries and that that remains the primary reason why Third World governments continue to promote it as an economic development option. (Few policy makers accept the notion that international tourism, particularly IFS tourism, promotes cultural understanding among peoples of the world.) With over 100 low-income countries currently undergoing some form of structural adjustment program, the International Monetary Fund (IMF) and other international bodies have placed enormous pressure on Third World governments to promote export industries that are often socially disruptive and environmentally destructive.

There is, however, an alternative to IFS tourism and even to IFS alternative tourism—one that may benefit local communities at the same time that it promotes tourism as an export industry and earns foreign exchange for financially strapped Third World governments (and their First World creditors). It is based on the fact that First World consumers have expressed a greater interest in recent years for "authentic" holidays in low-income countries, that such tourists generally spend more money per capita than traditional IFS tourists, and that a large supply of "authentic," informal-sector accommodation and other tourism-related facilities already exists in low-income countries. In other words, a viable tourism development strategy may be to combine what Marx and Engels call the "new wants [of bourgeois societies], requiring for their satisfaction the products of distant lands and distant climes" with the abundant supply of informal-sector tourism-related goods and services found in almost every "distant land and clime" in the world today. The result will generate foreign exchange at the same time as it empowers local communities and does away with the worst excesses of traditional mass tourism.

Afterword

During 2004 and 2005, I traveled halfway around the world and back two more times, returning to some very familiar places, such as Mexico City, Zipolite, New York, Los Angeles, New Delhi, Amsterdam, and Mumbai, visiting places I had not been to in quite a while, such as Chennai, Mahaballipuram, and Pondicherry, and going to other places for the first time, including the big

Island of Hawaii, the famous pilgrimage center of Tirupati in Andhra Pradesh and the Indian Ocean island nation of Mauritius, located several hundred kilometers off the coast of Madagascar. Although the places I visited were all very different, home to vastly different cultures, languages, and forms of social organization, they all had one thing in common: All were teeming with tourists. The types of tourists at each destination certainly differed, as did the organization of the industry and the nature of businesses people had set up to cater to tourists. Of the Third World destinations, all fit into one of the tourist destination types I set out to describe and explain in the pages of this book: IFS, IIS, DFS, or DIS tourism. Some were variations on a theme. Tirupati, for instance, is very much a formal-sector pilgrimage destination, the first I had encountered in years of traveling to India. Indeed, I cannot recall ever seeing a higher level of organization at any tourist destination I have visited in any country, Disney World included.

Despite the setbacks that international tourism industry officials, workers, and owners experienced after the 2001 terrorist attacks in New York and Virginia, the Bali nightclub bombing in 2002, the Madrid train bombing in 2003, and other forms of violence around the world that shorten peoples' journeys and keep them from becoming international tourists in the first place, international tourism has continued to trend upward. According to the World Tourism Organization (WTO 2005a; 2005b), there were 15 million more international tourists in 2002 than there were in 2000. Tourist spending was also up, increasing from U.S.$473.4 billion in 2000 to U.S.$474.2 billion in 2002. Tourist arrivals even increased by 600,000 in the Middle East, a region characterized by war and civil strife and one seemingly the least likely to attract international visitors and the most likely to register sharp decreases in tourist traffic (World Tourism Organization 2005f). The picture painted by the WTO is far from complete, because what the WTO figures do not capture is the extent to which other forms of travel, particularly domestic travel, increased over the 2000–2002 period. Despite recession, higher oil prices, and downwardly trending wage figures for many of the world's countries, more people than ever are traveling, if not internationally then certainly within the borders of their own countries. Their purposes may vary, as I hope this book has made clear, but if the processes I have described are even remotely accurate, the travel and tourism industry will continue to play an important economic, social, cultural, and political role in the years to come. Tourism is certainly here to stay, at least for the foreseeable future.

Notes

Preface

1. The Mughals were Muslim invaders who ruled large parts of India from the sixteenth to the nineteenth centuries.
2. The last time I visited New Delhi, in the winter of 2005, the Ashok Yatri Niwas was closed and under renovation.
3. The last time I visited New Delhi, in the winter of 2005, the Kanishka Hotel was closed and under renovation.
4. "Brown" is short for brown sugar, a form of heroin popular in India and Pakistan.
5. Some commentators have even suggested that the very concept of a "Third" World no longer has any meaning in a world of NICs, Asian tigers, and Mexican miracles (see, e.g., Harris 1987). However, I am not so sure they would make the same argument today in the wake of currency crises, financial collapse, and the draconian International Monetary Fund-style austerity that inevitably follows. I shy away from using the terms "developing world" and "developing countries" because they imply that the countries of Africa, Asia, and Latin America are in fact "developing," which many people equate with "getting richer." In many cases they are not, or at least the majority of the people in them are not. In fact, some people claim the United States and other "developed" nations, including the former Eastern Bloc nations (formerly a part of the Second World) are now taking on distinct Third World characteristics. Similarly, I prefer not to use the terms "developed" and "less developed" when referring to countries or societies because the terms imply an end state toward which people in all societies should aspire. It is not clear to me that a Western country, even in the economic sense, is any more advanced or "developed" than a non-Western society, many of which have been "developing" for thousands of years. In this book I use the terms "Third World country" and "low-income country" more or less interchangeably, although as I point out we may be better off following Jeremy Seabrook and using the term "Two-Thirds World," since more than two-thirds of the world's population lives in it.

Chapter 1: An Overview of Tourism in the 2000s

1. But not always, because there are often vast social and cultural differences among different groups within Third World countries. In Mexico, for example, Mexico City residents often do not understand the languages and cultural practices of the indigenous people from the south of the country and vice versa. The same is the case in India, where vast cultural and linguistic differences separate north Indians from south Indians and the *adivasis* (indigenous peoples) from the country's dominant cultural groups.
2. *Gurudwaras* are Sikh temples. A tenet of the Sikh faith is that any traveler, Sikh or non-Sikh, may stay overnight at any *gurudwara*, where they will receive a simple meal and cup of tea. *Dharamshalas*, *sarais*, and *chattis* are traditional Indian forms of lodging generally associated with the practice of *tirtha-yatra*, or pilgrimage. See chapter 6 for a further discussion of pilgrimage in India.
3. When Cook first brought English tourists to Carnarvon in Wales, there was only one person there who spoke enough English to act as guide (Rae 1891). In connection with Cook's new tours to Scotland, Rae (1891, 32–33) notes, "If the firm which he founded should now announce a personally conducted tour to the North Pole the public would not be more surprised."

Chapter 2: Conceptualizing Travel and Tourism in Third World Countries

1. Formal tourism establishments such as five-star hotels and upscale restaurants generally offer workers more job security, better working conditions, and higher wages. Formal-sector jobs in India are much sought after, although the experience of tourism workers in other countries is different. In the Mexican resort of Huatulco, for instance, room attendants prefer informal-sector employment because it affords them ample income-earning potential and better hours (Long 1989). My findings in Playa del Carmen and Cancún were somewhat mixed on this point. I will return to the issue in chapter 3.

2. I am begging the question, of course, as to whether tourism really is a discrete industry, an issue that has generated quite a bit of debate in academic circles (Smith 1998). A major point of contention involves the nature of tourism commodities. Tourism goods and services are unlike many other commodities in that the consumer must travel to where the goods and services are produced in order to consume them, which makes tourism more of a place-based industry than other, more traditional export industries, such as textiles or electronics. Although that fact gives tour operators an advantage when it comes to playing one "sea, sun, and sand" destination against another, it also makes it more difficult for tourism-related businesses to pick up and move or to threaten to pick up and move in order to gain concessions from workers and local and regional governments. Another inherent problem with identifying a tourism industry as distinct from other industries is that a tourism good or service is only a tourism good or service by dint of being sold to a tourist. If a resident eats in a restaurant, it does not figure into the tourism balance sheet, but if a traveler eats there, it does. In other words, in contrast to many other industries, the tourism industry is defined by the demand side of the equation, not the supply side, which is one of the reasons Fainstein, Hoffman, and Judd claim the industry has "vague boundaries" (Hoffman, Fainstein, and Judd 2003, 4).

Chapter 3: The International Formal Sector

1. A less common sight is a Western female tourist with a younger local man. See Meisch (1995) on Ecuador; Pattullo (1996) on the Caribbean; and Pruitt and LaFont (1995) on Jamaica.

2. Exceptions include Britton 1982; 1991; de Kadt 1979; Ioannides 1995; Mullins 1991; Munt 1994; Truong 1990; and Urry 1990. Although these authors adopt critical perspectives with respect to the tourism industry and how it relates to Third World countries, they concentrate almost entirely on the formal tourism sector. Their analyses largely ignore the millions of Western low-budget travelers and billions of Third World domestic tourists who demand tourism goods and services from informal-sector enterprises.

3. Like the other literature on tourism, however, the political economy literature deals almost entirely with the formal tourism sector of franchised hotels and restaurants, state-regulated transport facilities, and related tourist attractions. Although this approach undoubtedly captures a great deal (certainly the majority) of tourism activity in First World countries and some Third World countries (e.g., certain Pacific island and Caribbean microstates), it neglects what is by far the largest tourism sector in the Third World, the informal sector of small hotels, guesthouses, restaurants, and other unregulated activities falling outside the purview of state regulation.

4. Much of the worldwide growth in international arrivals is explained by a much greater propensity for Europeans to travel abroad.

5. As a result of continuing economic troubles, most recently the so-called peso crisis and associated economic collapse in 1994, Mexico's leaders are now more committed than ever to developing the country's tourism sector; in addition to the five coastal *turismo mega-proyectos* (tourism megaprojects) currently in various stages of completion, a new U.S.$300 million "Sea of Cortez—Copper Canyon Mega-Project" is on the drawing board for the northern state of Chihuahua. International tourist arrivals in the ecologically sensitive region are expected to increase from 80,000 to over 500,000 annually.

6. One part of Prebisch's argument is no longer valid; although many Third World countries continue to experience declining terms of trade, economists recognize that productivity gains in the rich countries are no longer translated into higher wages for workers. On the contrary, in the United States real wages have been declining or stagnating since the 1970s despite increases in

productivity, and the distribution of both income and wealth has become much more unequal. One result has been the increasing "Third Worldization" of the U.S. working class. See Harvey 1989; Wolff 1999.

7. Even higher-income Third World countries register low tourism multipliers. The primary reason stems from the franchise agreements with the international hotel chains that require "international-standard" accommodation and amenities in any hotel bearing their particular names or logos. Because even the more industrially diversified countries do not produce air-conditioning units, elevators, escalators, Scotch whiskey, limousines, and management personnel at the standards acceptable to the international hotel and resort firms, much of the physical plant, staff, and supplies of the five-star hotels and enclave resorts in the Third World are imported.

8. Author's interviews with tourism workers in Mexico, March 11–23 and April 6–11, 2005.

9. See Pattullo 1996. On the Bahamian island of New Providence (the country's most heavily populated), the last remaining stretch of publicly accessible beachfront land is slated for an upscale, gated tourist resort financed by the Bechtel family trust. As one Bahamian resident proclaimed, "Bahamians have to have a puddle in our backyards to swim." Quoted in Gonzalez 2000.

10. *Ecotourism* is a rather loosely defined term, the exact meaning of which varies from author to author. It generally connotes some form of nature- or culture-based travel experience but with an emphasis on sustainability. See chapter 7 for a discussion of ecotourism and its applicability to the four tourism sectors.

11. Author's interviews with tourism workers in Cancún, Mexico, April 10, 2005.

12. If we include both overnight visitors and excursionists (day visitors), Mexico hosted 92.9 million visitors, who spent approximately U.S.$7.6 billion dollars on tourism goods and services. The large number of tourists is attributable to the extensive cross-border traffic between Mexico and the United States, one of the busiest borders in the world. Similarly, total tourism-related spending varies considerably, depending on the methodology employed. The World Travel and Tourism Council (WTTC), using a broad-based definition of a tourism-related good or service, estimates Mexico's travel and tourism expenditures at close to U.S.$40 billion.

13. San Cristobal de las Casas, in the southern state of Chiapas, is the only major noncoastal tourist center in Mexico that attracts more international than domestic tourists, but unlike the six destinations mentioned here, it does not have an upscale tourism sector. Although the city is completely lacking in five- and four-star hotels, it has a large number of *posadas*, *casas de huespedes*, and other small-scale, informal tourist facilities. See van den Berghe 1994.

14. That is, *centros turisticos* (tourism centers) for which the Secretaría de Turismo (tourism ministry; SECTUR) publishes statistics; the actual number of individuals working in tourism establishments nationwide is much higher. Mexico's *Instituto Nacional de Estadistica e Informatica* (National Institute of Statistical Information; INEGI) estimates total employment in hotels and restaurants alone at over 1.5 million, and the WTTC estimates total travel- and tourism-related employment in Mexico at over 2.2 million. As we have seen in previous chapters, the methodological problems associated with measuring tourism employment are legion, and in this sense the Mexican case is no exception.

15. Indirect employment attributed to the tourism industry will significantly inflate the total. It is very difficult to measure the indirect effects of tourism activity in individual IFS resorts because detailed regional input-output tables are not available, either in Mexico or in other countries. Hiernaux-Nicolas and Woog (1990, 15) point out, however, that localities and even entire regions in Mexico are rarely self-sufficient and thus, "indirect employment generated by tourism is not likely to follow the same geographic pattern as direct employment."

Chapter 4: The International Informal Sector

1. A major exception is their air ticket(s) to the destination country, although even here many IIS tourists purchase cheap tickets from bucket shops (deep-discount travel agencies) in New York, London, Amsterdam, and other cities in the West. It is more common for an IIS than an IFS tourist to fly on a Third World airline than on a major carrier from the United States, Western Europe, or Japan.

2. What we do not know, however, is the number of international tourists to India who share all of these characteristics. In other words, it is possible that longer-staying foreign visitors are older than thirty, that visitors between the ages of seventeen and thirty earn more than U.S.$15,000

per year, and that students spend more than U.S.$20 per day. The survey of foreign tourists to India does reveal, however, that length of stay correlates strongly with daily expenditure. In other words, longer-staying tourists generally spend less money per day.

3. In constant (1999) dollars, each traveler spent about U.S.$2,000, and the total travel and tourism-related expenditure for the three-month period exceeded U.S.$2 billion.

4. See, e.g., Bhattacharya on India in general (1997); Edensor (1998) on Agra; and Hutnyk 1996 on Calcutta (1997).

5. Interview with author, March 29, 1997.

6. Joni Mitchell's lyrics capture the feeling of youth tourism in the 1960s and in particular the interchangeability of destinations: "Maybe I'll go to Amsterdam/Maybe I'll go to Rome. . . . I caught a plane to Spain/There were lots of pretty people there reading *Rolling Stone,* reading *Vogue*."

7. Curiously, Smith makes this claim on the basis of an extensive study carried out by Pam Riley (1988). Riley, however, arrived at precisely the opposite conclusion (see below).

8. The black market for hard currency is very well organized in Pahar Ganj. Rates for different currencies change daily. Most dealers will accept only dollars and pounds, with some offering relatively lower rates for German marks, French francs, Swiss francs, and other hard currencies. In recent years, black market currency transactions have declined in Pahar Ganj, due in large part to the International Monetary Fund (IMF)-dictated rupee devaluations since 1990.

9. Not the hotels' real names.

10. Even five-star, formal-sector hotels in Delhi ignore official zoning regulations. City officials delayed the opening of the new Radisson Hotel near Indira Gandhi International Airport on the grounds that the hotel did not conform to the city's building regulations. One upscale hotel manager explained to me, "It is really a game; you can never adhere to every regulation, even if you wanted to. It simply isn't possible. The city doesn't want you to either, since they know that you'll have to pay them something. So owners go ahead and build without the necessary permits and expect to negotiate later with city officials over the amount [of *baksheesh*] they'll have to pay."

11. I use "he" because tourism workers in Pahar Ganj are exclusively male. Sex workers are an important exception; most are women and girls.

12. Until recently (1989), foreigners were unable to own more than a 49 percent interest in any tourism establishment in India. The laws have since changed, and now foreigners are able to own more than a 50 percent interest in tourism projects, and in certain cases may retain a 100 percent ownership stake.

13. Investigating the illicit drug trade is fraught with difficulty. On several occasions, I was told in no uncertain terms to cease my investigations—or else. Thus, I have kept the following account of Delhi's drug trade intentionally vague.

14. The sample ($n = 30$) represented about 15 percent of the total number of foreign tourists staying at Zipolite.

Chapter 5: The Domestic Formal Sector

1. Third World tourism researchers have, of course, written about tourism in their own countries. Most are well aware of the fact that the vast majority of the tourists they write about are domestic and not international travelers. Yet even here, the distinction between an internationally oriented and a domestically oriented tourism destination is implicit and rarely drawn out. Similarly, tourism researchers in India have noted the long history of *rath yatra* (pilgrimage) but have not to my knowledge differentiated tourist destinations on the basis of their formal versus informal characteristics.

2. In the media industries, globalization almost always means commercialization, as privately owned, advertiser-based TV and radio broadcasting supplants traditional government monopolies. As Herman and McChesney (1997) point out, the benefits of the privatization process have been mixed: The end of government-owned monopolies means the air waves are no longer used as a state propaganda tool, but the types of programming that attract commercial advertisers (soap operas, sporting events, movies, game shows) and the commercial advertising itself are geared to the consuming classes and those with effective demand—a distinctly undemocratic outcome.

3. India's commercial broadcasting industry also provides a good example of how global, technologically advanced industrial sectors such as the mass media and telecommunications are often

enmeshed with and depend on informal-sector economic activities. Illegal cable operations proliferated rapidly after 1991, the year the country officially "opened up" to global trade and capital flows. Small-scale, unregulated cable operators "wire" their neighborhoods and villages with
cable, then broadcast satellite transmissions over their informal networks of subscribers. The process is largely unregulated and almost always illegal, but as Ninan (1995, 46) points out, "much
of the broadcasting revolution in India over the last four years [1991–1995] has ridden on this
illegal network of cable systems."

4. Whereas in 1991 the entire Kulu District had just 165 hotels, by 1998 the number had grown
    nearly threefold to 473, second in number within Himachal Pradesh only to Shimla, the capital
    district. Kulu registered an even greater growth in its high-end hotel sector of over 2,000 percent
    and a correspondingly lower rate of growth in the low end of 11 percent. One reason for Kulu's
    much higher rate of growth is the much smaller base of high-end hotels in 1991.

5. One local resident stated that one or two foreigners purchasing *charas* and staying with local
    people are more beneficial to the local economy than are 100 or more domestic tourists. He
    went on to say that foreigners are also more likely to respect local traditions than are domestic
    tourists.

6. In discussing tourism's sociocultural impacts, Singh (1989, 167) notes that scholars tend to focus
    on the social and economic contrasts between Western tourists and Third World residents but
    "such contrasts can also be possible in the case of domestic tourism." In Manali, such contrasts
    are readily apparent because most tourists are urban-based, educated, and middle class, and most
    of the local inhabitants are not.

7. Because most local people were not involved in tourism and were, even in the late 1970s, by-
    passed in favor of outsiders for tourism-related employment, the planners understood that bull-
    dozing agricultural land and apple orchards for hotel construction would put local people out of
    work and result in high rates of local unemployment.

Chapter 6: The Domestic Informal Sector

1. An estimated 1–2 million tourists visit Mecca each year. Millions more visit Jerusalem and
    Bethlehem. An estimated 7 million people traveled to the Holy Land for the 1999–2000 millen-
    nium celebrations. The Vatican named the Israeli airline El Al as the "official pilgrims' airline for
    millennium trips" (Anonymous 1998).

2. Nolan (1991) identified 6,150 pilgrim shrines in Western Europe and 937 in Central and South
    America.

3. Other international gatherings of Muslims attract just as many, if not more, pilgrims than the *hajj*
    (pilgrimage to Mecca). The Vishwa Ijtema (World Gathering) organized by the Tabligh Jamaat
    Bangladesh, for example, attracts millions of visitors every year. I witnessed the event firsthand a
    number of years ago when the Biman Bangladesh flight I was on from Brussels to New Delhi by-
    passed the scheduled stop in India and landed in Dacca, Bangladesh's capital city. Because airline
    officials could not put me on a connecting flight the same day, I had an opportunity to venture
    out of the hotel where I was staying and speak with quite a few Bangladeshis and travelers from
    other parts of the world who had come to Bangladesh to attend lectures on Islamic doctrine and
    practice.

4. The degree to which tourists and pilgrims utilize the *same* infrastructure depends on the locality,
    the region, and the country. In most places in the early twenty-first century, pilgrimage centers
    have become de facto tourist centers and, conversely, many tourist attractions, or at least those
    described by MacCannell (1973; 1976), have taken on characteristics of pilgrimage shrines. Thus,
    the questions of who are tourists and who are pilgrims is not easy to decipher on the basis of the
    attraction or destination alone.

5. The following discussion relates mostly to Hindu pilgrimage in India. Hindus are not, however,
    the only Indians who travel on pilgrimages. Many of India's 100 million Muslims go on pilgrim-
    ages as well. There are many Muslim *tirthas*, or holy sites, in India, such the *dargah* (shrine)
    of Hazrat Nizamuddin Aulia in Delhi and the *dargah* of Khwaja Moinuddin Chisti in Ajmer
    (both Sufi saints). The annual Urs festival celebrates the six days before Khwaja Moinuddin
    Chisti ascended to heaven. For millions of Muslims in India, like those in other countries, a
    hajj (pilgrimage) to Mecca (for those with the resources to undertake one) is a requirement of
    their religion.

6.   Roger Housden (1996, 17) provides another variation on the same theme:

> If you would like to circumambulate the Ganges, a well-known Sadhu pilgrimage of 3,000 miles, but do not have the time, you can stand on any spot of the Ganga, with hands raised in salutation, and turn on your axis once. That is the microcosm of the entire circumambulation.

If one sacred place contains all the others, if indeed one need not "go" anywhere to perform a *tirtha-yatra*, then why go on a pilgrimage at all? We go because, as Housden (1996) points out, that is simply the nature of human existence.

7.   Although most of today's pilgrims use some form of mass transportation, going on foot is still regarded as the highest form of pilgrimage (see, e.g., Housden 1996). Many *sadhus* (wandering holy men) have told me that walking is not only the best way of approaching *tirthas*, it is also a form of yoga in its own right.

8.   Popular accounts of Pushkar, what Joseph (1994) calls the "oral tradition," represent a mixture of historical fact and myth. To understand Pushkar as a pilgrimage center, it is important to place the mythical accounts of the town's origin and its place in the cosmos on an equal footing with what we know of its actual history because it is the mythical aspect, not the historical one, that draws pilgrims to the banks of its lake.

9.   Literally, Senior Pushkar, Middle Pushkar, and Ancient Pushkar. Jyestha Pushkar is clearly the most important of Pushkar's three lakes; few pilgrims visit the other two lakes (Madhya Pushkar is actually a brick-lined tank that runs dry during the summer).

10.   Tourist arrival statistics are periodically gathered on the basis of the toll tax that all visitors to Pushkar must pay (the tax is collected at a toll booth or, for tourists arriving by bus, it is figured into the ticket price). Foreign tourist arrivals are calculated on the basis of hotel ledgers and "Schedule C" forms that most foreign tourists are required to sign when they check into a hotel or guesthouse. It is important to stress that calculating tourist arrivals is not an exact science in India (or anywhere else, for that matter); the cited figures are estimates only.

11.   Pushkar is often the first and last stop. See Gold (1988) for an ethnographic account of a Rajasthani pilgrimage to Gaya (Bihar) and Puri (in Orissa).

12.   Not their real names.

13.   Many residents have expressed concern over what they perceive to be the *pandas'* excessive card playing, gambling, drinking, *bhang* (marijuana) eating, and womanizing.

14.   As Fuller (1992) points out, until fairly recently, pilgrims who departed from their villages on pilgrimages rarely expected to return.

15.   Other places include government and professional employment.

Chapter 7: An Alternative to the Alternative?

1.   IFS ecotourism destinations are places that cater overwhelmingly to foreign visitors and operate with significant levels of outside investment. Like traditional IFS tourism, IFS ecotourism is state-regulated and much more capital-intensive than informal-sector tourism destinations.

2.   See, e.g., Baudrillard 1984; Boorstin 1992; Debord 1992; Eco 1986.

3.   See chapter 3. See also Castells 1989; Harvey 1989.

4.   For an analysis of post-Fordist flexible specialization and its impact on the tourism industry, see Ioannides and Debbage 1998; Poon 1988; 1990; Urry 1990.

5.   See, e.g., Honey (1999) on Tanzania, Kenya, and South Africa; Pattullo (1996) on Dominica and Guyana.

6.   Who, exactly, "they" are who sell the Third World's nature resources on international markets is problematic; often, as in the case of Belize and Costa Rica, "they" are foreign investors who, for instance, presently own 90 percent of all coastal land in Belize. "They" are also domestic elite groups, as in the case of Manali (see chapter 5) and the Serengeti (see, e.g., Honey 1999).

7.   An official of Mexico's Secretaría de Turismo, who asked to remain anonymous, said that the interests of local communities have never entered into the government's calculus of costs and benefits regarding formal-sector tourism development. (He wished it did.)

List of Acronyms

BBC	British Broadcasting Company
BJP	Bharatiya Janata Party
CNN	Cable News Network
DFI	Direct foreign investment
DFS	Domestic formal sector
DIS	Domestic informal sector
EC	European Community
ECLA	Economic Commission for Latin America
EIU	Economist Intelligence Unit
FIYTO	Federation of International Youth Travel Organizations
FONATUR	*Fondo Nacional de Fomento al Turismo* (National Fund for the Promotion of Tourism)
GNP	Gross national product
GWP	Gross world product
HPTDC	Himachal Pradesh Tourism Development Corporation
IDB	Inter-American Development Bank
IFS	International formal sector
IIS	International informal sector
ILO	International Labour Organisation
IMF	International Monetary Fund
ITDC	Indian Tourism Development Corporation

INEGI *Instituto Nacional de Estadistica e Informatica* (National Institute of Statistical Information)

INFRATUR *Fondo de Promoción e Infraestructura Turística* (Fund for the Promotion of Tourism Infrastructure)

ISI Import substitution industrialization

ISKCON International Society for Krishna Consciousness

LIBOR London Interbank Offered Rate

MTV Music Television

NAFTA North American Free Trade Agreement

NIDL New International Division of Labor

NIC Newly industrializing countries

NRI Nonresident Indian

OECD Organization of Economic Cooperation and Development

PPP Purchasing power parity

RMB Renmimbi, the official currency of the People's Republic of China

RTDC Rajasthan Tourism Development Corporation

SECTUR *Secretaría de Turismo* (Tourism Ministry)

SES Socioeconomic strata analysis

TNC Transnational corporation

WTO World Tourism Organization

WTTC World Travel and Tourism Council

References

Adler, J. 1985. Youth on the Road: Reflections on the History of Tramping. *Annals of Tourism Research* 12: 335–354.

Aglietta, M. 1979. *A Theory of Capitalist Regulation*. London: Verso.

Aglietta, M. 1982. World Capitalism in the Eighties. *New Left Review* 136: 5–41.

Aguilar, A. G.. 1994. Ingreso y Mercado Laboral en Ciudades Turisticas. *Ciudades: Analisis de la Coyuntura, Teoria e Historia Urbana* 23: 10–17.

Alarcón, D. C. 1997. *The Aztec Palimpsest: Mexico in the Modern Imagination*. Tucson: The University of Arizona Press.

Alsop, K. 1972. Across Europe and out of Sight, Man. *Punch* 263: 130–131.

Amirahmadi, H., and D. Gladstone. 1996. Towards a Dynamic Theory of the State and Civil Society in the Development Process. *Journal of Planning Education and Research* 16 (1): 15–25.

Ankomah, P. K. 1991. Tourism Skilled Labor: The Case of Sub-Saharan Africa. *Annals of Tourism Research* 18: 433–442.

Anonymous. 1971. Rites of Passage: The Knapsack Nomads. *Time* 98 (3): 66–67.

Anonymous. 1996. Police Drive Against Illegal Guest Houses. *The Pioneer* (Delhi Edition), April 25, 1996, sec. 1, 2.

Anonymous. 1998. El Al Picked as Pilgrim's Airline. *Associated Press*, June 3, 1998; available at *The New York Times* Web site.

Anonymous. 1999a. Alaska Sues Cruise Line Over Pollution in State Waters. *Reuters*, August 15, 1999.

Anonymous. 1999b. Ecotourism Statistical Fact Sheet. Bennington, Vt.: The Ecotourism Society; available at the Ecotourism Society Web site.

Archer, B. H. 1989. Tourism and Island Economies: Impact Analyses. In *Progress in Tourism, Recreation and Hospitality Management*. Edited by C. P. Cooper. London: Belhaven Press.

Bahal, A. 1998. Travel: Outward Bound. *Outlook* 4: 56–62.

Bakken, B., ed. 1998. *Migration in China*. Copenhagen: Nordic Institute of Asian Studies.

Banerjee, A. C. 1980. *The Rajput States and British Paramountcy*. Rajesh Publications: New Delhi.

Banerjee, C. 2001. (Holi)day in Pink City. *The Sunday Tribune*, Spectrum Travel, March 25, 2001; available at www.tribuneindia.com/2001/20010325/spectrum/travel.htm. [cited November 2004].

Baran, P. 1957. *The Political Economy of Growth*. New York: Monthly Review Press.

Barber, B. 1992. Jihad vs. McWorld. *The Atlantic* 269 (3): 53–62.

Barry, T. 1995. *Zapata's Revenge: Free Trade and the Farm Crisis in Mexico*. Boston: South End Press.

Baudrillard, J. 1984. The Precession of Simulacra. In *Art After Modernism: Rethinking Representation*. Edited by B. Wallis. New York: The Museum of Contemporary Art.

Bhardwaj, S. M. 1973. *Hindu Places of Pilgrimage in India (A Cultural Geography)*. Berkeley, Los Angeles, and London: University of California Press.

Bhardwaj, S. M.. 1985. Religion and Circulation: Hindu Pilgrimage. In *Circulation in Third World Countries*. Edited by R. M. Prothero and M. Chapman. London, Boston, Melbourne, and Henley: Routledge & Kegan Paul.

Bhattacharya, D. P. 1997. Mediating India: An Analysis of a Guidebook. *Annals of Tourism Research* 24 (2): 371–389.

Bianchi, R. R. 2004. *Guests of God: Pilgrimage and Politics in the Islamic World*. Oxford and New York: Oxford University Press.

Boeke, J. H. 1978. *Economics and Economic Policy of Dual Societies, as Exemplified by Indonesia*. New York: AMS Press.

Bohlen, C. 1993. Russians Discover Capitalism's Harsher Realities. *The New York Times*, November 13, 1993, Section A, 3.

Boorstin, D. J. 1992. *The Image: A Guide to Pseudo-Events in America*. New York: Vintage Books.

Böröcz, J. 1996. *Leisure Migration: A Sociological Study on Tourism*. New York and Oxford: Pergamon Press.

Bourdieu, P. 1984. *Distinction: A Social Critique of the Judgment of Taste*. Cambridge: Cambridge University Press.

Breman, J. 1996. *Footloose Labour: Working in India's Informal Economy*. New York: Cambridge University Press.

Britton, S. G. 1982. The Political Economy of Tourism in the Third World. *Annals of Tourism Research* 9: 331–358.

Britton, S. G. 1983. *Tourism and Underdevelopment in Fiji*. Australia: Australian National University.

Britton, S. G. 1991. Tourism, Capital, and Place: Towards a Critical Geography of Tourism. *Environment and Planning D: Society and Space* 9: 451–478.

Britton, S. G., and W. C. Clarke. 1987. *Ambiguous Alternative: Tourism in Small Developing Countries*. Suva: University of the South Pacific.

Bromley, R., and C. Gerry, eds. 1979. *Casual Work and Poverty in Third World Cities*. Chichester, U. K. and New York: John Wiley & Sons.

Butler, R. W. 1980. The Concept of a Tourist Area Cycle of Evolution: Implications for Management of Resources. *Canadian Geographer* 24 (1): 5–12.

Butler, R. W. 1992. Alternative Tourism: The Thin Edge of the Wedge. In *Tourism Alternatives: Potentials and Problems in the Development of Tourism*. Edited by V. L. Smith and W. R. Eadington. Philadelphia: University of Pennsylvania Press.

Butler, R. W. 1999. Tourism—An Evolutionary Perspective. In *Tourism and Sustainable Development: Monitoring, Planning, Managing, Decision Making*. Edited by J. G. Nelson, R. Butler, and G. Wall. Waterloo, Ontario: University of Waterloo, Department of Geography.

Bywater, M. 1993. Market Segments: The Youth And Student Travel Market. *Travel and Tourism Analyst* 3: 35–50.

Camacho, M. E. 1996. Dissenting Workers and Social Control: A Case Study of the Hotel Industry in Huatulco, Oaxaca. *Human Organization* 55 (1): 33–40.

Castells, M. 1989. *The Informational City: Information Technology, Economic Restructuring, and the Urban-Regional Process.* Oxford, UK and Cambridge, MA: Blackwell.

Cater, E. A. 1994. Ecotourism in the Third World—Problems and Prospects for Sustainability. In *Ecotourism: A Sustainable Option?* Edited by E. Cater and G. Lowman. Chichester, U. K. and New York: John Wiley & Sons.

Chadee, D. and J. Cutler. 1996. Insights into International Travel by Students. *Journal of Travel Research* 35(2): 75–80.

Cheng, Li. 1998. Surplus Rural Labourers and Internal Migration in China. In *Migration in China.* Edited by B. Bakken. Copenhagen: Nordic Institute of Asian Studies.

China National Tourism Admininstration. 2005. Fact & Figure; available at www.cnta.com/lyen/2fact/index.htm. [cited July 2005].

Chossudovsky, M. 1997. *The Globalisation of Poverty.* London and Atlantic Highlands, NJ: Zed Books.

Christaller, W. 1963. Some Considerations of Tourism Location in Europe: The Peripheral Regions—Underdeveloped Countries—Recreation Areas. *Regional Science Association Papers* 12.

Clancy, M. J. 1996. Export-led Growth Strategies, the Internationalization of Services, and Third World Development: The Political Economy of Mexican Tourism. Ph.D. diss., University of Wisconsin.

Cohen, E. 1972. Toward a Sociology of International Tourism. *Social Research* 39: 164–182.

Cohen, E. 1973. Nomads from Affluence: Notes on the Phenomenon of Drifter-Tourism. *International Journal of Comparative Sociology,* 14(1–2), 89–103.

Cohen, E.. 1979. A Phenomenology of Tourist Experiences. *Sociology,* 13(2): 179–201.

Cohen, E. 1988. Traditions in the Qualitative Sociology of Tourism. *Annals of Tourism Research* 15: 29–46.

Cormack, B. 1998. *A History of Holidays 1812–1990.* London: Routledge/Thoemmes Press and the Thomas Cook Archives.

Crossette, B. 1989. India Loosens Travel Policies to Woo Tourists. *The New York Times,* April 9, 1989, 19.

Crossette, B. 1998. *The Great Hill Stations of Asia.* Boulder, CO: Westview Press; excerpt available at *The New York Times* Web site.

D'Amore, L. J. 1988. Tourism—A Vital Force for Peace. *Annals of Tourism Research* 15 (2): 269–270.

Daltabuit, M., and O. Pi-Sunyer. 1990. Tourism Development in Quintana Roo, Mexico. *Cultural Survival Quarterly* 14 (1): 9–13.

Das, Gurcharan. 2002. *India Unbound: From Independence to the Global Information Age.* Penguin Books: New Delhi.

Davidson, J. O. 1996. Sex Tourism in Cuba. *Race & Class* 38 (1): 39–48.

Debord, G. 1992. *The Society of the Spectacle.* New York: Zone Books.

de Kadt, E. J., ed. 1979. Tourism—Passport to Development? Perspectives on the Social and Cultural Effects of Tourism in Developing Countries. In *Joint Unesco-World Bank Seminar on the Social and Cultural Impacts of Tourism.* New York: Oxford University Press.

de Soto, H., and Instituto Libertad y Democracia. 1989. *The Other Path: The Invisible Revolution in the Third World.* 1st Perennial Library ed. New York: Harper & Row/Perennial Library.

220 • From Pilgrimage to Package Tour

du Toit, B. M. 1990. People on the Move: Rural-Urban Migration with Special Reference of the Third World: Theoretical and Empirical Perspectives. *Human Organization* 49 (4): 305–319.

Eade, J. 1992. Pilgrimage and Tourism at Lourdes, France. *Annals of Tourism Research* 19 (1): 18–32.

Eco, U. 1986. *Travels in Hyperreality.* San Diego and London: Harcourt Brace Jovanovich.

Economist, The. 1991. Thailand's Tourist Industry: Beached. *The Economist* 320 (7714): 72.

Economist Intelligence Unit (EIU). 1991. Indonesia. *International Tourism Reports* 3: 23–40.

Edensor, T. 1998. *Touring the Taj.* London and New York: Routledge.

Eickelman, D. F., and J. Piscatori. 1990. *Muslim Travellers: Pilgrimage, Migration, and the Religious Imagination.* Berkeley and Los Angeles: University of California Press.

Fainstein, S. S., Hoffman, L. M., and D. R. Judd. 2003. Introduction. In *Cities and Visitors: Regulating People, Markets, and City Space.* Edited by L. M. Hoffman, S. S. Fainstein, and D. R. Judd. Malden, MA and Oxford: Blackwell.

Fanon, F. 1963. *The Wretched of the Earth.* New York: Grove Press.

Flint, J. 1898. *Tramping with Tramps.* New York: The Century Company.

Freitag, T. G. 1994. Enclave Tourism Development: For Whom the Benefits Roll? *Annals of Tourism Research* 21 (3): 538–554.

Froebel, F., J. Heinrichs, and O. Kreye. 1979. *The New International Division of Labour: Structural Unemployment in Industrialised Countries and Industrialisation in Developing Countries.* Cambridge and New York: Cambridge University Press.

Fuller, C. J. 1992. *The Camphor Flame: Popular Hinduism and Society in India.* Princeton: Princeton University Press.

Ginsberg, A. 1970. *Indian Journals: March 1962—May 1963: Notebooks Diary Blank Pages Writings.* San Francisco: City Lights Books.

Gitlin, T. 1988. Hip-Deep in Post-modernism. *The New York Times,* November 8, 1988, Section 7, 1, 35.

Gladstone, D. 1998. Tourism Urbanization in the United States. *Urban Affairs Review* 34 (1): 3–27.

Gold, A. G. 1988. *Fruitful Journeys: The Ways of Rajasthani Pilgrims.* Berkeley, Los Angeles, and London: University of California Press.

Goldstein, A., S. Goldstein, and S. Guo. 1991. Temporary Migrants in Shanghai Households. *Demography* 28 (2): 275–291.

Goldstein, A., and S. Guo. 1992. Temporary Migration in Shanghai and Beijing. *Studies in Comparative International Development* 27 (2): 39–56.

Gonzalez, D. New Providence Journal; Bahamians Resent the Loss of Beaches to Luxury. *The New York Times,* February 29, 2000; available at the *The New York Times* Website.

Government of India Ministry of Tourism. 1989. Foreign Tourist Survey. New Delhi: Government of India Ministry of Tourism.

Graburn, N. 1989. Tourism: The Sacred Journey. In *Hosts and Guests: The Anthropology of Tourism.* Edited by V. Smith. Philadelphia: University of Pennsylvania Press.

Hall, M. 1995. Ecotourism or Ecological Imperialism? *Geographical* 67 (2): 19.

Halla, F. F. 1997. Institutional Arrangements for Urban Management: The Sustainable Dar-es-Salaam Project. Ph.D. diss., Rutgers University.

Hampton, M. P. 1998. Backpacker tourism and economic development. *Annals of Tourism Research* 25 (3): 639–660.

Hansen, T. B. 1999. *The Saffron Wave: Democracy and Hindu Nationalism in Modern India.* Princeton: Princeton University Press.

Harris, N. 1987. *The End of the Third World*. Harmondsworth, England: Penguin Books.

Harrison, D. 1994. Learning from the Old South by the New South? The Case of Tourism. *Third World Quarterly* 15 (4): 707–721.

Hart, K. 1973. Informal Income Opportunities and Urban Employment in Ghana. *The Journal of Modern African Studies* 11 (1): 61–89.

Harvey, D. 1989. *The Condition of Postmodernity: An Enquiry into the Origins of Cultural Change*. Oxford and Cambridge, Mass.: Blackwell.

Herman, E. S., and R. W. McChesney. 1997. *The Global Media: The New Missionaries of Global Capitalism*. London: Cassell.

Hiernaux-Nicolas, D. 1999. The Cancun Bliss. In *The Tourist City*. Edited by D. R. Judd and S. S. Fainstein. New Haven, CT: Yale University Press.

Hiernaux-Nicolas, D., and M. R. Woog. 1990. Tourism and Absorption of the Labor Force in Mexico. Working Paper No. 34, Commission for the Study of International Migration and Cooperative Economic Development, Washington, DC.

Himachal Pradesh Tourism Development Corporation. 2005. Latest data; available at hptdc.nic.in/hptdc.htm [cited July 2005].

Hirschman, A. O. 1958. *The Strategy of Economic Development*. New Haven: Yale University Press.

Holden, P., ed. 1984. *Alternative Tourism: Report of the Workshop on Alternative Tourism with a Focus on Asia, Chaing Mai, Thailand, April 26–May 8, 1984. Sponsored by the Ecumenical Coalition on Third World Tourism*. Bangkok: The Ecumenical Coalition on Third World Tourism.

Honey, M. 1999. *Ecotourism and Sustainable Development: Who Owns Paradise?* Washington, DC: Island Press.

Housden, R. 1996. *Travels Through Sacred India*. New Delhi: HarperCollins.

Hudman, L. E., and R. H. Jackson. 1992. Mormon Pilgrimage and Tourism. *Annals of Tourism Research* 19 (1): 107–121.

Human Rights Watch/Asia. 1995. *Rape for Profit: Trafficking of Nepali Girls and Women to India's Brothels*. New York: Human Rights Watch.

Hutnyk, J. 1996. *The Rumour of Calcutta: Tourism, Charity and the Poverty of Representation*. London: Zed Books.

India Tourism Development Corporation. 2005. Latest data; available at www.theashokgroup.com [cited July 2005].

Indian Railways. 1999. Latest data available at www.indianrailways.gov.in [cited June 1999].

Informationszentrum Dritte Welt (Information Center for the Third World). 1990. Don't Come to Goa. *Earth Island Journal* 5 (3): 12.

Inglis, F. 2000. *The Delicious History of the Holiday*. London and New York: Routledge.

International Ecotourism Society. 2005. What Is Ecotourism? Definition and Ecotourism Principles; available at http://www.ecotourism.org/index2.php?what-is-ecotourism [cited May 2005].

International Labour Office. 1972. *Employment, Incomes and Equality: A Strategy for Increasing Productive Employment in Kenya*. Geneva: International Labour Office.

Ioannides, D. 1993. Tourism, Information Technologies, and the Flexibility Debate. Paper presented at the 89th Annual Meeting of the Association of American Geographers, Atlanta, Georgia, April 10, 1993.

Ioannides, D. 1994. Tourism as a Sustainable Development Option: A Case Study of Alternative Development Strategies in Akamas, Cyprus. Paper presented at the 36th

Annual Meeting of the Association of Collegiate Schools of Planning, Phoenix, Arizona, November 5, 1994.

Ioannides, D. 1995. Planning for International Tourism in Less Developed Countries: Toward Sustainability? *Journal of Planning Literature* 9(3): 235–254.

Ioannides, D. and K.G. Debbage, eds. 1998. *The Economic Geography of the Tourist Industry: A Supply Side Analysis*. London and New York: Routledge.

Jafari, J., A. Pizam, and K. Przeclawski. 1990. A Sociocultural Study of Tourism as a Factor of Cultural Change. *Annals of Tourism Research* 17 (3): 469–472.

Jameson, F. 1984. Postmodernism, or the Cultural Logic of Late Capitalism. *New Left Review* 146: 53–93.

Jimenez, A. 1993. *Turismo: Estructura y Desarrollo*. Mexico City: McGraw-Hill.

Joseph, C. 1994. Temples, Tourists and the Politics of Exclusion: The Articulation of Sacred Space at the Hindu Pilgrimage Center of Pushkar, India. Ph.D. diss., University of Rochester.

Judd, D. R., and S. S. Fainstein, ed. 1999. *The Tourist City*. New Haven, Conn.: Yale University Press.

Kazmi, N. 1999. How Would You Like to be My Valentine? *The Sunday Times of India*, February 14, 1999, Section 1, 1.

Kermath, B. M., and R. N. Thomas. 1992. Spatial Dynamics of Resorts: Sosua, Dominican Republic. *Annals of Tourism Research* 19: 173–190.

Kerouac, J. 1991. *On the Road*. New York: Penguin Books.

Khan, S. Y. 1999. The Dangers of Being Thin and Beautiful. *The Sunday Times of India*, March 28, 1999, Section 1, 1.

Klein, R. A. 2002. *Cruise Ship Blues: The Underside of the Cruise Industry*. Gabriola Island, British Columbia: New Society Publishers.

Leheny, D. 1995. A Political Economy of Asian Sex Tourism. *Annals of Tourism Research* 22 (2): 367–384.

Lenin, V. I. 1975. *Imperialism, The Highest Stage of Capitalism*. Peking: Foreign Languages Press.

Lewis, W. A. 1958. Economic Development with Unlimited Supplies of Labour. In *The Economics of Underdevelopment*. Edited by A. N. Agarwala. Oxford University Press: London.

Lipietz, A. 1982. Towards Global Fordism. *New Left Review* 132: 33–47.

Lipietz, A. 1986. New Tendencies in the International Division of Labor: Regimes of Accumulation and Modes of Regulation. In *Production, Work, Territory: The Geographical Anatomy of Industrial Capitalism*. Edited by A. J. Scott and M. Storper. Boston: Allen & Unwin.

Lipietz, A. 1987. *Mirages and Miracles: The Crises of Global Fordism*. London: Verso.

London, J. 1907. *The Road*, available at http://sunsite.berkeley.edu/London/Writings/TheRoad/ [cited May 2005].

Long, V. 1989. Social Mitigation of Tourism Development Impacts: Bahias de Huatulco, Oaxaca, Mexico. *Tourism Recreation Research* 14 (1): 5–13.

Luxemburg, R. 1968. *The Accumulation of Capital*. New York: Monthly Review Press.

MacCannell, D. 1973. Staged Authenticity: Arrangements of Social Space in Tourist Settings. *American Journal of Sociology* 79 (3): 589–603.

MacCannell, D. 1976. *The Tourist: A New Theory of the Leisure Class*. New York: Schocken Books.

Mandelbaum, D. G. 1970. *Society in India*. 2 vols. Berkeley, Los Angeles, and London: University of California Press.

Mathieson, A., and G. Wall. 1982. *Tourism: Economic, Physical, and Social Impacts*. London and New York: Longman.

McDowell, E. 1998. Tourism slipping, along with Asian economies. *The New York Times*, March 8, V, 3.

McKinley, J. 1999. The Avante Garde: Follow That Backpack. *The New York Times*, August 8, V, 16.

Mehta, G. 1990. *Karma Cola*. London: Minerva.

Meijers, W. G. 1991. Rucksacks and Dollars: The Economic Impact of Organized and Non-Organized Tourism in Bolivia. In *Towards Appropriate Tourism: The Case of Developing Countries*. Edited by T. V. Singh, H. L. Theuns, and F. M. Go. Frankfurt am Main: Peter Lang.

Meisch, L. A. 1995. Gringas and Otavalenos: Changing Tourist Relations. *Annals of Tourism Research* 22 (2): 441–462.

Meriwether, L. 1887. A Tramp Trip: How to See Europe on Fifty Cents a Day. New York and London: Harper & Brothers.

Michener, J. 1971. *The Drifters: A Novel*. New York: Random House.

Milne, S. 1992. Tourism and Development in South Pacific Microstates. *Annals of Tourism Research* 19: 191–212.

Mishra, P. 1995. *Butter Chicken in Ludhiana: Travels in Small Town India*. New Delhi: Penguin Books.

Morinis, A. 1992. Introduction. In *Sacred Journeys: The Anthropology of Tourism*. Edited by A. Morinis. Westport, Conn.: Greenwood Press.

Mullins, P. 1991. Tourism Urbanization. *International Journal of Urban and Regional Research* 15: 326–342.

Munt, I. 1994. Eco-tourism or ego-tourism? *Race & Class* 36 (1): 49–60.

Naipaul, V. S. 1962. *The Middle Passage; Impressions of Five Societies: British, French and Dutch in the West Indies and South America*. London: Deutsch.

Nash, D. 1981. Tourism as an Anthropological Subject. *Current Anthropology* 22 (5): 461–481.

Nash, D. 1989. Tourism as a Form of Imperialism. In *Hosts and Guests: The Anthropology of Tourism*. Philadelphia: University of Pennsylvania Press.

Nash, D. 1996. *The Anthropology of Tourism*. Oxford: Elsevier Science.

Ninan, S. 1995. Transforming Television in India. *Media Studies Journal* 9 (3): 43–51.

Nolan, M. L. 1991. The European Roots of Latin American Pilgrimage. In *Pilgrimage in Latin America*. Edited by N. R. Crumrine and A. Morinis. New York and London: Greenwood Press.

O'Connor, J. 1973. *The Fiscal Crisis of the State*. New York: St. Martin's Press.

Oppermann, M. 1993. Tourism Space in Developing Countries. *Annals of Tourism Research* 20: 535–556.

Orwell, G. 1999. *Down and out in Paris and London*. London: Penguin Books.

Pagdin, C. 1996. *Assessing Tourism Impacts in the Third World: A Nepal Case Study*. Oxford and Tarrytown: Pergamon.

Parnwell, M. 1993. *Population Movements and the Third World*. London and New York: Routledge.

Pattullo, P. 1996. *Last Resorts: The Cost of Tourism in the Caribbean*. London: Latin American Press.

Pearce, D. G. 1995. *Tourism Today: A Geographical Analysis*. Harlow and Essex, England: Longman Scientific and Technical; New York: John Wiley & Sons.

Peppelenbosch, P. G. N., and G. J. Tempelman. 1972. Tourism and the Developing Countries. *Tijdschrift voor Economie en Sociale Geografie* 64 (1): 52–58.

Pereira, W., and J. Seabrook. 1994. *Global Parasites: Five Hundred Years of Western Culture.* Bombay: Earthcare Books.

Philipose, P. 1999. Forgotten Regions in the Nation's Mind: The Teflon Generation. *The Indian Express* (Chandigarh edition), March 17, 1999, 8.

Plog, S. C. 1974. Why Destination Areas Rise and Fall in Popularity. *The Cornell Hotel and Restaurant Administration Quarterly* (February): 55–58.

Poon, A. 1988. Tourism and Information Technologies. *Annals of Tourism Research* 15: 531–549.

Poon, A. 1990. Flexible Specialization and Small Size: The Case of Caribbean Tourism. *World Development* 18 (1): 109–123.

Port Authority of New York and New Jersey. 1994. *Destination New York–New Jersey: Tourism and Travel to the Metropolitan Region.* New York: The Port Authority of New York and New Jersey.

Portes, A. 1996. The Informal Economy. In *Exploring the Underground Economy.* Edited by S. Pozo. Kalamazoo, Mich.: W. E. Upjohn Institute for Employment Research.

Prinsep, H. T. 1972. *History of the Political and Military Transactions in India During the Administration of the Marquess of Hastings 1813–1823, Volume 1.* Shannon, Ireland and New York: Irish University Press and Barnes & Noble Books.

Pruitt, D. and S. Lafont. 1995. For Love and Money: Romance Tourism in Jamaica. *Annals of Tourism Research* 22 (2): 422–440.

Rachowiecki, R. 1995. *Southwest: a Lonely Planet Travel Survival Kit.* Melbourne, Australia and Oakland, Calif.: Lonely Planet Publications.

Rae, W. F. 1891. *The Business of Travel: A Fifty Years' Record of Progress.* London and New York: Thos. Cook and Son.

Rajotte, F. 1987. Safari and Beach Resort Tourism: The Costs to Kenya. In *Ambiguous Alternative: Tourism in Small Developing Countries.* Edited by S. Britton and W. C. Clarke. Suva: University of the South Pacific.

Ramani, P., and V. J. Thapa 1999. New Kicks on the Block. *India Today* 24 (14): 49–54.

Reimer, G. D. 1990. Packaging Dreams: Canadian Tour Operators at Work. *Annals of Tourism Research* 17: 501–512.

Reynoso y Valle, A., and J. P. de Regt. 1979. Growing Pains: Planned Tourism Development in Ixtapa-Zihuatanejo. In *Tourism—Passport to Development? Perspectives on the Social and Cultural Effects of Tourism in Developing Countries,* Edited by E, de Kadt. New York: Oxford University Press.

Richter, L. K. 1992. Political Instability and Tourism in the Third World. In *Tourism and the Less Developed Countries.* Edited by D. Harrison. London: Belhaven Press and Halsted Press.

Riley, P. J. 1988. Road Culture of International Long-Term Budget Travelers. *Annals of Tourism Research* 15: 313–338.

Robinson, W. I. 1996. Globalisation: Nine Theses on Our Epoch. *Race & Class* 38 (2): 13–31.

Schédler, A. 1988. *El capital extranjero en México: el caso de la hotelería* [The foreign capital in Mexico: The case of the hotel profession]. *Investigación Económica* (Mexico) 47: 137–178.

Schor, J. 1991. *The Overworked American: The Unexpected Decline of Leisure.* New York: Basic Books.

Seabrook, J. 1995. *Notes from another India.* London and East Haven, Conn.: Pluto Press.

Seabrook, J. 1996. *In the Cities of the South: Scenes from a Developing World*. London: Verso.

Secretaría de Turismo (SECTUR). 1996. *El Mercado de Turismo Doméstico en México: Segmentos y Comportamiento*. Mexico City: Secretaría de Turismo.

Shabab, D. 1996. *Kullu: Himalayan Abode of the Divine*. New Delhi: Indus.

Shacochis, B. 1989. In Deepest Gringolandia: Mexico: The Third World as Tourist Theme Park. *Harper's Magazine*, 42–50.

Singh, D. 1999. We Also Make Babies. *The Hindustan Times*, February 6, 1999, Lifestyle Section, 2.

Singh, T. V. 1989. *The Kulu Valley: The Case of Appropriate Tourism Development in the Mountain Areas*. New Delhi: Himalayan Books.

Singh, T. V., H. L. Theuns, and F. M. Go, eds. 1989. *Towards Appropriate Tourism: The Case of Developing Countries*. Frankfurt am Main and New York: Peter Lang.

Smith, S. L. J. 1998. Tourism as an Industry: Debates and Concepts. In *The Economic Geography of the Tourist Industry*. Edited by D. Ioannides and K. G. Debbage. London and New York: Routledge.

Smith, V. L. 1989. *Hosts and Guests: The Anthropology of Tourism*. 2nd ed. Philadelphia: University of Pennsylvania Press.

Smith, V. L. 1990. Geographical Implications of "Drifter" Tourism, Boracay, Philippines. *Tourism Recreation Research* 15 (1): 34–42.

Smith, V. L. 1995. Privatization in the Third World: Small-Scale Tourism Enterprises. In *Global Tourism: The Next Decade*. Edited by W. F. Theobald. Oxford and Boston: Butterworth Heinemann.

Spano, S. 1996. In Oaxaca, Reveling in the Exchange Rate. *The New York Times*, January 7, 1996, 56.

Srisang, K. 1989. The Ecumenical Coalition on Third World Tourism. *Annals of Tourism Research* 16: 119–121.

Strategy Research Corporation. 1995. *Latin American Market Planning Handbook*. Miami: Strategy Research Corporation.

Thomas, J. J. 1995. *Surviving in the City: The Urban Informal Sector in Latin America*. London and East Haven, Conn.: Pluto Press.

Truong, T. 1990. *Sex, Money and Morality: Prostitution and Tourism in Southeast Asia*. London and New Jersey: Zed Books.

Turner, L., and J. Ash. 1976. *The Golden Hordes: International Tourism and the Pleasure Periphery*. New York: St. Martin's Press.

Turner, V. 1973. The Center Out There. *History of Religion* 12 (3): 191–230.

Turner, V., and E. Turner. 1978. *Image and Pilgrimage in Christian Culture: An Anthropological Perspective*. New York: Columbia University Press.

Turshen, M., and C. Hill. Sex Tourism, The Military, and the Spread of AIDS in Asia. Unpublished manuscript. n.d..

Tuting, L., and K. Dixit, eds. *Bikas Binas [Development Destruction]*. Kathmandu: Ratna Pustak Bhandar, n.d..

Urry, J. 1988. Cultural Change and Contemporary Holiday-Making. *Theory, Culture & Society* 5: 35–55.

Urry, J. 1990. *The Tourist Gaze: Leisure and Travel in Contemporary Societies*. London: Sage Publications.

van den Berghe, P. L. 1994. *The Quest for the Other: Ethnic Tourism in San Cristobal, Mexico*. Seattle and London: University of Washington Press.

Varma, P. K. 1998. *The Great Indian Middle Class.* New Delhi: Viking Penguin India.

Visaria, P., and P. Jacob. 1996. The Informal Sector in India: Estimates of Its Size, Needs, and Problems of Data Collection. In *Unveiling the Informal Sector: More Than Counting Heads.* Edited by Bohuslav Herman and Wim Stoffers. Aldershot, U.K. and Brookfield, Vt.: Avebury Press.

Wahnschafft, R. 1982. Formal and Informal Tourism Sectors: A Case Study in Pattaya, Thailand. *Annals of Tourism Research* 9: 429–451.

Walker, C. 1995. The Global Middle Class. *American Demographics* 17: 40–46.

Wall, G. 1996. One Name, Two Destinations: Planned and Unplanned Coastal Resorts in Indonesia. In *Practicing Responsible Tourism: International Case Studies in Tourism Planning, Policy and Development.* Edited by Lynn C. Harrison and Winston Husbands. New York and Toronto: John Wiley & Sons.

Warren, B. 1973. Imperialism and Capitalist Industrialization. *New Left Review* 81: 3–45.

Watson, G. L., and J. P. Kopachevsky. 1994. Interpretations of Tourism as Commodity. *Annals of Tourism Research* 21 (3): 643–660.

Whelan, T. 1991. *Nature Tourism: Managing for the Environment.* Washington, D.C.: Island Press.

Wight, P. A. 1996. North American Ecotourists: Market profile and trip characteristics. *Journal of Travel Research* 34 (4): 2–10.

Wise, J. 1994. Is the Hippie Circuit Washed Up? *The New York Times Magazine*, November 13, 1994, 58.

Wolff, E. N. 1999. Recent Trends in Wealth Ownership, Conference volume, Benefits and Mechanisms for Spreading Asset Ownership in the United States, April 20, 1999.

Wood, R. E. 1979. Tourism and Underdevelopment in Southeast Asia. *Journal of Contemporary Asia* 9 (3): 274–287.

World Bank 1996. *From Plan to Market: World Development Report 1996.* Oxford and New York: Oxford University Press.

World Bank. 1998. Press Release: World Bank and World Tourism Organization Examine Role of Tourism in Development. News Release No. 98/1853/S, Washington, DC: The World Bank Group; available at the World Bank Web site.

World Bank. 2005. WDI Data Query; available at devdata.worldbank.org/data-query/ [cited July 2005].

World Resources Institute. 2005. Ecotourism and Conservation: Are They Compatible?; available at pdf.wri.org/wr2000_chapter1_box1.15_ecotourism.pdf [cited July 2005].

World Tourism Organization. 1986. *Annuaire des Statistiques du Tourisme* [Yearbook of Tourism Statistics]. Madrid: World Tourism Organization.

World Tourism Organization. 1994. *Global Distribution Systems (GDSs) in the Tourism Industry: A Study Prepared for WTO by Olivier Vialle.* Madrid: World Tourism Organization.

World Tourism Organization. 1996. *Annuaire des Statistiques du Tourisme* [Yearbook of Tourism Statistics]. Madrid: World Tourism Organization.

World Tourism Organization. 1997. *Tourism Market Trends: World, 1985–1996.* Madrid: World Tourism Organization.

World Tourism Organization. 1998a. *Annuaire des Statistiques du Tourisme* [Yearbook of Tourism Statistics]. Madrid: World Tourism Organization.

World Tourism Organization. 1998b. *Compendium of Tourism Statistics 1992–1996.* Madrid: World Tourism Organization.

World Tourism Organization. 2001. *Annuaire des Statistiques du Tourisme* [Yearbook of Tourism Statistics]. Madrid: World Tourism Organization.

World Tourism Organization. 2002a. Latest data; available at http://www.world-tourism .org/market_research/facts&figures/latest_data.htm [cited December 2002].

World Tourism Organization. 2002b. Methodological notes; available at www.world-tourism .org/market_research/facts&figures/menu.htm [cited December 2002].

World Tourism Organization. 2002c. World's top 15 tourist destinations; available at www .world-tourism.org/market_research/facts&figures/latest_data/tita01top15._07-02pdf.pdf [cited December 2002].

World Tourism Organization. 2005a. Facts & Figures; available at www.world-tourism.org/ facts/trends/inbound/arrivals/1950-2002.pdf

World Tourism Organization. 2005b. Facts & Figures; available at www.world-tourism.org/ facts/trends/inbound/receipts/ITR(1950-2002).pdf [cited July 2005].

World Tourism Organization. 2005c. World's Top Tourism Destinations; available at www .world-tourism.org/facts/tmt.html [cited July 2005].

World Tourism Organization. 2005d. World's Top Tourism Earners; available at www .world-tourism.org/facts/tmt.html [cited July 2005].

World Tourism Organization. 2005e. Methodological Notes; available at www.world-tourism .org/facts/metho.html [cited July 2005].

World Tourism Organization. 2005f. International Tourist Arrivals by Country of Destination; available at http://www.world-tourism.org/facts/trends/inbound/arrivals/ITAME02 .pdf [cited July 2005].

World Trade Organization. 2002. Trade Statistics; available at www.wto.org/english/res_e/ statis_e/statis_e.htm.

World Travel and Tourism Council (WTTC). 1996. Caribbean Travel & Tourism: Millennium Vision. London: World Travel and Tourism Council; available at the WTTC Web site.

World Travel and Tourism Council (WTTC). 1998. WTTC Hawaii Tourism Report: How Travel and Tourism Affects Hawaii's Economy. London: World Travel and Tourism Council; available at the WTTC Web site.

World Travel and Tourism Council (WTTC). 1999. *Travel and Tourism's Economic Impact.* London: World Travel and Tourism Council.

World Travel and Tourism Council. 2002. The Travel and Tourism Economy 2002: Special End of Year Update; available at www.wttc.org/measure/PDF/EOY_World.pdf [cited December 2002].

Zinder, H. and Associates. 1969. *The Future of Tourism in the Eastern Caribbean.* Washington, DC: H. Zinder and Associate.

Zurick, D. N. 1995. *Errant Journeys: Adventure Travel in a Modern Age.* Austin: University of Texas Press.

Index